THE CHEAP BASTARD'S® GUIDE TO

Boston

We would love to hear from you concerning your experiences with this guide and how you feel it could be improved and kept up to date. Please send your comments and suggestions to:

editorial@GlobePequot.com

Thanks for your input, and happy travels!

CHEAP BASTARD'S® SERIES

THE CHEAP BASTARD'S® GUIDE TO Boston

Secrets of Living the Good Life—**For Free!**

Second Edition

Kris **Frieswick**

gpp®
travel

Guilford, Connecticut
An imprint of The Globe Pequot Press

The information in this guidebook is subject to change. We recommend that you call ahead to obtain current information before finalizing your plans.

Text design by Sheryl P. Kober
Revised and updated by Paul Karr

ISSN: 1934-2586
ISBN: 978-0-7627-5022-1

Printed in the United States of America

10 9 8 7 6 5 4 3 2 1

CONTENTS

LAND **OF** THE **FREE**

Give us a good cheap twenty-four-hour day,
No part of which we'd have to waste.
—ROBERT FROST

Ever since the Puritans set foot on Massachusetts' rocky soil in 1620, Bostonians have spent a great deal of time and energy trying to live on the smallest amount of money possible. For centuries that meant eschewing the finer things in life and making do with only the basic necessities—and having the basic necessities patched, resewn, resoled, or shellacked when they eventually fell apart. The Puritans may be gone, but the Puritan ethic is still alive and well in the City on the Hill. Today, that ethic has created a new kind of Puritan—the Cheap Bostonian.

Unfortunately for anyone who didn't grow up here, though, the first rule of being cheap in Boston is to **not talk about being cheap in Boston.** We just find it unseemly to talk about money: either how much we spend, or how much we earn. We would much rather talk about an embarrassing medical condition. This makes it a lot harder for newcomers, visitors, and even longtime residents to find bargains. That is why this book was crying out to be written— to help everyone find the way toward Cheap Living. In a city that has seen prices skyrocket on everything from real estate to movie tickets in the past decade, it's getting harder and harder to find good stuff cheap or free. The good news is that it's out there for the taking.

Lots of Bostonians are cheap, but that doesn't mean we'll take any old thing just because it's free. We have standards, and I dare say they're fairly high. As such, this book is by no means a comprehensive overview of every single free or very cheap thing in the city—that would take volumes. What I've tried to do is to weed through as much of the free Boston universe as I could and to highlight things worth your time and effort. In fact, I like to think that what you hold in your hand is a guide to some of the best places, things, and experiences that the city of Boston has to offer. That they're free or cheap is a nice side benefit.

First, some definitions. Most of the listings in this book are free. By free, I mean that absolutely no money will change hands. But as anyone will tell you, there are two kinds of free: totally free, and free with strings attached. Strings, in this book, often involve some investment of something other than money to procure the object of your desire. Often that investment is your time—for instance, volunteer ushering to get theater tickets or arriving extra early to avoid a cover charge. And since time is money, I've made sure to call out any deals that come with a catch. (I've done that by boldly highlighting *The Catch* in any listing that has one.)

> But as anyone will tell you, there are two kinds of free: totally free, and free with strings attached.

The second type of listing in this book is for things that are obscenely, ridiculously cheap, things that are such a profound bargain that I thought you'd really want to know about them—like $25 massages or cut-rate mortgages. Sometimes, to get a true value, you must part with a little green.

I've tried to include listings that would appeal to everyone who finds themselves in Boston proper: vacationers who must offset the cost of their expensive hotel room by economizing on everything else, residents who want or need to economize, or just people who can't think of a good reason to spend more money than is absolutely necessary. Some listings will be more appropriate for full-time Bostonians—for instance, anything that requires a long lead time (like volunteer ushering)—but many other things are perfect for anyone who just needs a quick fix of free.

All the listings in this book are located in Boston proper unless otherwise indicated. The information contained here was accurate as of press time, but things are always changing. Make sure to call ahead to confirm dates, times, and whether the deal is still on offer before you venture out.

As you're experiencing all the free and cheap goodness that Boston has to offer, remember that half the fun of being a Cheap Bastard in Boston is uncovering bargain treasures that no one else knows about. If you do find some good cheap stuff that didn't make it into this book, please let us know about it or, at the very least, tell some friends.

We hope you enjoy this book, and that it helps you discover a whole new side of a city that is getting a bad rap as one of the most expensive places in the United States to live. That's true *only* if you don't know where to look and how to live.

Entertainment in Boston

BARGAIN BEATS:
MUSIC ON THE CHEAP

"Extraordinary how potent cheap music is."

—NOEL COWARD

Boston has long been an incubator for raw musical talent, thanks to the presence of the Berklee College of Music, the New England Conservatory, Longy School of Music, the Boston Conservatory, and strong music programs at our universities.

Our bars and lounges have hosted the fledgling incarnations of the best rock 'n roll the world has ever seen. There is also a dizzying variety of completely free outdoor concerts in the summer, featuring everything from alternative and jazz to classical and oldies.

What follows is by no means a comprehensive list, as lounges and bars are adding and subtracting live music from their mix all the time, sometimes depending on the season.

Below we've listed the places that are known for the high quality (and regularity) of the free tunes they showcase. Unless otherwise noted, venues listed here have no cover and no minimum. It's good to be a music-loving Cheap Bostonian.

ROCK/**POP**/FOLK/**ALTERNATIVE**

All Asia
334 Massachusetts Avenue
Cambridge
(617) 497–1544
www.allasiabar.com

The Catch Occasionally shows require a drink minimum and/or cover.

This longtime locals' favorite offers a number of no-cover musical acts nearly every night (music sometimes gives way to an open-mic or comedy night, so check the Web site before heading out). Acts range from modern rock to jazz to alternative. And when the munchies hit, there's Asian cuisine just a waitress away. In rare cases, this bar has a drink minimum and a cover.

Asgard

350 Massachusetts Avenue
Cambridge
(617) 577–9100
www.classicirish.com

The Catch Cover charge on certain holidays.

This renovated space partway between MIT and Central Square is open and airy but gets down with a wide selection of musical acts, including jazz, funk, pop, and rock. There's no cover, except on some holidays. The live music is on Saturday nights (sometimes Fridays, too), and shows begin around 9:00 p.m. Updated music schedules can be found on the Web site.

The Black Rose

160 State Street
(617) 742–2286
www.irishconnection.com

The Catch There's a $5.00 cover most nights.

This staple of Boston's Irish community features low- and no-cover traditional Irish music Sunday through Thursday. (U2 played here in the early '80s when they were virtually unknown in the States.) The bands start at 9:00 p.m. seven nights a week. On Saturday and Sunday there's also sometimes no-cover music in the afternoon from 4:00 to 7:00 p.m.

The Cantab Lounge

738 Massachusetts Avenue
Cambridge
(617) 354–2685
www.cantab-lounge.com

The Catch Cover charge $3.00 Thursday, variable Friday and Saturday.

The Cantab has been around forever and is a beloved, though noisy, local watering hole right in Central Square. Monday night features folk and acoustic music at 8:00 p.m.

Tuesday is bluegrass night, starting at 8:00 p.m. Sunday and Wednesday feature the blues, starting at 9:00 p.m. On Thursday night there's a soul review band that goes on at 9:00 p.m. On Friday and Saturday nights, Little Joe Cook and the Thrillers hold court at 9:30 p.m., as they have done for the past thirty years. Covers are variable but reasonable.

Dick's Last Resort
Quincy Market at Faneuil Hall Marketplace
(617) 267–8080
www.dickslastresort.com

If you don't mind noise, flying napkins, waiters sporting too much "flair," a warehouse-like ambience, and the hordes of ridiculously attired bachelorette parties that swamp this place on the weekends, you can actually hear some pretty good music seven nights a week. Shows begin between 8:00 and 8:30 p.m. and are typically acoustic guitar cover bands. Classic rock cover bands take the stage on the weekend, when shows start between 9:00 and 9:30 p.m.

The Green Dragon Tavern
11 Marshall Street (near Faneuil Hall Marketplace)
(617) 367–0055
www.somersirishpubs.com

The Catch Cover charge $5.00 Friday and Saturday nights.

This is one of the oldest continuously operating pubs in Boston, dating back to Revolutionary War days, and now it's a popular hangout for the young and restless professional crowd that flocks to this part of town for the nightlife. Free rock cover bands take the small corner stage on Tuesday, Wednesday, and Thursday at 9:00 p.m. and on Friday and Saturday at 10:00 p.m. Sunday features live-band karaoke at 10:00 p.m.—this is your long-awaited chance to front your own rock band, if only for one song. Leave that hairbrush at home, 'cause they let you use a real mic and everything. Though there's a small charge on weekends, if you're in the bar before 10:00 p.m., you can see the show free.

Hennessy's
25 Union Street
(617) 742–2121
www.somersirishpubs.com

The Catch Cover charge $5.00 Friday and Saturday.

Seven days a week, bands perform light rock, hits from the '70s, '80s, and '90s, and Top 40 covers at this hopping pickup joint in the Quincy Market area. Shows start at 10:00 p.m. on Friday and Saturday and at 9:00 p.m. on other nights.

Kinsale

2 Center Plaza (across from City Hall Plaza)
(617) 742–5577
www.classicirish.com/kinsale_music.html

Live shows without a cover occur on Tuesdays, Fridays, and Saturdays. On Tuesday the shows begin at 7:30 p.m. and feature Irish music. On Friday and Saturday the shows begin at 9:00 p.m. and are mainly cover bands.

Lucky's Lounge

355 Congress Street (corner of A Street)
(617) 357–5825
www.luckyslounge.com

This hip, happening underground bar (there's no sign, so look for the mysterious stairs on the corner of A Street and Congress Street going down into a basement) has a cool '60s vibe that attracts lots of artists and writer types from the surrounding Fort Point Channel arts community. Appreciative of the fact that they're mostly starving artists, Lucky's offers up free live music on every night except Monday and Tuesday, all without a drink minimum. On Wednesday it's usually jazz at 9:00 p.m. On Thursday Lucky's features 1960s, 1970s, and soul music at 9:30 p.m. Friday night features local bands at 10:00 p.m., and on Saturday there's a jazz trio at 10:00 p.m. But save yourself for the big daddy of them all—Sinatra Sunday, starting at 8:30 p.m. Yes, p.m. It runs past midnight.

Matt Murphy's

14 Harvard Street
Brookline
(617) 232–0188
www.mattmurphyspub.com

It's not Matt "Guitar" Murphy of Blues Brothers fame, unfortunately. But this teensy Irish bar does boast free live music Thursday through Tuesday nights, starting at 10:30 p.m. It is definitely one of the better free-music venues in town. On offer are jazz, reggae, fusion, and everything else in between. Side note: unbelievably, Esquire mag said this joint serves some of the best sandwiches in America. Wha?

Get there early or prepare to stand, possibly in someone else's back pocket. This place really packs 'em in. And remember: it's out in Brookline. Allow extra transit time.

Middle East

474 Massachusetts Avenue
Cambridge
(617) 492–9181
www.mideastclub.com

The legendary Middle East is actually four spaces in one: **Upstairs, Down-stairs, the Corner,** and **ZuZu.** Upstairs and Downstairs are stages featuring absolutely top-notch national and local acts. Ticket prices vary from $10 to $15, which is still quite a deal. The ZuZu and Corner spaces serve up eclectic Middle Eastern food and host a variety of free live music and other types of entertainment, like art openings and belly dancing with live musi-cal accompaniment on Wednesday nights. Dates and times vary, and there is sometimes a small cover charge, so check the Web site before venturing out. The shows start around 10:00 p.m., the pay-per-view shows generally an hour or two earlier.

Mr. Dooley's Boston Tavern

77 Broad Street
(617) 338–5656
www.somersirishpubs.com

This is a fun place. Traditional Irish music fills the pub on Friday from 5:00 to 9:00 p.m. and on Friday and Saturday around 8:30 or 9:00 p.m., when there's a small cover charge. An Irish *seisuin,* a traditional Irish music gath-ering, happens on Sunday from 4:00 to 7:00 p.m. Other nights of the week, bands sometimes show up, too—last time we checked in, on a Thursday, a Johnny Cash tribute band was hitting the stage.

Paddy O's

33 Union Street
(617) 263–7771
www.somersirishpubs.com

The Catch There's a $5.00 cover on Friday and Saturday evenings after 9:00 p.m.

Light rock, blues, and Top 40 covers are on tap at this small locals' place on Wednesday and Thursday at 9:00 p.m. and on Friday and Saturday at 10:00 p.m., and an Irish *seisuin* happens on Sunday from 4:00 to 7:00 p.m.

Toad

1912 Massachusetts Avenue
Cambridge
(617) 497–4950
www.toadcambridge.com

This great little bar, with live music all seven nights of the week, is so small that it's sometimes necessary to ask the bass player in the band to "move it on over" should you actually want to use the bathroom behind the stage. Now that's intimate. The quality of the music at this place never ceases to amaze—you'll encounter lots of Berklee grads trying out new stuff, for starters. And there is never a cover. Repeat: never. Get there early and claim your spot at the door end of the bar. Rock, jazz, and blues are the staples here; shows start after 7:00 p.m. and the bar stays open until at least 1:00 a.m. every night. Check the bar's Web site for nightly details.

JAZZ/**BLUES**

Bristol Lounge

The Four Seasons Hotel
200 Boylston Street
(617) 351–2052
www.fourseasons.com/boston/lounge_35.html

This swanky bar at the opulent Four Seasons (known as "Boston's living room," or so they claim) is a hidden gem when you're looking to hear some high-quality jazz for free in a pinch. The drinks here are pricey, but there's never a cover or a drink minimum (that would be so gauche); nurse that glass o' wine carefully. Surprisingly for these swank digs, the bar menu leans toward Red Sox–themed small plates. And, best of all, there's free jazz on Friday and Saturday nights in the lounge from 6:00 p.m. to 10:00 p.m. One tip: Come looking nice, or stay home.

Good Life Downtown
28 Kingston Street
(617) 451–2622
www.goodlifebar.com

Renovation has left this bar/restaurant without much of its previous Rat Pack cool, but the music is still pretty hot and cheap to hear. Mostly it's hip-hop and house DJs, if that's your thing, or cover bands.

Les Zygomates
129 South Street
(617) 542–5108
www.leszygomates.com

This gorgeous French bistro was one of the first restaurants to colonize the previously dodgy "Leather District" of Boston, and it helped raise this area to its current hip level. Most nights, things are standing room only here despite a snooty staff. The stage features live jazz music, often with a vocalist, Wednesday through Saturday from 8:00 p.m. to midnight. Sit at the bar and relax: There's no drink minimum (though there is an excellent wine list, if you feel so inclined). Tables are reserved for diners.

Top of the Hub
Prudential Tower
800 Boylston Street
(617) 536–1775
www.selectrestaurants.com/tophub/index.html

Everyone in Boston knows about the Top of the Hub, but not everyone knows it offers live jazz seven nights a week. The lounge has the best view in town—from the fifty-second floor of the Prudential Center, second-tallest building in the city. Shows begin around 8:30 p.m. during the week, 9:00 p.m. on Friday and Saturday, and 8:00 p.m. on Sunday.

Wally's Cafe Jazz Club
427 Massachusetts Avenue (near Huntington Avenue)
(617) 424–1408
www.wallyscafe.com

Since 1947 Wally's, a dingy, dubious-looking hole-in-the-wall in a not-great section of Massachusetts Avenue, has been the undisputed king of the Boston jazz club scene. It's just right. Wally's has live music seven nights a week and never a cover. It also happens to regularly host some of the best jazz, funk, Afro, and Latin musicians in the world, plus each new crop of Berklee grads (the world-famous jazz school is just a couple of blocks up Mass. Avenue). If there's a top jazz or blues musician in town, chances are excellent that he or she will make the required pilgrimage down to Wally's.

Music starts at 9:00 p.m. each night, with cool jazz jams on Saturday at 5:00 p.m. and on Sunday at 4:00 p.m.

CLASSICAL/**CHAMBER**/EARLY MUSIC

Boston Lyric Opera
45 Franklin Street, fourth floor
(617) 542–4912
www.blo.org

You can see the BLO at many of the Waterfront Performing Arts Series nights in Columbus Park during the summer (see below). But here's a little secret: You can also attend the company's opera performances for free at other times during the season—if you are willing to volunteer a little time. Cool, huh? The opera actively seeks volunteers in their administrative and ticket offices, at performances, and to staff their gala fund-raising events. Contact the BLO directly to let them know you're interested in helping out.

Boston Symphony Orchestra Community
Chamber Concert Series
(617) 638–9300
www.bso.org

BSO does free concerts out of the goodness of its heart, Sundays at 3:00 p.m., at various sites in the metro area about once a month from October through May. Admission is free, but you must reserve your tickets two weeks prior to the concert. Also note that most of the performance venues are not in downtown Boston, but rather in outlying communities up to an hour away that usually require a car to reach. A few performances are right in town. Call or e-mail for exact dates, times, places, and tickets.

Emmanuel Music at Emmanuel Church

15 Newbury Street
(617) 536–3356
www.emmanuelmusic.org

Each Sunday at 10:00 a.m., Emmanuel Music, an orchestra and choir started three decades ago by New England Conservatory students, offers a free Bach cantata immediately after the church service. The cantata lasts about twenty to thirty minutes. What's a cantata? An atmospheric, fugue-like musical piece with interspersed series of solos, duets, and group sections. That's what. Very moving stuff.

King's Chapel

64 Beacon Street
(617) 227–2155
www.kings-chapel.org

The Catch Suggested donation of $3.00. But you don't have to. Really.

This Beacon Street Unitarian Universalist (UU) chapel offers free recitals on Tuesday at 12:15 p.m. They run about thirty to forty minutes and feature all types of music—jazz, folk, classical, world music. Not a die-hard Christian? Worry not: Unitarian Universalism is among the most diversity-accepting faiths on the planet.

MIT Chapel

84 Massachusetts Avenue
Cambridge
(617) 253–2826
www.mit.edu/mta/www/music/events.html

There are free noontime performances each Thursday in this hauntingly beautiful chapel designed by world-renowned architect Eero Saarinen. The music is mostly classical or baroque.

Newton Free Library
330 Homer Street
Newton
(617) 796–1360
www.newtonfreelibrary.net

Now this is an amazing find. At Newton's library, every single Sunday-afternoon concert is free and open to the public, and there are some tasty licks indeed being served up: jazz, folk, handbell ringers, classical pianists. You'd pay big bucks to hear any of these performers out in the field, yet here it's free; all you need to do is show up before they fill up. The classical concerts are typically at 2:00 p.m., but check the Web site for times of special events. Oh, and mute that cell phone. Please.

Old South Meeting House
310 Washington Street
(617) 482–6439
www.oldsouthmeetinghouse.org

In addition to a good slate of lectures and other cultural offerings, some musical events offered at this historic church are free or cheap (figure $5.00 per person). Check the Web site for full information. Musical styles vary from classical violin to acoustic guitar with Latin rhythms. Very global, very eclectic.

Rutman's Violin Shop
11 Westland Avenue
(617) 578–0066
www.rutmansviolins.com

The Catch Donations accepted. Make one.

Russian emigree Ilya Rutman's store, which specializes in string instruments, doubles as an impromptu performance space; do these folks love music or what? In its tiny recital area, which holds up to fifty people, you can see the classical stars of tomorrow today. Performers are often students from Berklee or the New England Conservatory. The easiest way to find out what's coming up is to check the Web site, which is updated regularly, rather than calling. Only call if you want to perform. Ilya? Take a bow! (Get it? Never mind . . .)

PUBLIC **CONCERTS** AND **FESTIVALS**

Walking through Boston in summertime sometimes seems a little like walking through a concert hall; there's music almost everywhere—downtown, along the river, tucked into plazas, sometimes even inside a subway or bus station at the peak of rush hour. Most public concert series begin in mid-June, when the weather finally turns consistently warm, but Boston's outdoor music lovers know that no matter what the weather is doing when you leave your house, you always pack backup rain gear anyway. These public concerts are enormously popular in Boston—especially the ones that take place on the Esplanade—so go early, bring a folding chair and something to chow on or sip, and enjoy all these gloriously free tunes! This is one of the facts of Hub life (along with the Red Sox's World Series victories) of which locals are secretly proudest.

Cambridge River Festival

Memorial Drive
Cambridge
(617) 349–4380
www.cambridgeartscouncil.org/community_river.html
Second or third Saturday in June, noon to 6:00 p.m.

A revered annual event in Boston, the River Festival occurs along a mile-long stretch of Memorial Drive between JFK Street and Western Avenue that is closed down especially for the party (be prepared for traffic snarls). It features music from around the globe, arts, crafts, and food, all by the side of the Charles River. The festival is organized by the Cambridge Arts Council.

Fourth of July Celebration

The Hatch Memorial Band Shell
Charles River Esplanade (access by Fiedler Footbridge off Mugar Way at Beacon and Arlington Streets)
www.july4th.org
Concert at 8:30 p.m. on both July 3 and July 4

This is the big daddy of outdoor concerts, the one that attracts over a million people who line both sides of the river just to be near the annual Fourth of July concert by the Boston Pops Orchestra, the dramatic cannon finale of the "1812 Overture," and, of course, the world-class fireworks display. John

Williams would be proud. The concert is broadcast around the world and has come to be known as "America's Fourth of July Celebration"; the event caps off a week-long series of happenings throughout the city. (If you don't like crowds, on the other hand, it's a good week to get out of town.)

Die-hards who want to be as close as possible to the performance by the Pops and their special guests arrive at the Hatch Shell well before 9:00 a.m. to snag one of 8,000 wristbands given out that allow in-and-out access to the Oval, the grassy seating area immediately in front of the Hatch Shell. Once the wristbands are gone—and they usually are by mid-morning—everyone else must find seating outside the Oval. But don't fret: the view of the fireworks from the Oval isn't so great. The best of all worlds is to find a seat *farther down* the Esplanade, where you will have a clear view of the sky directly over the river (where the fireworks explode) as well as the show. Small blankets and low beach chairs are allowed in the Oval, as are coolers, but alcohol is *strictly* prohibited throughout the Esplanade, and yes, security guards do check.

For those who are in it just for the music, the Pops does almost the exact same concert at the Hatch Shell a night earlier (on July 3), also starting at 8:30 p.m. This one, of course, lacks the "1812 Overture," cannons, and fireworks, but is a fine evening of free classical music anyway.

Harborfest
Locations throughout Boston
(617) 227–1528
www.bostonharborfest.com

It's a precursor to the big Fourth of July celebration (see above), and it takes over the city for about a week leading up to July 4 (and sometimes contin-ues until a day or so after the holiday). Harborfest takes place all along the Boston Harbor waterfront, from the Charlestown Navy Yard to Castle Island. There are Revolutionary reenactments, tall ship tours, walking tours, and concerts. Many of the events—lectures, walks, short kayak trips—require a fee, but most of the concerts are free. Venues include a stage set up on the plaza in front of Boston's uglyrific City Hall. Consult the Web site for time and location information.

Waterfront Performing Arts Series
Christopher Columbus Park
Atlantic Avenue (North End) and elsewhere
(617) 635–3911
www.cityofboston.gov/arts/default.asp
Tuesday evenings during summer, 6:00 to 8:00 p.m.

This series actually runs year-round, though few realize it; there are a smattering of events in Dorchester and at downtown's Strand Theatre, and a good annual Martin Luther King Day performance at changing venues. But this fest kick into a higher gear in summer, when you can expect nearly once-weekly free evening music by the harborfront. Local performing arts organizations such as the Boston Lyric Opera, Boston Pops Ensemble, ballet troupes, and the White Heat Orchestra are showcased during the popular outdoor concert series.

WBOS Copley Square Concert Series
Copley Square
www.wbos.com
Thursdays at 6:00 p.m., mid-July through mid-August.

I give this one a gold star, just because it's so improbable. Thanks to local rock station WBOS, some of the cooler alternative and pop artists in the country—folks like Martin Sexton, Fountains of Wayne (love them!), Howie Day, Aimee Mann, and Tracy Bonham—have taken the stage in the middle of Copley Square for this wonderful concert series that draws thousands of alt-rock groupies to the Hub of the Hub. It also seriously gnarls up the local traffic patterns (shocker) around Newbury Street and environs. Save yourself the hassle and take the T (subway) Green Line to the Copley stop; you'll emerge directly across the street from the stage.

WBOS EarthFest
The Hatch Memorial Band Shell
Charles River Esplanade (access by Fiedler Footbridge off Mugar Way at Beacon and Arlington Streets)
(617) 822–9600
www.earthfest.com

EarthFest is a free annual concert that started out to celebrate Earth Day, but since April 22 is usually cold and rainy in Boston, the sponsoring radio station began holding this event in late May instead. I wonder if the Earth even noticed. It starts at about 10:00 a.m. and goes on until 6:00 p.m. The day is filled with popular live music acts (both for kids and adults, on separate stages), food-sampling opportunities, and education. There are more than a hundred booths set up on the Charles River Esplanade for the purpose of educating people about the environment and nonprofit ecological organizations. You'd be surprised who they rope in to perform at this thing: in 2008, the lineup included acts like Cracker, the BoDeans, and the English Beat, most of whom hadn't been heard from since approximately 1986. What, R.E.M. wasn't available? Still, it's completely gratis. Baby boomers, rejoice!

THE **WORLD** IS **YOUR** RADIO: **MORE** FREE **MUSIC**

The proliferation of competitive music schools in the Boston area means that it is a veritable embarrassment of riches for cheap-but-hip music lovers. Local music schools and university music departments regularly host student recitals, and these aren't your garden-variety students—think Itzhak Perlman in his younger days. There are also frequent instructor recitals, as well as workshops offered by visiting musicians. All of the schools listed below hold frequent free performances. Dates and times vary, so check out the Web sites for the latest offerings.

Boston Conservatory
8 The Fenway
(617) 912–9222 (box office)
www.bostonconservatory.edu

The Conservatory offers lots of free performances from students, faculty, and visitors. Senior projects are also free and open to the public.

Boston University

Tsai Performance Center
685 Commonwealth Avenue
(617) 353-8725 (box office)
www.bu.edu/tsai

The Tsai hosts frequent student and school-organized musical performances and competitions (largely classical, it should be added), and most of them are free. If you love classical music, their events calendar should be one of your go-to Web sites on a weekly basis.

Longy School of Music

1 Follen Street
Cambridge
(617) 876-0956
www.longy.edu

Little known even by locals, Longy is right in Harvard Square. Concerts typically take place at the Edward M. Pickman Concert Hall at 27 Garden Street in Cambridge, though they sometimes take place in the Longy recital rooms, also located on Garden Street.

New England Conservatory

Jordan Hall
30 Gainsborough Street
(617) 585-1260
http://concerts.newenglandconservatory.edu

The Conservatory's Jordan Hall is a lovely combination of opulence and intimacy, and it is arguably one of the most beautiful places to hear classical music played by those who have made it their life. Yes, these wonderful events are free.

WFNX Concert Series

City Hall Plaza
Cambridge Street
(781) 595-6200
www.fnxradio.com
Various dates, usually 6:00 to 9:00 p.m.

Love alt rock, new music, and heavy metal? These concerts are just packed with your musical compadres, and things can get mighty lively when the

New Year's without Tears

First Night Boston
36 Bromfield Street, Suite 204
(617) 542–1399
www.firstnight.org

When it comes to city-wide Festivus-type events, First Night Boston takes the cake: it's a universe unto itself. The nation's first coordinated New Year's celebration, Boston's event has grown by leaps and bounds since it started out in 1976. Most Bostonians wouldn't miss it today, thanks to the tons of performances and events in the hours leading up to the big bang moment at midnight: children dancing, composers conducting, puppets cavorting, artists being obscure, and so forth.

Yet it's hardly a cheapie's dream: a button to get you into many of the events now costs a stiff $18 per adult. Of course, you are supporting the arts, and that's good. And you could argue that the unlimited nature of the button makes it a cheap deal. Fair enough. But here at *CB Boston*, we're after more of a bang per non-buck. So, in addition to (or instead of) buying the button, consider these options.

Volunteer a little of your precious time to help out with the myriad tasks (planning, setting up music stages, organizing, publicizing, trash pickup . . .) involved in the massive First Night effort. As your reward, you'll get free entry on the Big Night (though you might be busy, you'll also meet some cool folks). To volunteer, call First Night directly at the number listed above.

Fireworks occur not once but twice on New Year's Eve, and obviously they're free, because they're up in the sky. First, at 7:00 p.m. on Boston Common, the mayor of Boston concludes a parade and initiates a twelve-minute (why twelve? who knows?) family fireworks display keyed to families with young 'uns who might be fast asleep by the midnight hour.

Then, at the actual turning of the calendar (midnight), another set of fireworks—this one packed by professional Italian guys, the best in the world—blasts off over Boston Harbor. Cool! Total price for the dual displays? Nada.

Boston Common becomes a field of **outdoor sculptures** (some of them in ice!) and art installations in the days leading up to December 31. Yet you don't need a button—and you don't need to brave thousands of semi-inebriated revelers—to see this art if you don't wait until the last moment. Check areas of the Common like the Frog Pond, the Visitor's Center, and the Soldiers and Sailors Monument. Or simply stroll around.

Finally, if you do break down and **buy a button,** fear not: that money isn't thrown away at the stroke of the new year. Not at all. In fact, the button *keeps* working as a cheapie's stealth discount card through the winter, scoring you anything from discounted (by as much as 50 percent) tix to string ensemble performances around town to $2.00 off at the Gardner museum, $10.00 off certain haircuts, half-price New Year's Eve parking in certain garages, and free cookies (with purchase of a coffee) at the Seaport Hotel's bakery. Use it or lose it, baby—that's what we say.

speakers get turned up to 11. Each show features several bands. WFNX's largest free show is the Disorientation Tour—a welcome-back concert for students in September. The event kicks off in the early afternoon and is filled with music and booths—an alternative festival. Check the Web site for updates on artists and times.

WODS Concert Series

The Hatch Memorial Band Shell
(617) 787–7000
www.oldies1033.com
Mid-June through mid-September. June shows Saturday 7:00 p.m.; July through September shows, usually Wednesday 7:00 p.m.

Each year for the past two decades, Oldies 103.3 has held their free summer concerts at the Hatch Shell. There are typically five concerts per summer, and they feature the "oldies but goodies" of the '50s and '60s. Past shows have featured Gloria Gaynor, Frankie Valli, and KC and the Sunshine Band. Station officials and (compact?) disc jockeys are at the Hatch Shell as early as 2:00 p.m. giving away free goodies, so you can even make a day of it. Bring blankets and lawn chairs. Shows run about two hours. Check the station's Web site for info on dates and performers.

THE PLAY'S
THE (CHEAP) THING:
FREE AND CHEAP THEATER

"If you must have motivation, think of your paycheck on Friday."

—NOEL COWARD'S ADVICE TO ACTORS

Boston's theater scene has exploded in the past few years. Once the province of a few well-known theaters that hosted traveling productions of Broadway favorites, the city is now home to a slew of new, smaller theaters featuring homegrown productions—a trend powered by local elites hungry for more homegrown "cultcha." The city is now packed with brand-new and refurbished historic theater spaces, some ornate and some basic.

Today, there is something out there for everyone who loves theater, especially if you are a Cheap Bastard. That's because much of the best is free. When it's not free, it's available on the cheap. If you are willing to usher during a performance, the universe of free Boston shows grows even larger. Ushering is a great way to sample all the diversity (and, sometimes, perversity) in Boston's vibrant, eclectic, and active theater scene.

IT'S **SHOWTIME!** UM, **WHEN,** AGAIN?

The best way to figure out what shows are heading your way is to consult one of the many Web sites devoted to Boston theater. Among the most comprehensive is from **Stage Source** (www.stagesource.org), operated by the Boston Theatre Alliance, which maintains a quarterly listing of every performance going on in the area. It tells you the hottest coming attractions and their performance dates, too, so you can get your name on that volunteer list in advance. Other good resources for keeping yourself in the know are **Theatre Mania** (www.theatremania.com/boston), Boston Theatre Scene (www.bostontheatrescene.com), and the Web sites of the daily newspaper the **Boston Globe** (www.boston.com), and the hip weekly the *Boston Phoenix* (www.thephoenix.com).

VOLUNTEER **USHERING**

Can you walk and chew gum at the same time? If so, you're already halfway to a lucrative part-time career as a volunteer theater usher. Most of the theaters and performance troupes in Boston are actively seeking people to help out in a variety of ways, and, in exchange, they're willing to let you stick around and see the show for free.

Note that some of the most well-known spaces in town, such as the Wang Theatre, Wilbur Theatre, Colonial Theatre, and Opera House, use unionized ushers (who knew?) and do not accept volunteer help. However, most of the rest of the city's stages welcome volunteer ushers with open arms. The job couldn't be much easier, given the perks: After helping paying ticket holders (those poor suckers) to their seats, the ushers are often allowed to fill whatever seats are left empty once the doors are closed, lights fall, and the curtain rises. If no extra seats are available, many theaters will make folding chairs available. In rare instances, ushers do have to stand during a performance. But that's a small price to pay to watch award-winning thespians do their thing, right?

The dress code varies by venue from formal to casual. Ushers are usually required to show up about an hour before the show to learn the seating plan, get familiar with the layout of the theater, and get other basic information so that they can answer theatergoers' questions—and then it's go time. Some theaters also ask that volunteers participate in some light cleanup after the show (darn!), so don't make any early dinner plans. And it's bad form to simply skip out on this simple chore. Cheap doesn't mean immoral.

There's a very active ushering subculture in the city of Boston, so if you're interested in joining this crowd, make your interest known well in advance. Ushering slots usually fill up quickly, especially for the most popular shows (like musicals). Most theaters that use ushers have a hotline, or an e-mail address, and will let you reserve a preferred date and performance up to three weeks in advance if it's available for ushering. Some will even allow you to book entire parties of ushers for a particular night, a terrific way for a gang of friends to go to a show for a grand total of . . . nada. And that's right in your price range, isn't it?

If the show or company you're interested in isn't listed here, try giving them a call anyway (most administrative offices open at or after 10:00 a.m.).

Theaters are constantly changing their policies, so you never know when they might start using volunteer ushers. There might also be other volunteer opportunities (such as administrative or marketing positions) that could also net you free seats for shows.

Above all, don't be the least bit shy about asking!

Actors Shakespeare Project

191 Highland Avenue, Suite 2E
Somerville
(617) 547–1982 (house manager)
www.actorsshakespeareproject.org
ushers@actorsshakespeareproject.org

The Catch Ushers per performance: 3–4

This Shakespearean troupe performs in a variety of spaces throughout the city (mostly in Cambridge), winning awards and accolades from far and wide, including kudos from such unlikely observers as *New York* magazine (which cited actor Alvin Epstein's performance as King Lear as "The Best Performance New York Missed" in 2005). If you don't want to miss it, too, make sure to call or e-mail the house manager at least a month in advance. The house manager keeps a database of ushers that they've used in the past, and contacts them several weeks before a new performance starts to see who is interested. That's a list you want to be on.

American Repertory Theatre

Loeb Drama Center
64 Brattle Street
Cambridge
(617) 496–2000, extension 8817 (volunteer usher hotline)
www.amrep.org

The Catch Ushers per performance: 2–4

The grande dame of local theater, the ART has been offering award-winning plays in Cambridge since 1979. Founding director Robert Brustein and creative director Robert Woodruff have earned the ART a reputation as "one of the best three theater companies in the country," according to a review in *Time*. Classic theater and cutting-edge premieres are the name of the game here, and there's a long list of regular ushers who make it a point to get in early for upcoming shows—in other words, don't dawdle if you want to see the ART for free. Ushers don't even need to seat people at this venue; they merely hand out programs, take tickets, greet guests, and answer questions.

Call the volunteer usher hotline two weeks before a show opening to reserve your spot; leave a message on the machine, and wait for them to (hopefully) call you back. Make sure to leave open two potential dates that you can usher. The house manager checks the hotline on Monday mornings.

Another Country Productions

P.O. Box 560192 (administrative offices)
West Medford, MA 02156
(617) 939–4846
www.anothercountry.org

The Catch Ushers per performance: 1–4

Another Country Productions, which is in residence at the Devanaughn Theatre (see listing below), is a fringe theater favorite in Boston. Creators of SLAMBoston, a monthly, high-octane, short-play competition, ACP features regular productions that deal with diversity, inclusion, and gender issues. Contact the company's artistic director, Lyralen Kaye, to volunteer for an usher spot. ACP prefers to hear from volunteers up to a month before a scheduled show, but Kaye encourages people to call at any time, as usher vacancies sometimes crop up at the last minute.

Blue Man Group

Charles Playhouse
74 Warrenton Street
(617) 426–6912
www.blueman.com

The Catch Ushers per performance: 12

They're wacky, they're rhythmic, they're blue. This show, which defies description, has been packing the Charles Playhouse with delighted, slightly confused audiences for nearly twenty years. Although the theater uses a lot of ushers, make sure to call well in advance, as some shows (weekends, holidays) book up fast. Ushers must wear all black, but there are also some special considerations: Don't wear anything that you don't mind getting drenched with paint and other drippy stuff. Open-toed shoes are also verboten. Arrive an hour before showtime to get a briefing on the seating situation, usher for about half an hour, then enjoy the show—and keep your head down! Volunteers have to stay behind to help the house staff clean for about twenty minutes after the show, as well.

Boston Theatre Works

325 Columbus Avenue, Suite 11 (administrative offices)
www.bostontheatreworks.com
volunteer@bostontheatreworks.com

The Catch Ushers per performance: 2

The Boston Theatre Works has become a vibrant, important, and acclaimed player on the local theater scene. With shows like *Pulp,* a musical that explores the world of 1950s lesbian pulp fiction, to *Take Me Out,* about a baseball player's coming out, the BTW pushes the theatrical envelope while also embracing classics such as *Othello* (which it staged in cooperation with the lauded Shakespeare & Company of Lenox, Massachusetts). But BTW doesn't just act—it makes you think, with after-show discussions and Q&A sessions with actors. Once a year, the BTW also stages BTW Unbound, a festival of new plays featuring local writers. Ushers should contact the theater two to four weeks in advance by e-mailing the volunteer coordinator.

Note: This theatre company was on hiatus at press time. Call ahead to check on the status.

Cambridge Multicultural Arts Center

41 Second Street
Cambridge
(617) 577–1400
www.cmacusa.org

The Catch Ushers per performance: varies

Theater and dance troupes, jazz musicians, and comedians perform regularly at this renovated former courthouse. The building also houses an art gallery with a rotating schedule of exhibits. The performance space manager books ushers for about half the shows that take place here. Check the Web site for the current performance schedule.

Company One

539 Tremont St.
(617) 292–7110
www.companyone.org

The Catch Ushers per performance: 2

Company One bills itself as a "diverse fringe theatre for young diverse urban audiences." Launched in 1998 as a creative project by five friends, the company now regularly performs in the Boston Center for the Arts performance spaces—that's the big time here in Boston. The group polished its fringe cred when it started the Boston Fringe Festival, which brings together smaller theater companies to perform short, one-act plays that push the limits of human experience in works both familiar and original. Ushers should contact the house manager directly at the company's main number.

Devanaughn Theatre and Theatre Company
The Piano Factory
791 Tremont Street
(617) 247–9777
www.devtheatre.com

The Catch Ushers per performance: 2

The Devanaughn is home to its own fringe theater group (called the Devanaughn Theatre Company), which has tackled everything from Chekhov to Pinter and focuses its productions on works that dig down deep into the human psyche and look hard at whatever one finds there. Call the main number and leave your contact information for the executive director two weeks in advance to reserve an usher spot. Other theater companies also use the Devanaughn stage, and they generally arrange for their own ushers.

The Footlight Club
Eliot Hall
7A Eliot Street
Jamaica Plain
(617) 524–6506
www.footlight.org

The Catch Ushers per performance: 4 or more

The Footlight Club has been performing in Eliot Hall for almost 125 years, making it the oldest community theater in America. (The hall is listed in the National Register of Historic Places.) The company welcomes ushers for its five or so shows a year, which include productions of Broadway hits and at least two musicals. Visit the club's Web site and e-mail your interest in ushering at least two weeks in advance of the show you want to see. Ushers are asked to stay after the show to help with some light cleanup.

The Gold Dust Orphans

The Theater Machine (aka the Ramrod Center for the Performing Arts)
1256 Boylston Street
(617) 266–8511

The Catch Ushers per performance: 2

This all-male comedy drag troupe, fronted by writer/performer Ryan Landry, creates some of the funniest and most irreverent interpretations of the Great Canon of American Theater that you're likely to find in town, such as their critically acclaimed production of *Death of a Saleslady*. Landry and his posse perform in a small theater downstairs from a gay bar, the Ramrod, ensuring an entertaining and provocative night. Call at least two weeks before the show for which you want to usher; opportunities go fast, so call sooner rather than later.

The Huntington Theatre Company/ Boston University Theatre

264 Huntington Avenue
(617) 273–1666 (house manager)
www.huntingtontheatre.org

The Catch Ushers per performance: 8–10

The Huntington Theatre Company has received multiple Tony Award nominations for productions staged here and transferred to Broadway, and a half-dozen Elliot Norton Awards for Outstanding Production. As one of the premier theater companies in the country, the Huntington has produced over fifty American and world premieres by big guns like Tom Stoppard, as well as reinventing productions of works by Shakespeare, Molière, Cole Porter, and Steven Sondheim. Needless to say, it's one of the most coveted volunteer usher opportunities in the city. Call early. Call often. Phone the house manager's line for volunteer details.

Jewish Theatre of New England

333 Nahanton Street
Newton
(617) 558–6580 (main office)
www.lsjcc.org

The Catch Ushers per performance: 6–8

This local theater space hosts four to six shows by visiting performers each year, including musicals, drama, cabaret, comedy, and dance. Most feature a Jewish theme or Jewish performers. Past events have included monologist Rain Pryor, comedian Judy Gold, and the Klezmer Conservatory Band. Volunteers are asked to call the main office number to make usher reservations.

The Longwood Players
Cambridge Family YMCA Theatre
820 Massachusetts Avenue (Central Square)
Cambridge
(617) 566–3513 (Longwood Players house manager)
www.longwoodplayers.org
info@longwoodplayers.org

The Catch Ushers per performance: 2–4

The Longwood Players bring the biggest musical hits to Cambridge, including *La Cage aux Folles, West Side Story,* and *Singing in the Rain.* Call or e-mail no more than one month before a performance to reserve your ushering spot.

The Lyric Stage Company of Boston
140 Clarendon Street (2nd floor)
(617) 585–5675 (box office)
www.lyricstage.com

The Catch Ushers per performance: 4

The Lyric Stage performance company puts on seven shows a season, including musicals and at least one play written by a Bostonian. The Lyric has routinely garnered the top awards from the Boston Theatre Critics Association and the Independent Reviewers of New England for its productions of such eclectic plays as *The Underpants,* by comedian Steve Martin, and *Sunday in the Park with George.*

Ushers will greet, seat, and help patrons negotiate their way across the stage during intermission—a logistical necessity at this intimate performance space. Call the main box office number between noon and 5:00 p.m., and they'll put you on the list.

The Metro Stage Company

Cambridge Family YMCA Theatre
820 Massachusetts Avenue (Central Square)
(617) 524–5013 (administrative offices)
www.metrostagecompany.com/volunteer.html

The Catch Ushers per performance: 2–4

This newish theater company is looking for volunteers for all of its performances, which have included *Godspell* and *Nunsense*. It is also willing to accommodate groups of friends or family members who want to usher together, as space allows. Call the administrative offices to reserve an ushering spot, or complete the online form on the Web site.

The New Repertory Theatre

The Arsenal Center for the Arts
321 Arsenal Street
Watertown
(617) 923–8487 x101
www.newrep.org

The Catch Ushers per performance: 9

The New Rep, now in its second decade, has received numerous awards for its productions of locally written plays as well as the classics. It is the resident theater company at the newly built Arsenal Center for the Arts in Watertown, just west of Boston. Its first season included productions of *Romeo and Juliet, True West,* and *Ragtime.* The company needs a good supply of ushers, and you can reserve your spot as soon as the lineup for the new season is announced, usually in early March. (The season starts in September.) The best way to reserve is via e-mail. Couples or groups that want to usher together are very welcome. Public transportation is available to the Arsenal Square area from downtown Boston.

The Nora Theatre Company

c/o Central Square Theater
450 Massachusetts Avenue
Cambridge
(617) 576–9278 (house manager)
www.thenora.org
cph@centralsquaretheater.org

The Catch Ushers per performance: varies

The Nora Theatre Company created its own theater in Central Square and uses ushers for some, but not all, of its performances; call or e-mail several weeks before a show opens to determine if there's a need or not. Try to usher on a Wednesday when the company hosts its free post-performance wine tastings. Post-play discussions take place after Thursday shows. You're not required to stay for either, but it's a nice way to end your theatrical evening.

Queer Soup Theatre

(617) 824-4297
www.queersoup.net
queersoup@gmail.com

The Catch Ushers per performance: 1–2

This fringe theater company performs locally written plays, mostly comedy, about gay, lesbian, bisexual, and transgender issues. It has made a name for itself as a creative, edgy, extremely funny company that performs at the Black Box Theatre at the Boston Center for the Arts, the Boston Playwrights' Theatre, and other spaces throughout the city. To reserve an ushering spot, contact the company via e-mail.

The Regent Theatre

7 Medford Street
Arlington
(781) 643-4488
www.regenttheatre.com

The Catch Ushers per performance: 4

This ninety-year-old theater space was built as an E. M. Loew's vaudeville house, so it has showbiz in its very bones. The newly formed CORE Stage Company, which specializes in musicals like The Who's *Tommy,* took up residence here last year.

The Regent also hosts musical and traveling company performances. In 2004 the Regent made local headlines with the performance of *Sin: A Cardinal Deposed,* a play about the sexual abuse lawsuits against the Archdiocese of Boston, performed by the Bailiwick Repertory of Chicago. In a real rarity for these parts, the Regent has free parking across the street. Ushers should call between noon and 5:00 p.m. during the week to reserve a spot. Join the e-mail list for a monthly newsletter of upcoming events and bargain ticket opportunities.

Roxbury Center for the Arts at Hibernian Hall
184 Dudley Street
Roxbury
(617) 849–6324 (performance space manager)
www.rcahh.org

The Catch *Ushers per performance: varies*

The refurbished Hibernian Hall is home to the Roxbury Center for the Arts, which hosts several small local theater companies that specialize in African-American–themed performances. The space manager at the RCA coordinates some, but not all, of the usher opportunities at the Hibernian, so call ahead to find out which shows they're booking ushers for. If they're not booking ushers for a particular show you want to see, the RCA's manager is happy to direct you to the correct volunteer contact person at the theater company staging the performance.

Stuart Street Playhouse
200 Stuart Street
(617) 426–4499, extension 13
www.stuartstreetplayhouse.com/usher.html
info@stuartstreetplayhouse.com

The Catch *Ushers per performance: varies*

Housed in the Radisson Hotel on Stuart Street, the Stuart Street Playhouse and company have distinguished themselves in the past ten years by performing and hosting an eclectic selection of off-Broadway hits (such as *Stomp* and *Forever Plaid*), provocative social commentary (like the long-running *I Love You, You're Perfect, Now Change* and *Menopause, the Musical*), and standards (*Jacques Brel Is Alive and Well and Living in Paris*). They need ushers for every show (get there an hour early, and dress nicely), but check ahead to make they don't already have enough on hand. Call the house manager or e-mail your ushering desires.

Súgán Theatre Company
75 Garfield Street (administrative offices)
Cambridge
(617) 497–5134
www.sugan.org
peter@sugan.org

The Catch *Ushers per performance: 1*

Introducing Boston audiences to Celtic- and Irish-themed theater, as well as Irish and Celtic writers, directors, and actors, is the mission of the Súgán Theatre Company. Considered one of the best local theater companies in the city, the Súgán has earned rave reviews for its productions of *Tom Crean—Antarctic Explorer, Talking to Terrorists,* and *Women on the Verge of HRT.* Ushers are encouraged to sign up one to two weeks before the show is scheduled to begin. To reserve a spot, e-mail the company's managing director, Peter O'Reilly.

The Theatre Offensive
29 Elm Street #2
Cambridge
(617) 661–1600
www.thetheateroffensive.org
joinus@thetheateroffensive.org

The Catch Ushers per performance: 2–4

They're here, they're queer, and they're on the offensive. The Theater Offensive, a resident company at the Boston Center for the Arts, has been celebrating gay, lesbian, bisexual, and transgender culture and politics for over fifteen years, gathering an impressive lineup of local theater awards along the way. It also produces the OUT ON THE EDGE Festival of Queer Theatre, Plays at Work, new works by queer and local artists, True Colors Out Youth Theater, and A Street Theater Named Desire. Ushers should contact the company's office phone number or e-mail them.

Turtle Lane Players
283 Melrose Street
Newton
(617) 244–0169
www.turtlelane.org

The Catch Ushers per performance: up to 3

The Turtle Lane Players do one thing and do it well: musicals. This small local theater troupe has previously performed everything from Gilbert and Sullivan's works to *The Full Monty.* They love volunteer ushers (weekday shows start at 8:00 p.m., Sunday shows at 2:00 p.m.) To reserve a spot, call the box office between 11:00 a.m. and 5:30 p.m. on weekdays. Ushers will be asked to help clean up after the show.

Up You Mighty Race Performing Arts Company

8 Pleasanton Street (administrative offices)
Dorchester
(617) 427–9417

The Catch Ushers per performance: 2–4

This company, which derives its name from a quote from civil rights leader Marcus Garvey, focuses on black classic theater. The company was founded by Akiba Abaka, a local woman who was discouraged by the lack of outlets for black-themed theater in the Boston area. The company has staged performances of August Wilson's work, as well as Joe Turner's *Come and Gone, Raisin,* and other classic plays written by renowned black playwrights. The company also does pro bono and reduced-price performances. Contact Abaka directly at the main office number at least three weeks in advance to reserve an usher spot.

Wheelock Family Theatre

180 The Riverway
(617) 879–2000 (main number)
(617) 879–2147 (volunteer usher coordinator)
www.wheelock.edu/wft

The Catch Ushers per performance: 4–8

The WFT has won just about every award that a family-themed theater company can win, with its lively productions of *Tuck Everlasting, Alice in Wonderland,* and *Pippi Longstocking*. The company also produces at least one musical and one adult drama during the season. Ushers' dress code is casual. Call the volunteer usher coordinator directly to make a reservation.

Zeitgeist Stage Company

116 West Newton Street (administrative offices)
(617) 759–8836
www.zeitgeiststage.com
zeitgeiststage@aol.com

The Catch Ushers per performance: 1–2

The Zeitgeist Stage Company has been electrifying Boston audiences since 2002 with plays that explore controversial subjects like racism, mental health, and war. The company is in residence at the Boston Center for the Arts, where it performs mainly in the complex's Black Box Theatre. Ushers should e-mail the artistic director to reserve a spot two to three weeks in advance of the desired production. The earlier the better—ushering opportunities here are one of the hottest tickets in town.

SCORING **CHEAP** TICKETS: **MORE** TIPS 'N TRICKS

Free is da bomb, but cheap is good, too. If ushering isn't your bag, there are still plenty of ways to see theater in Boston—including the most popular productions—at a reduced price.

Bostix Ticket Booths

www.artsboston.org

The Catch Tickets available at booths are cash-only.

Copley Square window (corner of Boylston and Dartmouth Streets)
Hours: Monday through Saturday, 10:00 a.m. to 6:00 p.m.; Sunday, 11:00 a.m. to 4:00 p.m.; closed Patriots Day, Thanksgiving, and Christmas.

Faneuil Hall Marketplace (Congress Street) window
Hours: Tuesday through Saturday, 10:00 a.m. to 6:00 p.m.; Sunday, 11:00 a.m. to 4:00 p.m.; closed Monday, Thanksgiving, and Christmas.

Bostix, operated by ArtsBoston, is the best way to score half-price, same-day tickets to some of the city's most coveted shows. You must show up in person on the day of the show to take advantage of the half-price deal. Lines can be long, so bring a cup of coffee, something to read, and a fistful of dollars. If you hate lines, check out the Bostix Web site at www.bostix.org, where you can buy half-price advance (but not day-of-performance) tickets for future shows. Sign up on the Web site for an e-mail newsletter to receive a sneak peek at the next day's bargain theater opportunities before anyone else.

Stage Source

88 Tremont Street, Suite 714
(617) 720–6066
www.stagesource.org

The Catch Membership in the Circle of Friends costs $50 per person.

Although it was created to band together and service the local theater community—performers, artists, and theaters—Stage Source has become the theater lover's best friend, too. By joining its Circle of Friends program, you receive a special membership card that will get you two-for-one ticket deals for over fifty different theater companies in the metro-Boston area. It's even tax deductible! Stage Source also maintains a list of all theater performances in Boston, and members get a heads-up on free or reduced-price performances throughout the year.

Wheelock Family Theatre

180 The Riverway
(617) 879–2000 (main number)
www.wheelock.edu/wft

Because it's a family-oriented theater company and understands that taking the entire brood out for a night of theater can put a strain on the ol' wallet, Wheelock Family Theatre has a policy of never turning away anyone because of inability to pay. Cool. Translation? They won't ask for any proof, but this offer should really only be used by those who really need it. The theater also offers half-price deals for members of many local organizations (and employees of certain local companies), so call ahead if you fall into one of those categories to find out whether you qualify for a deal.

ALWAYS **FREE**

Commonwealth Shakespeare Company
Boston Common
270 Tremont Street (administrative offices)
(617) 532–1252
www.commshakes.org

It has become an annual ritual as beloved as the Fourth of July—free Shakespeare on Boston Common. For three glorious weeks each July into August, the Commonwealth Shakespeare Company performs one of the Bard's classics for all to enjoy. The performances draw thousands to the grass of the Common (on the Charles Street side), and the entire park becomes a glorious al fresco theater for three hours.

If you plan to attend, though, come early. Shows start promptly at 8:00 p.m. on Tuesday through Saturday and at 7:00 p.m. on Sunday (on Monday they rest); by late afternoon, the most devoted fans are already staking their claims at the front of the stage. Bring a low chair or a blanket (chair rentals are available), picnic supper, and non-alcoholic beverages (booze is forbidden), then bask in the glory of great free theater.

If free isn't good enough for you, O Cheap One, then volunteer to help the CSC put on their mammoth productions and you'll get special VIP seating at one performance for yourself and a guest. For more information about volunteering, e-mail the group.

FREE (AND FREE-FORM) DANCE

"Your love for yourself is only shown when you are dancing freely."

—ANONYMOUS

Whether it's to keep warm during the cold winter months, or to pay homage to the blessed arrival of spring and summer, Bostonians are always dancing. There's an enormous culture of dance in the city, with dozens of tiny dance companies holding free performances at venues great and small, and free dance festivals scheduled throughout the year. Clubs and impromptu participatory dance events are easy to find, and their motto is always the same— the more the merrier. For those who picture themselves as the next Nureyev, dance education at many of the studios and schools in the area is also free for the asking for those willing to put in some hours in trade. So strap on your dancing shoes and enjoy all this great dance city has to offer.

FREE **AND** CHEAP
DANCE PERFORMANCES

Big Moves Boston
(617) 869–2970
www.bigmoves.org/boston.html

The Catch Volunteers, especially those willing to put up show flyers, can see shows for free.

This irreverent organization welcomes people of all sizes for classes in most forms of dance and movement. Big Moves also fields a dance troupe of fifteen dancers who perform hip-hop, modern, jazz, and ballet at spaces around town . . . plus some almost bawdy shows, too. Big Moves does not have a home studio, but a schedule of classes and shows, with locations, is available on its Web site or by emailing the address listed above. Send e-mail to the same address to volunteer.

BoSoma Dance Company

50 North Beacon Street (administrative offices)
Brighton
(978) 500–3057
www.bosoma.org

The Catch Ushers and volunteers can see the shows for free.

BoSoma has made a name for itself with its modern, highly athletic form of dance that blends classical ballet, Indian, West African, and jazz to push the limits of the human body. Its shows are always a popular ticket in town, and the company uses volunteer ushers when it performs at such prestigious venues as the Tsai Performance Center at Boston University.

Volunteers are also needed to help with marketing and publicity and to get the word out to the community about this innovative troupe. Contact the company through its Web site to find out more about ushering or volunteer opportunities.

The Boston Conservatory

31 Hemenway Street (main stage theater)
(617) 536–6340
www.bostonconservatory.edu

Founded in 1867, this preeminent fine arts school hosts several free full-length student performances each year—two in the spring and several more in the fall. Check the Web site for dates and times.

Cambridge Dance Month

Venues throughout Cambridge
(617) 547–9363, extension 15
www.dancemonth.com

The Catch Although some events are free, volunteers attend every event for free. Call in early February to sign up.

The mayor of Cambridge and the Dance Complex, a local teaching and performance studio that promotes dance throughout the area, host this month-long celebration of movement every May. The events kick off at a special ceremony on the first Saturday of May, when the mayor declares it Dance Month. Dance events include free classes, performances, and studio open houses. The most compelling part of Dance Month is "Dance Distractions," which event organizers call "outbreaks of movement in an unusual or choreographically underused location, a spontaneous frolic evoking a joyous response." Such locations have included bank lobbies, city council meetings, and major intersections during red lights. Most Dance Month events are free or suggest a small donation. The rest vary, mostly between $5.00 and $20.00. The annual Dance Month calendar is posted at the beginning of April.

Charles River Dance Festival
The Dance Complex
536 Massachusetts Avenue
Cambridge
(978) 239–1135 (volunteer coordinator)

The Catch Call in early February. Volunteer before the event to see the shows for free.

This two-day event has featured many of the best small dance companies in town, like Dance Edge, BoSoma, Amara, Caroline Patterson, and Synergy Dance Company. Tickets are usually around $15.00, but the event's organizers need lots of help before the show to get the festival off the ground. To volunteer, contact organizers directly in February at the number listed above.

Collage Dance Ensemble
16 Braeland Avenue (administrative offices)
Newton Centre
(617) 795–2468
www.collageusa.org

The Catch Ushers and volunteers can see the shows for free.

This acclaimed performance company, which blends folk and contemporary dance, performs at some of the largest theatrical spaces in town, so they're always looking for ushers. They're also eager for help in all aspects of production—everything from running lights and ironing costumes backstage to writing grants and marketing. Not only do ushers and volunteers get to see the shows for free, but volunteers are also allowed to take classes with the dance troupe, a unique treat reserved only for those who are part of the dance company's organization.

Monkeyhouse Dance Company

www.monkeyhouselovesme.org
monkeyhouselovesme@gmail.com
Various times and venues throughout the city.

This innovative, humorous modern dance trio does free performances through-out the city as part of its Princess Pamplemousse Project. The princess is a character that Monkeyhouse founder Karen Krolak invented to help explain dance choreography to audiences. The troupe also presents regular free per-formances for those who want to skip the lesson and get straight to the narrative-driven, sometimes zany dance for which this company is known. And even though its shows are free, you can also volunteer administrative help on Wednesdays.

Prometheus Dance

536 Massachusetts Avenue, Studio 6 (The Dance Complex)
Cambridge
(617) 576–5336
www.prometheusdance.org

The Catch Ushers see the shows for free.

This award-winning and highly acclaimed modern dance ensemble actually consists of two groups: the main troupe and the elders ensemble, composed of fifty-somethings and above who give the youngsters a run for their money. Both troupes do free shows around town from time to time. A listing is avail-able on their Web site. Rehearsals are also open to the public. The main troupe rehearses on Tuesday and Thursday from noon to 2:00 p.m. The elder group's rehearsal times vary, so call ahead for information. The main troupe uses ushers for its paid performances, which have taken place at the Boston Conservatory Theatre and the Dance Complex. Call the house manager at the main number if you want to see the show for free as an usher.

Sayat Nova Dance Company of Boston

Newton
(617) 923–4455
www.sayatnova.com

Armenian folk dance is a swirl of colors and emotions celebrating the ances-tral home of many Bostonians. This award-winning company, which tours the world, does a number of local shows at such prestigious venues as the Emerson Majestic Theatre. Sayat Nova uses ushers frequently for its Boston-area performances. The job requires taking tickets, selling items at the company's concession stand in the front of the house, and seating guests. Volunteers should call about a month before a show to participate. (Volunteers are also needed year-round to get the word out about this company's activities.) And, of course, volunteers and ushers get to see the show for free.

FREE **AND** CHEAP **DANCE** CLASSES **AND** EVENTS

Boston Swing Dance
The St. James Armenian Church
465 Mt. Auburn Street (corner of School Street)
Watertown
(617) 924–6603 (volunteer line)
www.bostonswingdance.com
Usually second Saturday of the month, September through June; lessons at 8:00 p.m.; social dance 9:00 p.m. to midnight.

The Catch Volunteer for one hour at a dance to get in free.

This monthly event is very popular with the Boston swing dance community, thanks to a combination of great live swing bands and a fantastic wood floor. It's about $13 to take part, but you can dance and take lessons for free if you volunteer to sell tickets and drinks for an hour during the night.

Contact the volunteer coordinator, and he'll put you on a list of volunteers. There are a lot of regulars, but eventually your name will be called up and you'll be assigned a one-hour shift. Check the Web site for the full schedule.

Free Swing at Copley Square
Dartmouth Street at St. James Street
www.fiveguysnamedmike.org; www.itsallswing.com
Every other Sunday, June through September, 1:00 to 4:00 p.m.

This free swing dance happening is an impromptu event pulled together by the local swing dance community, spearheaded by five guys from Boston named Mike who love swing dancing. Updates on dates of the events, scheduled deejays, and rain dates are available on their Web site or on www.itsallswing.com, another swing dance Web site for local hoofers.

MIT Folk Dance Club

Massachusetts Institute of Technology Student Center
84 Massachusetts Avenue
Cambridge
(617) 253–3655
http://web.mit.edu/fdc
Second and fourth Tuesday of the month, 8:00 to 10:30 p.m.; Wednesday and
Sunday, 8:00 to 11:00 p.m.

The Catch The suggested donation for non-students is $5.00.

The Folk Dance Club at the Massachusetts Institute of Technology, started
more than forty years ago by students, offers three different types of folk
dances to keep you in touch with the motherland. Dances from around the
world can be found on Sunday night, Israeli dances on Wednesday night,
and America's homegrown contra dances every other Tuesday night. The
dances are usually held in the fourth floor of the MIT student center but are
subject to change, so check the Web site before venturing out. Organizers
say that the donation is "just a suggestion." It helps pay for the cookies and
lemonade that are available at some of the dances. Beginners are welcomed,
and introductory lessons are given at the start of each class.

MIT Lindy Hop Society

Massachusetts Institute of Technology Student Center
84 Massachusetts Avenue (various classrooms) Cambridge
http://web.mit.edu/swing
http://mit-swing.blogspot.com
Wednesday night, 8:30 to 11:30 p.m.

The Catch The dance is free, but they sometimes ask all participants for
donations.

Lindy hop, swing, and sometimes even salsa are the raison d'être of this
student-run dance club. Introductory classes usually start at 7:30 p.m., and
the social dance starts after that. The room location changes from week to
week, and sometimes so does the lesson start time, so check the Web site for
up-to-the-minute scheduling info.

Tango by Moonlight

Weeks Pedestrian Bridge (intersection Memorial Drive and DeWolfe Street)
(617) 699–6246 (tango line)
www.bostontango.com
Full-moon nights from May through September, 7:30 to 11:00 p.m.

Imagine the sight of more than a hundred people, locked in the classic tango embrace, swirling across a historic footbridge over the Charles River in the moonlight. Even if you don't tango, it's a sight worth seeing. This magical dance event, organized by the Tango Society of Boston, has become a blockbuster event that draws people from all over the metro area. A fifteen-minute tango lesson precedes the festivities. The society's Web site (listed above) also lists other, year-round tango club events and lessons in the metro area.

MORE RESOURCES: DANCE ORGANIZATIONS

With all the options, keeping track of what's happening in the dance community in Boston can be a daunting task, but several good Web sites will keep you up to date. Visit these sites for great information on free and low-cost dance events going on all over town.

The Boston Dance Alliance
www.Bostondancealliance.org

This is the premier dance advocacy organization in Boston promoting dance. Here you'll find a list of upcoming performances and links to most of the area's dance organizations, troupes, and performance spaces.

Have to Dance
www.havetodance.com

There's a very comprehensive monthly calendar of all Boston dance events on this Web site, as well as links to dance clubs and studios throughout New England. One-stop shopping for all your dance needs!

West African Dance in Boston (WADaBo)
www.wadabo.com

This organization promotes West African dance and culture in the Boston area and maintains a list of free performances taking place around the city. It's also an online gathering place for teachers of African dance.

DOING THE WORK-STUDY THING

Dance Complex
536 Massachusetts Avenue
Cambridge
(617) 547–9363 (volunteer line: extension 11)
www.dancecomplex.org

The Dance Complex has more than seventy classes a week in all forms of dance in its six studios. It has a formalized work-study program that awards students one class-hour credit or one hour of rehearsal space for each hour worked. There's a four-week training period for work-study participants, for a total of about eight hours, after which the studio asks for a minimum sixteen-week commitment of two to three and a half hours per week. Yes, really. They also ask that you commit to the same time each week and make arrangements to have your shift covered if you can't make it.

There are two main types of volunteer positions available: the front desk and facility maintenance. The front-desk position involves answering phones, taking reservation requests for classes and performances at the Dance Complex, and handling all cash transactions. The facility-maintenance job involves cleaning and maintenance of the building. There is usually a waiting list for both of these positions, but there is turnover, so the sooner you get on the list, the sooner you can start hoofing!

CHEAP LAUGHS:
FREE AND CHEAP COMEDY

*"Always laugh when you can . . .
it is cheap medicine."*

—LORD BYRON

Who knew? Boston's a funny place! The city has spawned more than its fair share of world-class comics: Jay Leno, Conan O'Brien, Denis Leary, Janeane Garofalo, Dane Cook, Paula Poundstone, and Steven Wright all hail from here . . . and they all started by working the comedy clubs in Boston. Sadly for Cheap Bastards, free laughs in this town are hard to find, though. Most clubs charge at least $8.00 to $10.00 for a show (and most of the time, the comics see very little of it . . . ah, such is showbiz). Still, some of the best and most innovative humor in the city can be had for free, sometimes with a catch, sometimes without. Either way, you've got a very good chance of catching a rising star at one of these comedy shops.

COMEDY **CLUBS** AND **NIGHTS**

Comedy MeetUps
http://comedy.meetup.com/cities/us/ma/boston

The Catch Must be eighteen or older to register.

Sometimes, the best laughs come from just hanging around with funny people. If you'd like to connect with some funny people in Boston, then MeetUp is the best way to do it for free. MeetUp.com, a Web site that facilitates in-person gatherings for people with similar interests, has a very active Boston comedy meetup group. Register on their Web site, and then log into one of the many Boston comedy meetups (there's one each for sketch comics, improv comics, and stand-up comics). The group moderator will schedule the meetups off-line, and if you're registered, you'll be in the know. You're not required to say funny things when you meet up with comics, but they're all theoretically Cheap Bastards too, and if you don't hold your own you could get stuck with the tab.

The Green Dragon Tavern

11 Marshall Street (near Faneuil Hall Marketplace)
(617) 367–0055
www.somersirishpubs.com
Monday at 10:00 p.m.

Comedians duke it out in an open-mic format for cash prizes at this historic pub in the heart of the Quincy Market/Faneuil Hall area.

Mystery Lounge at the Comedy Studio

Upstairs at the Hong Kong Restaurant
1236 Massachusetts Avenue
Cambridge
(617) 661–6507
www.mysterylounge.com
Every Tuesday, 7:00 to 8:00 p.m.

The Comedy Studio, just outside Harvard Square, has been called the greatest comedy club in the world. While we can't prove this conclusively (a laugh-o-meter? anyone? dang, we forgot ours at home), we can prove that it's the only place in town to see a live magic cabaret show. The Mystery Lounge, started by local magicians in 1997, takes place in the Comedy Studio on Tuesday nights at 8:00 p.m. and costs $10. But you can get a sneak peek at the magic to come by heading to the second-floor lounge to see one hour of jaw-dropping "close-up" magic—card tricks, pulling things out of people's noses—for absolutely free. There is no drink minimum. And who knows, maybe one of the close-up magicians will pull $10 out of your ear so you can go upstairs and see the stage show, too.

Sally O'Brien's Bar

335 Somerville Avenue (Union Square)
Somerville
(617) 666–3589
www.sallyobriensbar.com
Titters Comedy Club, Monday at 7:30 p.m.

"Hungry comedians will joke for food" is how this night of free comedy (also known as the Cheapshots Comedy Club) is sold to the masses. A roster of local comics compete for a free dinner, and the audience votes on who wins. With a free meal at stake, suffice it to say that some of these guys will never be funnier. And there's never a cover! (But tip the 'tender, dude.) Sweet.

A **COMEDY** FESTIVAL

Boston International Comedy and Movie Festival
119 Braintree Street (administrative offices)
Allston
(617) 782–8100
www.bostoncomedyfestival.com
One week in mid-September.

Although most of the performances and movie screenings surrounding this acclaimed comedy festival, which was launched in 2000, cost money (and the tickets are becoming harder to get every year), the festival plans at least one large, free event to bring comedy to the downtrodden masses. The location and the date vary, so check the Web site for details. The schedule is usually posted by early August.

IMPROV **ON** THE **CHEAP**

So you think you're funny? The smell of the greasepaint, the roar of the crowd, the humiliation of running out of funny things to say—welcome to the dicey world of improv. Improvisational comedy is one of the most popular types of entertainment in this city. The shows pack 'em in night after night, with some improv troupes doing two or more shows, six nights a week. And now you—yes, you—can be part of this phenomenon. In exchange for a few hours of work a week, two local improv groups will make you part of their slightly dysfunctional families. They'll let you watch as much improv as you can stomach, and maybe even teach you the tricks of the trade.

ImprovBoston

1253 Cambridge Street Cambridge
(617) 576–1253
www.improvboston.com
www.improvboston.com/training/scholarship.html (Matt Carey Scholarship)

One of the best improv troupes in the city, ImprovBoston is looking for people to work in the box office for a minimum of three shows per month and do some light office work. Not only will you get a small stipend (that's right, they're paying you), but you will also get an ImprovBoston membership card that will let you see as many shows as you want for free. The troupe performs two to three shows a night (except for Mondays). ImprovBoston also offers an annual scholarship in honor of former member Matt Carey, who tragically died in 2004 at the age of just 23. The scholarship bearing his name covers the cost of workshops and a master class for an undiscovered improv talent in training.

The Tribe

Tribe Theater
67 Stuart Street
(617) 510–4447
www.tribeboston.com
Shows typically begin at 8:00 p.m.

The Catch You must be nineteen or older to attend shows at The Tribe Theater.

This improv and sketch comedy group has an innovative work-study program for people interested in learning improv. You'll need to enroll in the program and work at least eight hours per week (as an usher, member of the stage crew, box office staff, or intern in other departments). In return, you can see an unlimited number of shows for free and even take free improv training classes. The Tribe offers four different levels of training, and you need to log at least twelve hours of work per level. Shows are on Thursday and Friday, with other shows on occasional Saturdays and Sundays.

CELLULOID ZEROES:
MOVIES ON THE CHEAP

"We're so poor, we don't even have a language! Just a stupid accent!"

—MEL BROOKS, *ROBIN HOOD: MEN IN TIGHTS*

You probably don't even remember when a family of four could head to the local drive-in to see the latest Hollywood blockbuster for, like, just five bucks a car! In spite of conventional wisdom that it costs an arm and a leg to see a film in Boston, there are still plenty of ways to see movies for free or dirt cheap.

Take your pick of the cherished classics, latest releases, even those impenetrable foreign films throughout the city of Boston. Most places, especially the outdoor venues, encourage you to bring your own snacks, so you'll spend as much for a big night out as you would have if you'd just stayed home on the couch in front of the tube—again. Films are a lot more enjoyable when you see them on the really big screen, like their makers intended, and even more so when they're free!

ALWAYS-FREE **FILMS**

Boston Public Library
700 Boylston Street (Copley Square)
(617) 536–5400
www.bpl.org/news/UpcomingEvents.htm

You could spend the next month in the Boston Public Library and still find new things to do every day. It hosts a variety of film series throughout the year featuring diverse cinematic offerings. Founded in 1848, the Boston Public Library was the first large free library in the United States, which makes it a hallowed place near and dear to our cheap little hearts. In addition, the following branch libraries have regularly scheduled adult and children's films. Many other branches have randomly scheduled films, so check the main BPL Web site listed above for the latest schedules for each branch.

Charlestown
179 Main Street; (617) 242–1248; children's films on Tuesday at 10:30 a.m.

Dorchester
Lower Mills Branch, 27 Richmond Street; (617) 298–7841; children's films on Friday at 10:30 a.m. (schedule varies; consult Web site for details).

East Boston

276 Meridian Street; (617) 569–0271; children's films on Friday at 10:00 and 11:00 a.m.

Jamaica Plain

Connolly Branch, 433 Centre Street; (617) 522–1960; children's films on Wednesday at 10:30 a.m.

Mattapan

10 Hazelton Street; (617) 298–9218; children's films on Thursday at 10:30 a.m.

North End

25 Parmenter Street; (617) 227–8135; children's films on Monday at 11:00 a.m.; grown-up films Wednesdays in summer and other dates throughout the year.

Roslindale

4238 Washington Street; (617) 323–2343; preschooler films on Monday at 10:30 a.m.

Roxbury

Egleston Square Branch, 2044 Columbus Avenue; (617) 445–4340; preschooler films on Monday at 11:00 a.m.; grown-up films on Thursday at noon.
Parker Hill Branch, 1497 Tremont Street; (617) 427–3820; preschooler films on Friday at 10:30 a.m.

South Boston

646 East Broadway; (617) 268–0180; children's films every other Wednesday at 10:30 a.m. and noon; grown-up films on Thursday at 6:00 p.m.

South End

685 Tremont Street; (617) 536–8241; preschooler films on Monday at 10:30 a.m.

Film Series at the Scandinavian Living Center

Nordic Hall
206 Waltham Street
Newton
(617) 527–6566
www.slcenter.org
First Thursday of each month at 7:30 p.m., September through June.

The Catch These are free, but donations are "gratefully accepted." C'mon. Cough up.

And you thought Scandinavians were all about glögg and saunas? Well, there's also some mighty fine cinema coming out of those chilly little countries, and much of it can be seen for free at the Scandinavian Living Center, an assisted living community.

If you attend one of these monthly free film screenings (held in the library), you will notice that most of the people in the room will not need to read the graciously provided subtitles, which will lend the whole experience some elusive authenticity in a world gone ersatz.

Free Friday Flicks

Hatch Shell (at the Esplanade along the Charles River, next to the Arthur Fiedler Footbridge)
(617) 787–7200 (movie hotline)
www.wbz1030.com
Starts at sunset every Friday, mid-June through August.

The Catch Because of copyright issues, WBZ can't release the name of the film until the Monday before the show.

This free, kid-friendly film series, hosted by local radio station WBZ 1030 AM, has become a Boston institution. Movies begin at sunset. Bring a picnic, a blanket, and the kids. Remember that, as in all public parks in the city, alcoholic beverages are not allowed.

Free Radicals: Film Night Takes a Left Turn

If the man is getting you down, you'll find lots of like-minded company at the **Lucy Parsons Center Radical Movie Night.** Although Parsons, a strident activist, early anarchist, eventual communist, and prolific writer, died in 1942, her spirit lives on at this small, collectively run bookstore devoted to direct citizen action. Every Wednesday, the center screens a film that deals with progressive, activist, or radical issues. Come angry or stay home.

Lucy Parsons Center; 549 Columbus Avenue; (617) 267–6272; www.lucyparsons.org; Every Wednesday night at 7:00 p.m.

Movies by Moonlight
Boston Harbor Hotel
70 Rowes Wharf
(617) 439–7000
www.bhh.com/special_summer.htm
Begins at sunset every Friday, mid-June through August.

What a great freebie! Just as the glow from another spectacular sunset fades over Boston Harbor, the opening credits begin to roll on the huge portable movie screen assembled in front of the lovely Boston Harbor Hotel's outdoor cafe. You can enjoy the movie for free if you sit along the docks on either side of the cafe seating area, which is reserved for people who plan on eating or drinking something off the cafe's menu. Come early and bring a chair—this annual film series is one of the most popular public events in the city. Most movies are classic comedies and dramas geared for an adult audience (the 2008 card included *Planet of the Apes, The Hustler,* and *Harold and Maude*). Check the hotel's Web site for the listing of films.

PRE-SCREENING **HOLLYWOOD** BLOCKBUSTERS? **AHEAD??** FOR **FREE!?**

The powers that be in Hollywood have identified Boston as a prime location to get intelligent feedback before movies go into general release; these marketers' cluelessness about what makes good cinema thus becomes our gain. There are a number of ways to score free tickets to these screenings. In most cases, even though you will be holding a free ticket, seating is on a first-come, first-served basis on screening nights. So make sure to arrive at least one hour prior to movie time to ensure that you and your date will snag seats.

Another tip for movie lovers: If there's a movie coming out that you know you want to see, go to the promotional Web site for that movie (usually the name of the film with a dot-com added at the end, but a simple Web search will usually find the link to the studio's official movie Web site). Many of these studios' sites also offer free advance-screening tickets.

Entertainment Weekly Free Screenings
www.ew.com/ew/freescreening

Brought to you by *Entertainment Weekly,* this site periodically has free tickets to local advance screenings. You'll have to check back frequently, because the site goes dark when a screening is over or all the tickets have been given away.

Free Movie Screenings
www.freemoviescreenings.net

This Web site compiles and lists the Web site links to movie studios' free screening offers. Most of the ticket links allow you to print out the tickets directly. Some tickets require you to enter personal information to qualify to be entered into a free-ticket drawing.

Wild About Movies
www.wildaboutmovies.com/screenings/index.php

This great movie lovers' site has reviews, a critics' forum, and access to free screening tickets. Unlike other sites, it even has a listing of upcoming films for which it will be offering free screening tickets, so you can plan way ahead. You'll have to search out listings for free screenings in the Boston area, but there are plenty of them in there. The site also has links to win free DVDs.

VOLUNTEERING **AT** THE **MOVIES**

The Harvard Film Archive
Carpenter Center
24 Quincy Street
Cambridge
(617) 495–4700
http://hcl.harvard.edu/hfa

What a great resource for film buffs! The Harvard Film Archive, part of Harvard University's Library of Fine Arts, is a rare and precious gem for film lovers. Its archives are among the most exhaustive and well preserved in the country, and it is recognized nationwide as a leader in the study of film. The HFA hosts frequent screenings, forums, and director lectures by groundbreaking talents such as Atom Egoyan, British director Terence Davies, actor-directors John Malkovich and Tommy Lee Jones, and the "Father of African Cinema," Ousmane Sembene. Its bulletin, available online, gives in-depth overviews of screenings and a listing of other upcoming events.

The HFA hosts frequent free events, and when they're not free, screenings are $8.00, and special events are just $10.00. If that's too rich for your blood, the HFA does also use some volunteer ushers. By ushering at screenings one night a week, volunteers get free admission to all HFA screenings. Contact the volunteer coordinator directly to sign up. If you love film, this is the volunteer gig of a lifetime.

Museum of Fine Arts
465 Huntington Avenue
(617) 369–3040 (volunteer line)
www.mfa.org

The Museum of Fine Arts hosts some of the most exciting film series and director lectures in the city every year, including series featuring international women's films, French films, and gay and lesbian films, but they're not cheap. The best way to get in on the action for free is by volunteering to become a movie usher. All volunteer candidates are required to fill out an application (the link is provided above). The museum will send you a list of volunteer opportunities—if their current needs include theater ushers, you're golden. The museum operates with a staff of more than 1,200 volunteers and is looking for a fixed time commitment from those who want to join the ranks.

FREE VERSE:
CHEAP READINGS AND LECTURES

*"No entertainment is so cheap as reading,
nor any pleasure so lasting."*

—MARY WORTLEY, LADY MONTAGU

Boston is a city that lives by the belief that the pen and mouth are mightier than the sword. We like to think we came up with the idea, actually. Our Old South Meeting House was one of the first places where the natural right to free speech was tested—the result was the Boston Tea Party and the Revolutionary War. (You might have heard of those.) So it's no surprise that you can find readings and lectures at venues large and small throughout the metro area, featuring people exercising their precious right to say whatever the heck they want as long as it doesn't incite a riot. As becomes free speech, most of these events are free, although some come with a small price tag. On any given night you can hear some of the most accomplished writers, thinkers, and movers and shakers in the country. Boston has long been known as the Athens of America, and it ain't because we wear togas.

BOOKSTORE **READINGS**

Most bookstores in the Boston area host readings from time to time, but we've weeded through the many to present you with this list of gems, known for both the frequency and quality of their events.

Barnes and Noble, Boston University
660 Beacon Street
(617) 267–8484
www.bu.bkstore.com

This bookstore dominates Kenmore Square, near Fenway Park, and serves the tens of thousands of Boston University students who descend on the area each September. But there are plenty of treats here for non-students, too. The store hosts readings and author discussions in its special reading room, usually at 7:00 p.m., on various dates throughout the year. The volume drops off a bit after May, when the hordes return to wherever it is they're from, but the quality of the events suffers not a whit. Some events are hosted off-site at the Boston University School of Management at 595 Commonwealth Avenue, and for those events, tickets are sometimes required. They can be obtained (they're often free) at the School of Management building after 5:00 p.m. the day of the event.

Brookline Booksmith

279 Harvard Street Brookline
(617) 566–6660
www.brooklinebooksmith.com

Brookline Booksmith, which has been around for over forty years, was one of the first bookstores in the area to make author readings look like celebrity events. The names they draw in are so large that the bookstore often moves the festivities to nearby Coolidge Corner Theatre, where admission is a paltry $2.00 for author events, and that's just to cover the cost of renting the theater.

Harvard Book Store

1256 Massachusetts Avenue Cambridge
(800) 542–READ
www.harvard.com/events

Harvard Book Store was founded in 1932 by Boston native Mark Kramer with $300 he borrowed from his parents. Since then, it has become one of the most well-known and prolific sources of author readings, discussions, and literary events in the city. It hosts events at its store, as well as at locations throughout Cambridge. Some off-location events, such as those at the Brattle Theatre in Harvard Square, cost $3.00. There is something happening at the Harvard Book Store nearly every day of the week, so check the events calendar frequently to see what's new.

The Harvard Coop Author Series

Harvard Coop
1400 Massachusetts Avenue
(617) 499–2000
www.thecoop.com

Students started the Harvard Coop (pronounced co-op, short for Cooperative) back in 1882, and today it's one of the coolest sports in Harvard Square to grab a book or a coffee. Locals often refer to it simply as the "coop"—as in chicken coop. In the beginning it was simply a place to buy school supplies and coal or wood for those cold Cambridge winters. But now it's one of the biggest bookstores in the state and hosts author readings and discussions nearly every day. Reading times and locations vary, so check the Web site for details.

Newtonville Books in the Attic Series

www.newtonvillebooks.com
296 Walnut Street; Newton; (617) 244–6619
107 R Union Street; Newton Centre; (617) 964–6684

The owner of Newtonville Books, Tim Huggins, has taken book readings up a notch. He hosts a bunch of author readings, discussions, and book signings in a special room at his bookstore, predominantly featuring local writers, with a nationally touring writer thrown in from time to time. This is truly a great place for bibliophiles to hang out.

Porter Square Books

Porter Square Shopping Center
25 White Street Cambridge
(617) 491–2220
www.portersquarebooks.com
Readings throughout the week, check Web site for updates.

This independent bookstore and coffee shop prides itself on featuring the works of local writers, and there is an entire section devoted to the works of Boston's own talent. This store is located right at the Porter Square T stop on the Red Line and offers plenty of free parking.

SALONS AND SLAMS

Cantab Lounge

738 Massachusetts Avenue Cambridge
(617) 354–2685
www.slamnews.com/cantab/schedule.html
Poetry slams Wednesday at 8:00 p.m.

The Catch Cost to watch or participate is $3.00, and you must be eighteen or older with valid photo ID.

The Cantab (short for Cantabrigian, which is what you are if you live in Cambridge) hosts a weekly poetry slam, a fast-paced, winner-take-all competition in which members of the audience judge the competing poets on their performed poetry. Poetry Slam International rules are always in effect:

Poems are the poet's original work of three minutes or less, no props, no costumes, no musical accompaniment.

Center for New Words
7 Temple Street Cambridge
(617) 876–5310
www.centerfornewwords.org

This feminist organization is a hotbed of grrrrl power and gives authors and thinkers a forum to showcase their work. Free readings take place throughout the week and include talks with authors and "Feminism & Dessert" (a salon with sweets).

Four Stories
The Enormous Room
567 Massachusetts Avenue (Central Square)
Cambridge
www.fourstories.org

The Catch The series goes on summer hiatus from mid-April to September. *You must be twenty-one or older to get in.*

Started by local writer Tracy Slater in 2005, the Four Stories reading series rapidly became one of the hottest gatherings in the city. Built around the idea of a salon, Four Stories features a happening deejay, a cool club space, hip locals, and readings by four accomplished authors on the first Monday of every month. Each reading has a theme (such as Down and Out in Chestnut Hill, or Light and Dark). Be sure to get there early as you can—they fill to capacity nearly every night they run.

Grub Street, Inc.
160 Boylston Street
(617) 695–0075
www.grubstreet.org

This literary organization is the center of writers' life in the city of Boston. Its membership and faculty reads like a who's who of Boston literary elite. Throughout the year it offers courses, free workshops, seminars, and free readings at venues throughout the city, as well as at its headquarters on Boylston Street. Check out their Web site for a complete listing of upcoming events.

Out of the Blue Art Gallery
106 Prospect Street Cambridge
(617) 354–5287
www.outoftheblueartgallery.com

This art gallery/social gathering place for the alternative crowd is also an active participant in Boston's rich literary landscape. It hosts a variety of evening reading, art, and music events; all either request a donation or charge a flat fee. Open Bark, an open-mic night every Saturday at 8:00 p.m., allows just about any form of expression.

MUSEUM **AND** LIBRARY
READING SERIES

Boston Public Library
700 Boylston Street (Copley Plaza)
(617) 536–5400
www.bpl.org/news/upcomingevents

What better place to go for a free reading than the first free large public library in the country? There are readings, discussions, and lectures nearly every day at the library's main Copley Square location; most are held in the roomy Rabb Lecture Hall. All of the library's neighborhood branches host author events as well. For a complete listing of events at all branches, see the Web site listed above (see Appendix B for a list of addresses and phone numbers for all branches).

The French Library and Cultural Center
53 Marlborough Street
(617) 912–0400
www.frenchlib.org

The Catch You must RSVP for free public events. Many other events are free only to members. Membership costs $70 a year.

Love the French? Bostonians do. The French came to New England to help out in that little clash with the British back in the 1700s, and we never forgot the favor. There are statues of our French heroes all over town. The

French Library, which occupies two historic mansions in the Back Bay, is a cultural and educational institution that seeks to perpetuate the love affair, through parties, readings, and other events, many of which are free to all. Others require a membership. Readings occur on no set schedule, so consult the French Library's Web site for more information.

John F. Kennedy Presidential Library and Museum
Columbia Point
Dorchester
(866) JFK–1960
www.jfklibrary.org

The Catch Attendees must register in advance for all forums. Seating in the main hall is first-come, first-served. Doors open an hour before the forums begin.

It is a sobering yet uplifting sight—the gleaming white John F. Kennedy Presidential Library and Museum, standing by the shore where the Neponset River meets the Atlantic. The museum is not only a fitting tribute to our late president, who was born in Brookline, but also the home of the Kennedy Library Forums, a series of political, historical, and cultural "conversations" that feature some of the most powerful and influential voices in our country. Forum events are free and happen on selected Mondays from 5:30 to 7:00 p.m. Note that you are required to register in advance.

Museum of Afro-American History
14 Beacon Street, Suite 719 (administrative offices)
46 Joy Street (museum galleries)
(617) 725–0022
www.afroammuseum.org/events.htm

The Catch Admission is $3.00. The series takes a break from June through August.

Between 1800 and 1900, the north side of Beacon Hill was home to most of the black population in the city of Boston. From there, they worked to help free their brothers and sisters in the rest of the country in the years before Emancipation. That proud history is captured at the Museum of Afro-American History. Frequent free lectures, readings, and educational gallery tours are available to all comers.

LITERARY **LECTURES**

Blacksmith House
Cambridge Center for Adult Education
56 Brattle Street
Cambridge
(617) 547–6789
www.ccae.org

Some of the best poets and authors from, or coming through, town make a stop to read at the Blacksmith House Poetry Series on Mondays at 8:00 p.m. The readings take place at the historic site of Cambridge's village smithy (also the inspiration for Longfellow's 1839 poem "The Village Blacksmith"). Tickets may be purchased forty-five minutes prior to the reading.

Cambridge Forum
3 Church Street
Cambridge
(617) 495–2727
www.cambridgeforum.org

Cambridge Forum is one of public radio's longest-running public affairs programs. It is recorded live every week in Harvard Square for broadcast by WGBH radio. Dates, locations, and times vary, so check the Web site for more information. Topics run the gamut from Saudi oil reserves to gay marriage. Tapings are free and open to the public.

Ford Hall Forum
716 Columbus Avenue, Suite 565 (administrative offices)
(617) 373–5800
www.fordhallforum.org

The Ford Hall Forum, founded in 1908, claims to be the nation's oldest free lecture series. It schedules a wide variety of lectures and debates in venues around the city, including at the Old South Meeting House, Suffolk University's law campus (near Boston Common), and the Walsh Theatre on Temple Street (which is behind the State House). Previous speakers have included Al Gore, Noam Chomsky, Robert Frost, Henry Kissinger, Martin Luther King Jr., Rosa Parks, Ayn Rand, Robert Reich, Eleanor Roosevelt, Pete Seeger, and Malcolm X— talk about heavy hitters. All the lectures are free and open to the public, and likely always will be. Check the Web site for a calendar of upcoming events.

The Old South Meeting House

310 Washington Street
(617) 482–6439
www.oldsouthmeetinghouse.org

The Catch Many events are free; some require museum admission ($5.00).

Angry about a tax on tea, 5,000 colonials gathered on December 16, 1773, at the Old South Meeting House to devise a way to make sure their displeasure was duly noted by King George. Someone suggested tossing all that tea into the ocean, people seemed to like the idea, and the rest is history. Ever since, the Meeting House has been a forum for spirited debate and history-making. A National Historic Landmark now, it continues to host regular discussions and lectures on events that shape our world today, just as it did more than 200 years ago. As always, check the Web site for a calendar of upcoming events.

The Write Stuff: Cheap Books

There are tons of used-book stores in and around Boston, just as you'd expect; this is Student Central, after all. But my very favorite bookery in town is the grandpappy of them all: the wonderful **Harvard Book Store** just east of the square and its T station. (Exiting the station, make a beeline for Au Bon Pain, pass it, and keep going a few more blocks east.) Don't bother with the new titles on the main floor, the hoodies, or any of the other merch; instead, head down to the bargain basement, where the philosophies of Kant mix with Neruda poetry, oversized art books, chick lit, popular science tomes, outdated text-books, Zen handbooks from the '70s, and a whole lot more. All of it used and cut-rate, but in good condition. Knock yourself out. They buy books, too. (You've also got to love the fact that these guys— rather than the ivory tower wonks across the street—have locked up the harvard.com domain for, probably, eternity.) They're open daily, year-round, until at least 10:00 p.m. each night, and until midnight on weekends. I love this place.

1256 Massachusetts Avenue; (617) 661–1515; www.harvard .com.

Visiting and Living in Boston

CHEAP SLEEPS:
BEDDING DOWN AS
A VISITOR

"Vacation, all I ever wanted; vacation, have to get away!"

—"VACATION," THE GO-GOS

Coming for just a short stay? I've got news for you. You won't find free beds in Boston (unless you're packing a VW van and a resident-parking sticker . . . then, who knows?).

But this city *is* blessed with an abundance—even an overabundance—of students for nine months out of the year. That means for *three* months out of the year, tons of boardinghouses, hotels, and other digs in and around the city are literally empty—and some of them can be rented out by non-students and/or non-Bostonians and/or transitionally-moving-to-the-city-but-too-busy-to-find-a-roomie-on-Craigslist-yet for a song. Yes, really.

The cheapo digs generally fall into three or four categories: ultra-cheap flophouses (we'll ignore those); boardinghouse-style digs; hostels; and budget hotels and motels.

BOARDINGHOUSES

You must be careful when thinking about renting out boardinghouse-style digs in any U.S. city, and that's also true in Boston. If you're still determined, remember the rules: you will probably have to share a bathroom. Characters coming and going may be full of character, but they also might be up to no good; you never can tell. There might or might not be double or triple locks on the insides of the doors.

If you're still determined to save as much as possible, rather than wandering around Chinatown picking up leaflets, try giving give a call to some of the local short-term options (some charge as little as $60 per night, single occupancy). Here's a list of some popularly recommended digs for area students, culled from housing officials at various hoity-toity graduate programs around town. And no, I haven't stayed in them. It's buyer beware:

Beacon Guest House
1047 Beacon Street; Brookline; (617) 232–0292

Beech Tree Inn
83 Longwood Avenue; Brookline; (617) 277–1620

The Brigham Guest House
698 Huntington Avenue; (617) 566–8947

Constitution Inn
150 Third Avenue; Charlestown; (800) 495–9622

Huntington Avenue YMCA
316 Huntington Avenue; (617) 536–7800

Irving House at Harvard
24 Irving Street; Cambridge; (800) 854–8249

YWCA Berkeley Residence
40 Berkeley Street; (617) 375–2524

HOSTELS

They don't really call them "youth hostels" anymore; anyone can stay, and they're dirt-cheap and usually safe and clean.

In summertime, there are at least three hostel options available in Boston, and two of them are really good: the **Boston International Hostel** (12 Hemenway Street, 617–536–9455) near Back Bay, and the **Fenway Hostel** (575 Commonwealth Avenue; 617–267–8599) in the Fenway/Kenmore area. Both are managed by **American Youth Hostels (AYH),** a nonprofit organization based in the Washington, D.C. area.

There's also one backpacker-style hostel, **Boston Backpackers** (234 Friend Sttreet, 617-723-0800) close to the North End and Quincy Market. It's somewhat more down-at-heel, but it's incredibly cheap, with free beer and meals included.

For a fuller, more opinionated review of all the hostels in Boston (and New England, and the U.S.), check out Paul Karr's *Hostels USA* (Globe Pequot Press).

BUDGET **HOTELS** AND **MOTELS**

There are plenty of chain hotels and motels around the outskirts of Boston. Normally you can't expect to pay less than $100 or $150 per night, even for one with a "6" or an "8" in its name, but there are exceptions . . . if you know how to play the game. (The downside is that you will need a car to stay at almost all of these places.) How to play the game? Like this: First, come on the weekend. Believe it or not, prices on the outskirts really plunge on weekends (except during special-event weekends and holidays like Memorial Day or Columbus Day). You can get a night in a king bed at a Westin hotel— a pretty good brand, and a pretty good bed—for $60 to $90 per night in nort hern 'burbs like Waltham. Next, look for new properties, which pop up all the time in 'burbs like Lexington, Waltham, and the like—most just a twenty-minute drive from the city center under ideal conditions.

If you're without a car, try another strategy. A clutch of chain properties on Routes 1A and 60 near Logan Airport offer free airport pickup shuttles and free rides to the Blue Line T station, for instance. Prices here tend to be pretty low. (The hotels right *at* the airport, though, are pricey.) Over on the Cambridge side of things, you can snag free shuttles at several properties in Cambridge and nearby Soldiers Field Road (which is actually in Boston, just across the bridge from Cambridge). Check out the **Hyatt Regency–Cambridg**e (575 Memorial Drive; 617-492-1234), the **DoubleTree Guest Suites** (400 Soldiers Field Road; 617–783–0090), and the **Royal Sonesta Cambridge** (40 Edwin Land Boulevard; 617-806-4200), among others.

Here are a few affordable, close-to-town chain hotels and motels to get you started; check around online and with locals to get a feel for their current quality level. For even more options (and deals) farther out from the center or near the airport, check online booking engines such as **Orbitz, Hotels.com, Kayak, Expedia,** and hotel-chain sites like **Starwood.com** and **Choicehotels.com.** You can usually sort by neighborhood, quality level, or—the biggie—price.

Best Western Terrace Inn
1650 Commonwealth Avenue; (617) 566–6260; www.bostonbw.com

Comfort Inn Boston
900 Morrissey Boulevard; (617) 287–9200

Howard Johnson–Fenway
1271 Boylston Street; (800) 267–8300

La Quinta–Somerville
23 Cummings Street; Somerville; (617) 625–5300

Midtown Hotel
220 Huntington Avenue; (617) 262–1000

LIVE FREE OR DIE:
SAVING ON THE RENT

*"The house came to be haunted by
the unspoken phrase:
There must be more money!
There must be more money!"*

—D. H. LAWRENCE

With real estate prices in metro Boston among the highest in the continental United States, it can be as hard to find affordable housing as it is to find a local who properly pronounces his r's. The elimination of rent control and eviction protections for most city residents in the 1990s put a real crimp in the budgets of middle- and lower-income tenants. Many residents simply moved out of town, exchanging high in-town housing costs for commutes from the suburbs, a mixed blessing at best (some consider the Southeast Expressway a kind of manifestation of hell on Earth). Others have found creative ways to realize their dreams of home ownership or rentership by staking their claims in less desirable parts of the city. With rents for studio apartments running about $1,000 a month, and the median price for a 1,000-square-foot condo cresting above $400,000, creativity and patience seem like a small price to pay.

Fortunately, the city of Boston and the Commonwealth of Massachusetts are keenly aware of the pain that working stiffs feel trying to pay the monthly rent here. A host of agencies have been developed specifically to help residents find affordable slices of Boston to call their own.

LOW-COST **APARTMENTS** AND **MORTGAGE** PROGRAMS

Boston Fair Housing Commission Metrolist
1 City Hall Plaza, Room 966
(617) 635–3321

The Commission keeps an updated list of below-market-rate and subsidized rentals and homes for sale at discounted rates. All residents of Boston can search the list, but many of the listings have a waiting list or low-income qualifications. Contact the BFHC directly to learn about gaining access to the list.

Boston Housing Authority
52 Chauncy Street
(617) 988–3400
www.bostonhousing.org

The Catch Income limits vary according to type of housing.

The city of Boston, through the Boston Housing Authority, is the largest landlord in the city, responsible for housing more than 10 percent of the city's residents. It administers dozens of public housing projects. The BHA also provides rent subsidies (through Section 8 voucher program). The housing developments include facilities for the elderly, people with disabilities, and families. Again, income limits apply, and residents are expected to pay about a quarter of their household income for rent. The turnaround time from application to approval can be long, from eight to ten weeks, so it's important to apply as early as possible.

Department of Neighborhood Development
(617) 635–HOME
www.cityofboston.gov/dnd/default.asp

This department administers a number of assistance programs for home buyers, including educational programs, financial assistance, grants, and help in finding city-subsidized real estate. If you qualify, you can even get money for a down payment and closing costs. To qualify for some of the DND's loan programs, assets and income must not exceed certain guidelines. If you qualify, however, the program can get you into your first Boston home with a far smaller up-front investment, and at lower total cost, than would have been possible otherwise.

MassHousing (Massachusetts Housing Finance Agency)
1 Beacon Street
(617) 854–1000
www.masshousing.com

MassHousing is the state's affordable housing bank. Founded in 1966, MassHousing has funded the construction of over 60,000 units of mixed-use rental housing throughout the state. MassHousing also makes construction loans to developers as long as they agree to offer at least 25 percent of the construction units for sale to lower-income households. Finally, it provides these households with mortgages that are far below conventional mortgage rates. Income and asset limits apply and vary with the specific program.

MassHousing also offers reduced-rate mortgage programs for people holding full-time jobs as employees of nonprofit organizations, the state or the county, government, education, social services, or health care. Employees in these fields are eligible if they don't earn more than 135 percent of the area's median average wage. In another innovative program, anyone who regularly uses public transportation to get to work or is a member of Zip-Car (a car timeshare service) is eligible for a no-down-payment, no-points, adjustable-rate loan through the MassAdvantage program. (The only catch is that you have to buy a home near public transportation, and take the T to work regularly.)

UP-AND-COMING
(SOMETIMES-CHEAP) NABES

One of the best ways to find a cheap place to live is to work the laws of supply and demand. The most desirable neighborhoods are nearly untouchable by the workaday masses who didn't inherit Brahmin wealth. If you make too much to qualify for a low or moderate-income rental program, but not enough to pay full price in one of the city's swank neighborhoods, you need to focus your search on one of the less-swank parts of town.

Here's a list of some up-and-coming Boston neighborhoods, and why you should check them out. Two-bedroom apartments can still be had in all of these neighborhoods for around $1,000 a month, which is virtually unheard of in other sections of the city. All are accessible by public transportation and are convenient to major highways.

ARLINGTON: Somerville has always been a hotbed of good-priced apartments, so much so that it's no longer cheap at all, except maybe in pockets near the Davis Square area. Instead, head for a place called Arlington, which is a little farther west and has a decent supply of brick-townhouse apartments mixed in with the single-family homes; a cute little main street with Asian eateries and a back-to-the-'50s feel; and good grocery stores.

CHINATOWN: High-rises and factory buildings are being converted to condos and lofts here, but there are still some bargains amidst the noodles, culture, and nightlife—a stone's throw from the city's downtown core. Students and artists are the trailblazers scooping up cheap rentals in this area, which had long been almost exclusively Asian, but beware: luxury hotels and condos are moving in fast.

DORCHESTER/SAVIN HILL: They say you can tell when a neighborhood is on the verge of becoming the next big thing when the gay community starts buying property there—and that's just what started happening a couple of years ago in Dorchester and the Savin Hill area. Long a bastion of working-class and immigrant families, this area is experiencing a swing toward the trendy, with new restaurants opening up regularly. Real estate prices and rents are slowly creeping up, so get in now if you want to take advantage of another potential "It" neighborhood.

EAST BOSTON: This 'hood, with a strong Italian history, has become a haven for immigrant families looking for a community to call their own. The rest of Boston is slowly catching on to the cultural diversity of this section of the city, which is most famous for its outstanding mom-and-pop restaurants, nearly indecipherable Boston accents, and proximity to Logan International Airport. If you like watching airplanes land and take off (I do), it's kinda cool.

MALDEN: East of the city center, Malden is my pick for the next working class-going-upscale 'hood in Boston. High-rise towers have begun to appear here, helped by a convenient Orange Line station that runs you downtown in about 20 minutes. (For something totally off the wall, check out an even bluer-collar suburb like Everett—close to the city, yet miles away in attitude (and pricing) from Newbury Street.

SOUTH BOSTON: Southie, as it's known in these parts, is a literal island jutting into the sea southeast of downtown. It's an isolated little spit of land that has been undergoing profound changes—more high-end nightlife and restaurants, fancy new condo developments, a more diverse population—ever since it made national headlines during the busing crisis there in the 1970s. Once a predominantly Irish, working-class neighborhood, yuppification has seriously taken hold; it can't be considered a bargain any longer, especially on stylish Telegraph Hill. If you want in, look for apartments closer to the area's beaches (which are pretty good, by the way); along alphabetized streets A through K; and between 1st and 5th streets. Don't bother with Fort Point Channel, though—it's long gone to high-end developers marketing a patina of grit.

O, Pair! Living for Free

If you are willing to work for your housing, then taking a job as a nanny, domestic worker, or household manager (the modern term for a butler) is a great way to get free housing and a tidy salary. High-end assignments often include health care, vacation, other perks, and, in some cases, housing for your immediate family. Full-time live-in nannies in Boston can expect to make anywhere between $400 and $750 a week, and household managers can make up to $100,000 for the really juicy, multi-estate assignments.

Word of mouth is the best way to land a job like this. Be aware that most agencies won't touch you if you're not a U.S. citizen (or don't have some kind of a work visa). Also, the IRS gets mighty testy if you don't pay taxes on your salary, especially if that salary is paid entirely in cash. Complex tax rules apply both to those who hire full-time domestic help and those who offer themselves for this type of work. If you go through an agency, most of these details will be fleshed out by your employer—make sure this happens, or else you could be stuck with paying what's owed.

Note that a live-in service job isn't for everyone, and the standards for admission into the profession are high and getting higher. People who can afford live-in help will expect you to have previous experience, and most nanny or domestic-help agencies run exhaustive background and criminal checks and require numerous stellar references from previous employers. Some even require a certificate from a doctor attesting that you are in good health and not the possessor of any unpleasant communicable diseases. However, if you've got the service pedigree, here are a few local and national placement agencies, and other resources, that can help you on your way to rent-free living.

Household Management

Cass & Company
60 State Street; (888) 453–2277; www.casscompany.com
Specializes in domestic help, household managers, and nannies.

International Guild of Professional Butlers

www.butlersguild.com

The International Butlers Guild is the real deal, a Netherlands-based association for those who have chosen a personal-service profession as a way of life. The group's Web site lists job openings and hosts a butler chat room, and there's even a cool napkin-folding tutorial page.

Starkey International Institute for Household Management, Inc.

1350 Logan Street; Denver, CO 80203; (800) 888–4904; www.starkey intl.com

This high-end-placement household management school specializes in training the butlers of tomorrow. It also assists clients and students in finding appropriate placements.

Nanny Agencies

American Nanny Company

P.O. Box 600765; Newtonville, MA 02460-0007; (800) 262–8771; www.americannannycompany.com

Beacon Hill Nannies, Inc.

825 Beacon Street, Suite 19; Newton; (617) 630–1577, (800) 736–3880; www.beaconhillnannies.com

Boston Nanny Centre

135 Selwyn Road; Newton; (617) 527–0114, (800) 456–2669; www.bostonnanny.com

Nannies' Nook

P.O. Box 661; Hingham, MA 02043; (781) 740–4595; www.nannies nook.com

Nanny Poppins Inc.

165 U New Boston Street, Suite 272; Woburn; www.nannypoppins .com

CHAMPAGNE BOSTON ON A SAM ADAMS BUDGET: SOME CHEAP TRICKS

"The wealthy man is not he who has money, but he who has the means to live in the luxurious state of early spring."

—ANTON CHEKHOV, 1892

It's one of the enduring ironies of Boston life that those with the most money often get the most free stuff. Dinner parties, grand openings, art shows, swag bags—you name it, they get it, usually without so much as a penny changing hands. Free parties and other events are the lifeblood of the social scene in Boston, and the best-kept secret in the city is that you don't have to be rich to get invited (although it helps a lot). It's all about who you know. Or who knows you.

The good news is that Boston's social world isn't nearly as tough to crack as it was in the last century, when all the good stuff was reserved for Mayflower-lineage types with names like Cabot or Lodge or Cabot Lodge. Our newly meritocratic society has thrown open those previously closed doors, and today you'll find people from all walks of life and economic strata rubbing elbows at house parties, club openings, debut balls, and networking events. The high-society parties that the public sees are $1,000 fund-raisers with impossible-to-score tickets, but the best free parties are actually invisible to the public.

The trick to scoring an invite to one of these free shindigs is getting on the social radar.

Once you do, all sorts of unpublicized entertainment and party opportunities begin to drift your way (provided you're not a self-important jerk—Bostonians have limited patience for such individuals, unless they're very, very, very rich). The key to tapping into the mother lode of Boston freebies can be summed up in a word: networking.

WORKING THE NETWORK

Everyone has a "cohort," a group of people with whom they are naturally affiliated.

You probably are already familiar with the common affinity groups, like your alumni club or your professional organization. And I assume that if you're interested in increasing your social network, you already belong to one or more of these organizations.

But you may not be aware of another social phenomenon that has emerged in Boston in recent years—the networking group. These make no pretense of charity or fund-raising (although they occasionally hold benefits). Their only point is to help you meet and greet your way to fun. There is a near turf war raging between the city's networking organizations, each vying to increase its membership (which allows it to sell access to marketers and advertisers at top dollar—which is how they all fund the free and cheap parties they run). Events hosted by these organizations are either free or very inexpensive or offer a significant discount off regular prices.

Plus, you'll meet lots of new people, and that's when the serious networking begins!

Boston Ski & Sports Club
(617) 789–4070
www.bssc.com

The Catch Membership is $65 a year.

With something like 30,000 local members, this organization hosts every type of sports and outdoor adventure imaginable. The group also hosts a number of social events, including everything from private wine-tasting parties to weekends on the Vineyard. Many evening social events are free to members, and events with a fee are often marked way down from the retail cost charged to the public. The crowd tends to be in their late twenties to mid-thirties and single, although the organized sports leagues bring out a little bit of every demographic.

Boston Young Professionals Association
www.bostonypa.com
Boston Professionals Association
www.bostonpa.com
(617) 591–1400

The Catch Memberships $50 and up.

Basic membership in these two groups is free, and premium membership begins at $50 per person, but this membership gets you into up to twenty-four networking events and parties for free in a year. The BYPA limits membership to those between twenty-one and forty, and there is no age limit with the BPA. Both groups offer parties, trips at home and abroad, special opening events, sports packages featuring pregame cocktail parties, and at least one big annual party.

Downtown Women's Club
www.downtownwomensclub.com

This nationwide women's networking organization, started here in Boston by Diane Danielson, boasts members who are generally age thirty-five and older, earn over $75,000, live in urban areas, and are actively pursuing a career. The DWC sponsors free networking events throughout the month, usually with a cash bar, as well as some larger educational and social events that charge a small fee. Premium membership costs $49.99 per year, but it's not necessary.

The Society of Young Professionals
(781) 444–7771
www.bostoneventguide.com/events/syp.htm

With over 25,000 members, this organization, which is affiliated with the Boston Events Guide, sponsors trips, parties, and charity events. Membership is free. Most of the group's social networking events carry a small fee—most also have complimentary appetizers (but a cash bar). You must be twenty-one to join. The crowd trends to twenty-five- to thirty-five-year-olds, people who would prefer to mingle over cocktails than to jam into a crowded nightclub (although they like to do some of that once in a while, too). A favorite is the weekly mixer, which costs $5.00 for members and features $2.00 martinis. (The entrance fee is occasionally waived.)

DOING GOOD (AND SAVING A BUCK)

For the more philanthropically oriented, nearly every museum, house of worship, hospital, and cultural organization in the city has a volunteer fund-raising organization attached to it, and it is around these that the city's charity event scene revolves.

The major cultural institutions in the city, like the Boston Symphony, the Boston Ballet, the Museum of Fine Arts, and most of the biggest hospitals, have in-house fund-raising groups, and they staff their fund-raising committees and boards with big-money donors and other connected movers and shakers who are privately invited to participate. Still, there are a few organizations that allow Cheap Bastards to participate in boards, committees, and fund-raising event planning, just because we want to help.

The galas these groups plan are very expensive affairs—some top out at over $1,500 a ticket—but you don't have to go to the main event to get the benefits of your involvement.

Just helping out will get you networked with great people, who, in turn, throw lots of private parties that most people never hear about. Plus, these volunteer organizations usually throw a number of smaller parties that lead up to the big event, usually held for members of the fund-raising committee and friends (as a thank-you, for networking, and often just to boost enthusiasm for the big party to come). There will be plenty of work involved if you join one of these fund-raising committees, and a membership is usually required (where applicable), but the networking benefits, not to mention the satisfaction of working for a very worthy cause, are unparalleled.

Listed below are some of the philanthropic organizations in town that will let you take part in their fund-raising committees without requiring you to make a major donation, be a mover or shaker, or have a personal invitation from the board of directors.

Associates of the Boston Public Library
Boston Public Library
700 Boylston Street
(617) 536–3886
www.bpl.org

The Catch You must be a member in order to participate. Annual membership is $55 for an individual and $100 for a family.

The Associates and their various fund-raising committees host three major fund-raising gala events per year, as well as monthly events at the library, most of which are free or have a small fee. The only requirements are that you have paid your membership fee and that you have convinced the committee members that you're going to work hard for the library.

Brattle Theatre Foundation
50 Brattle Street
Cambridge
(617) 876–8021
www.brattlefilm.org

This nonprofit group is spearheading the fund-raising campaign for the Brattle Theatre, which for over 115 years has sought to elevate film to its rightful place as a fine art. The Brattle has faced near financial death several times in the past few years but has managed to raise the funds necessary to stay open each time. It eagerly welcomes those who want to join the foundation as a member and take part in the many fund-raising committees that are working hard to keep this treasured theater alive and vital for many years to come. Call the foundation directly for information on how you can become involved.

Young Professionals Group
The Boston Public Library Foundation
700 Boylston Street
(617) 247–8980
www.bplf.com

The Young Professionals Group of the BPLF doesn't have a specific age requirement (they take the young and young at heart). It's free to join, and all you have to do is call the BPLF and get on their mailing list. They sponsor many free networking events throughout the year as well as several parties leading up to the two major fund-raising galas they host annually. The group is very involved in a variety of philanthropic activities in the city, including literacy, mentoring programs, and two big fund-raisers each year sponsored by the Young Professionals Group. Benefit committee volunteers are expected to sell tickets to the fund-raisers and buy at least a couple for the big shindig, but as long as you are a productive volunteer, you probably won't get kicked out if you don't go to the big bashes.

JOINING **SOCIAL** NETWORKS

If you live in the city of Boston, you probably already have frequent contact with some of the most connected people in town: hairdressers, waitresses, bartenders, maître d's, concierges, artists, interior designers, art gallery owners, personal trainers, and other wealth intermediaries, as they are called by sociologists. Maybe you use their services, or maybe they're personal friends, but either way, they are the people who help the wealthy spend their money, and they are the best social networking resources you have.

Now I know what you're thinking: It's just downright crass to befriend people just because of what they can do for you. You're right. I'm not suggesting you do that. Nor will these people *let* you do that: They can spot a brown-nosing hanger-on a mile away. I seek only to inform you that these people, who some view only as "service industry" folk, have a better lock on what is happening in Boston than nearly anyone else. It's just worth your while to get to know them. They're people you'd want to be friends with anyway, and they, in turn, probably know lots of other nice people—some of whom will throw great events and parties.

Courageous Sailing Center
1 First Avenue (Charlestown Navy Yard)
Charlestown
(617) 242–3821
www.courageoussailing.org

If you like to sail, this is a great organization to meet like-minded people and help a great cause. This nonprofit provides free sailing instructions to kids, as well as paid memberships and classes to adults. It sponsors a number of fund-raising events throughout the year and is always looking for volunteer committee members who want to help with the planning. You don't have to be a member of Courageous to get involved. In fact, joining the events committees, and doing a good job, is a great way to get invited to join the high-powered board of directors of Courageous, one of the city's great philanthropic organizations.

The Esplanade Association
10 Derne Street
(617) 227–0365
www.esplanadeassociation.org

The Catch Membership begins at $45 for individuals, but membership isn't required to volunteer.

This organization is the caretaker of one of the city's most precious resources, the Esplanade, a manicured park that runs for over 2 miles on the Boston side of the Charles River. Members and volunteers are a vital part of this organization, and they not only get their hands dirty helping to keep the Esplanade looking good, but also help plan the big fund-raising events that pay for all the upkeep. If you're interested in participating, call the association directly or fill out the online volunteer form on the group's Web site. They're eager to have new faces.

The Institute of Contemporary Art
The New Group
100 Northern Avenue
(617) 478-3100
www.icaboston.org

The Catch *Annual membership is $65 for an individual, $95 for a couple or family.*

ICA, Boston's fantastic contemporary art museum/association, moved into provocative, roomy new headquarters in 2006 after years of fund-raising efforts, and the New Group was an important player in that effort. The New Group is an affiliate group within the ICA's membership that seeks to introduce members to new artists through seminars and lectures. Its members are a vibrant collection of Boston professionals, age thirty and older, who are passionate about art. (They're not just about art, though. The group is known to throw some of the best parties in the city.) The New Group hosts a variety of free networking and educational seminars for members throughout the year. And volunteering for the New Group events committee will give you the chance to help plan the two major fund-raising benefits that the group sponsors each year. This is one of the most inclusive cultural organizations in the city—and membership dues have recently been slashed dramatically.

THERE IS SUCH A THING AS A FREE LUNCH: FREE AND CHEAP EATS AND DRINKS

"Eat breakfast like a king, lunch like a prince, and dinner like a pauper."

—ADELLE DAVIS

Boston is such a foodie town that it's almost embarrassing. While our biggest celebrities have always been and always will be sports heroes (Big Papi is the current king of that throne; Tom Brady's right there, too), local chefs like Ming Tsai, Todd English, and Barbara Lynch aren't far behind in popularity. It seems a new edgy restaurant opens up somewhere in town nearly every week. All this haute cuisine usually comes at a steep price, but the ardently cheap can still unearth plenty of places to eat for free (or cheaply) at area restaurants, markets, stores, and events. Whether you want an entire free meal, or just a taste of something sweet, Boston is happy to share its culinary wealth with Cheap Bastards.

WHAT'S **LEFT** OF **HAPPY** HOUR

In a fit of Puritan madness in the mid-1980s, Massachusetts legislators banned the traditional happy hour, at which thirsty Bostonians could drink cheap or free at their favorite bar for two precious hours after work. Sadly, the local bar scene hasn't exactly embraced the next obvious thing, free happy-hour appetizers. A few places have dipped their toes in—some more than others. It's a lot more common to find half-price appetizers, and there are some great deals to be had on full meals. If you do partake of free chow at one of the establishments listed below, you'll be expected to buy a drink. If you're eating a meal half-price, you don't have to buy a beverage, but remember to figure your tip based on the full price of whatever you ordered. It's always nice to find new ways to save a few bucks, but cheaping out on the waitress is not one of them.

Bukowski's Tavern

1281 Cambridge Street; Cambridge; (617) 497–7077
50 Dalton Street; (617) 437–9999

The Catch *Bukowski's takes cash only.*

What's not to love about a bar named for a poet who wrote some of his best work while completely sloshed? It has one of the most awe-inspiring beer menus we've seen in town, and is locally renowned for its burgers. Yeah, this place is cheap: You can sample a Buck Burger or a Dollar Dog for about what it costs to feed the meter any weekday from noon through 8:00 p.m. (Another menu item is called White Trash Cheese Dip.) You get the point: nothing fancy here, just beer and grub, cheaply. There's one in the Prudential Center neighborhood, one in Cambridge's Inman Square.

Cactus Club

939 Boylston Street
(617) 236–0200
www.cactusclubboston.com

The Catch *Must buy a drink to get the free deals.*

Cactus Club, a hoppin' Mexican restaurant and lounge that fills up with twenty-somethings every night of the week, has some pretty sweet freebies and cheapies, even if it will set you back the cost of a margarita. First, the free stuff—they lay out an All You Can Eat Taco Bar Sunday nights, sometimes until midnight, and it isn't half bad. Sometimes you can also score cheap appetizers at the bar during weekday happy hours.

Fritz Lounge

26 Chandler Street (South End)
(617) 482–4428
www.fritzboston.com

Fritz Lounge is a gay sports bar (only in Boston) popular with the South End's sizable gay community, plus patrons from other walks of life too. They come to enjoy free appetizers weekdays from 6:00 to 6:30 p.m. These aren't just chips and salsa—expect to find quiches, pizza, buffalo wings, and other hearty fare. But don't call it a happy hour. We don't use that term in Boston.

McCormick and Schmick's
34 Columbus Avenue (Park Square)
(617) 482–3999

Half-price appetizers pack this high-end seafood place with hungry patrons every night from 3:30 to 6:30 p.m. and again from 10:00 p.m. to midnight. The menu changes nightly, but you can't lose with their thick, juicy $1.95 cheeseburger, which is available most nights.

News Café
150 Kneeland Street
(617) 426–6397
www.newsboston.com/events.html

Sometimes it pays to be a girl. The News Café, one of the trendier boîtes in downtown Boston, has dubbed Wednesday night Ladies Night, and this is just a fabulous deal. Women dine free on a three-course meal—salad, entree, and dessert—from 5:00 to 10:00 p.m. in the lounge. (Pay for a drink.) There's even a vegetarian entree if you need one. You may even see one of the local sports stars who frequent this joint.

Noir at the Charles Hotel
1 Bennett Street (off Harvard Square)
Cambridge
(617) 661–8010

Every weekday from 5:00 to 7:00 p.m., this sultry bar offers a "nibbles" menu that counts down thusly: $5.00 flatbreads, $4.00 sandwiches, $3.00 snacks, $2.00 salads, $1.00 sweets, and free nuts. See what they did there? Cute idea, with one caveat: you've gotta purchase $6.00 minimum in total.

Whiskey's Food & Spirits
885 Boylston Street
(617) 262–5551

Whiskey's makes the cut in this book on the strength of its 15-cent buffalo wings alone; it also serves cheap chicken fingers, mozzarella sticks, and other bad-for-you food. Appetizers are about $2.50 during happy hour. But points off for the college-dorm atmo of the place. Not for grown-ups.

> ## Boston's Best for Less
>
> Boston's Best for Less (bos-cc.boston-deals.com) sells $50 gift cer-
> tificates to restaurants in the city for just $25 dollars (plus a $3.50
> shipping and handling fee per certificate) each. Each Friday at 9:45
> a.m., the Web site begins selling that week's featured restaurant
> certificate, and once the allotted certificates have been purchased
> (online through a secure server), they're gone. The number of certifi-
> cates varies from week to week. Some go very fast. The hook-up is
> a service marketed to listeners of three Boston radio stations owned
> by Clear Channel Entertainment: Kiss 108 (FM), Jamn 94.5 (FM), and
> Rumba 1200 (!) AM. Note that the quantity and quality of offers seem
> to be declining recently, though.

LOADING **UP** ON **FREE** SAMPLES

Boston is packed with bakeries, coffee shops, farmers' markets, and other
purveyors of delectable treats, and most are more than happy to offer free
samples. All they ask is that you don't abuse the privilege. If you don't
want to become rapidly known (it's a small town) as "that guy who eats
our samples all the time but never buys anything," please keep things in
proportion, patronize these shops with your cash when you taste something
you like, and help keep them in business so they can live on to offer free
samples for another day.

Big Sky Bread Co.
105 Union Street
Newton
(617) 332–4242
www.panoramabakery.com

This small bakery offers samples of some of their delicious artisan breads.

Faneuil Hall Marketplace
Between State Street and Atlantic Avenue, across from Government Center
(617) 523–1300
www.faneuilhallmarketplace.com

Where once colonial revolutionaries fomented rebellion, today there stands a gourmand's paradise. Faneuil Hall, built in 1742, anchors the general area now known as Faneuil Hall Marketplace, which also includes three long stone warehouses used for centuries as merchant markets—now transformed into one of the most visited tourist attractions in the city of Boston. The warehouses house dozens of pubs, restaurants, shops, and small storefronts selling every food known to man. It is also Cheap Bastard paradise. Most of the food storefronts have samples available during normal business hours, but on the first Wednesday of every month, you'll find "A Taste of Quincy Market" (the historic name for the merchants' warehouses), in which food stores showcase their signature cuisine from 5:00 to 7:00 p.m. Favorites include Boston Chipyard, Boston Chowda, Boston & Maine Fish Co., Carol Ann's Bake Shop, and Steve's Ice Cream.

Flour Bakery
www.flourbakery.com
1595 Washington Street (South End); (617) 267–4300
12 Farnsworth Street (Fort Point Channel); (617) 338–4333

One of the best bakeries in the city, Flour always has some samples on display for you to try. It was founded by a Harvard grad! There's now a second location in the burgeoning Fort Point Channel neighborhood, near the children's museum and several pricey hotels.

Formaggio Kitchen
244 Huron Avenue
Cambridge
(617) 354–4750
www.formaggio-kitchen.com

JP Licks
www.jplicks.com
352 Newbury Street; (617) 236–1666
1312 Massachusetts Avenue (Harvard Square); Cambridge; (617) 492–1001
311 Harvard Street (Coolidge Corner); Brookline; (617) 738–8252
4A College Avenue (Davis Square); Somerville; (617) 666–5079
46 Langley Road; Newton Centre; (617) 244–0666
One Brigham Circle; 1618 Tremont Street (Mission Hill); (617) 566–6676
661 VFW Parkway (West Roxbury); (617) 325–1516

JP Licks has some of the most intriguing ice cream flavor combinations going—potato pie, mint Irish lace, Bailey's cheesecake—and they're happy to let you sample.

New England Soup Factory

www.newenglandsoupfactory.com
2–4 Brookline Place; Brookline; (617) 739–1899 (soupline); (617) 739–1695
244 Needham Street; Newton; (617) 558–9988 (soupline); (617) 558–9966

As you might guess, these shops are all about the soup. Small samples are available for tasting.

Peet's Coffee & Tea

www.peets.com
176 Federal Street; (617) 439–3177
100 Mount Auburn Street; Cambridge; (617) 492–1844
285 Harvard Street; Brookline; (617) 734–4725
776 Beacon Street; Newton Centre; (617) 244–1577

Peet's wants you to love coffee as much as they do, and they're out to convert the world, one coffee drinker at a time. Most stores will offer sample cups of their coffees, and they often have samples of pastries or candies.

South End Formaggio

268 Shawmut Avenue
(617) 350–6996
www.southendformaggio.com

These stores have been serving up the finest in gourmet and artisan cheese, meats, and other delicacies for over twenty years. There are always cheeses and other nibbly things displayed for your sampling pleasure. The store hosts wine tastings as well, often paired with an appropriate cheese selection. Call the store for more info on tasting times, dates, and products scheduled to be tasted.

Trader Joe's

www.traderjoes.com
899 Boylston Street; (617) 262–6505
1317 Beacon Street; Brookline; (617) 278–9997
748 Memorial Drive; Cambridge; (617) 491–8582

This great grocery store specializes in wholesome offerings and snacks for people with discerning palates; they stock organics, kosher, vegetarian, vegan, gluten-free, and sugar-free, but regular foods, too, like chocolate bars and ice cream. Best of all, there's always a free sample of a food and drink—coffee, fruit juice, mac n' cheese. Whatever it is, it's bound to be good.

Whole Foods Markets

www.wholefoodsmarket.com
Charles River Plaza; 181 Cambridge Street; (617) 723–0004
15 Westland Avenue; (617) 375–1010
15 Washington Street; Brighton; (617) 738–8187
115 Prospect Street; Cambridge; (617) 492–0070
200 Alewife Brook Parkway; Cambridge; (617) 491–0040
340 River Street; Cambridge; (617) 876–6990

This high-end grocery store, which specializes in organic and chemical-free foods, knows that discerning shoppers want to try before they buy (especially at these prices). That's why there are sampling events at every local branch of Whole Foods Markets. Each store has an in-store demo coordinator whose job is to offer tastings of various products throughout the store. You can try everything from tofu hotdogs, gourmet pastries and cookies, and artisan cheese to wholesome packaged foods. All stores are open 8:00 a.m. to 10:00 p.m. daily.

RESTAURANT **WEEK** FOR THE RESTAURANT-WEAK

Once a year, for two weeks, Boston does something that's very bad for your waistline but good for your wallet and taste buds: a collection of its restaurants (including some of its best) slash prices for three-course *prix fixe* meals to just $20 per meal at lunch and $33 for dinner (2008 prices)! That's amazing. You don't get to pick from the full range of a restaurant's menu, but you do get to save big bucks. In 2008, the event took place over two weeks (ten days) in mid-August; they don't extend the deal to Saturdays or Sundays. Of course, you want to reserve your table ahead if at all possible by calling the restaurant once the annual list of participating chefs hits the airwaves each July. (And if you reserve, show up or call to cancel. Otherwise you're just an ass.)

FOOD **FESTIVALS**

Bostonians love to get together and eat, and the more the merrier. Food festivals are legendary in Boston, at which tens of thousands of people strap on the old feedbag, sometimes for a charity, sometimes just 'cause it's so yummy. The rule of thumb for all of these festivals is to get there early— it's no fun standing around in the hot sun (or the rain) with several thousand hungry Bostonians, especially when you're one of them. Some of these events charge a fee to get in—they're listed here because I think they're worth it, especially if you bring a big appetite.

Boston Vegetarian Food Festival
Reggie Lewis Athletic Center
1350 Tremont Street
(617) 424–8846 (administrative office)
www.bostonveg.org

The Boston Vegetarian Food Festival is a completely free event that brings together exhibitors of vegetarian natural foods from across the country. The festival offers the opportunity to talk to food producers, see and taste the latest vegetarian products being introduced to the marketplace, and hear from a variety of national experts on health and nutrition, who lecture throughout the day. There's even a children's activity area. It is the longest-running event of its kind in the country.

Chowderfest
City Hall Plaza
(617) 227–1528
www.bostonharborfest.com/chowderfest

The Catch Admission is $10.00 and worth it.

Who makes Boston's best clam chowder? Wars have been waged over lesser questions. Finding the city's best chowder is the sole focus of the 10,000 people who swarm City Hall Plaza for one day in the summer for Chowderfest, part of the city's Fourth of July Harborfest celebration. Dozens of the city's top restaurants vie for the honor, as determined by the masses who stand in line for hours to taste as many chowders as they can. Between tastings, musical performances, jugglers, and all manner of distractions, the

Plaza resembles a clam-besotted Woodstock, but it is one of the defining events of our fair city. Get there early to avoid the huge lines. Wear comfortable shoes and bring a hat and bottled water. City Hall Plaza is a mass of concrete and can get very hot in July.

The Jimmy Fund Scooper Bowl
City Hall Plaza
(617) 632–4215 (volunteer line)
www.jimmyfund.org/eve/event/scooper-bowl

The Catch Volunteer to get in free. Tickets are about $7.00 for adults, $3.00 for kids ages three to ten, free for kids under three.

The Jimmy Fund Scooper Bowl, the nation's largest all-you-can-eat ice-cream festival, is held in City Hall Plaza every June. Here you can taste ice cream from ten of the nation's leading ice-cream companies while raising money for the Jimmy Fund, which supports cancer research and treatment at Dana-Farber Cancer Institute. To get in free, call the volunteer line. Volunteer shifts are about three hours long. You'll be asked to collect tickets, scoop ice cream, and sell T-shirts—but then you'll be free to eat ice cream to your heart's content (although I'm not sure you'll want to after scooping it out for three hours).

FREE SPIRITS:
FREE WINE AND
BEER TASTINGS

*"Good wine warms people's faces;
good money warms their hearts."*

—CHINESE PROVERB

Boston is packed with wine and liquor stores (could it be the long, cold winters?), and most of the best wine shops in town have been around for generations.

The proprietors know the ins and outs of plonk, Châteaux Petrus, and everything in between, and they are eager to share their knowledge with sophisticated and neophyte wine lovers alike. Wine tastings can be formal affairs, presented by the vintners who actually produced the wines, or more informal tastings in which a shop puts out a variety of wines for you to try, without much fanfare or discussion. In either case, most shops will open wines that share a theme (Italy, Burgundy, ice wine) so that you can educate your palate. Boston is also home to two breweries making some of the finest specialty beers in the world (and they have the awards to prove it). Maybe we should thank those long winters after all.

FREE **WINE** TASTINGS

Auburndale Wine and Spirits
2102 Commonwealth Avenue
Newton
(617) 244–2772
Tastings Saturday, noon to 4:00 p.m.

and

Upper Falls Liquors
150 Needham Street
Newton
(617) 969–9200
www.thepostscript.com
Tastings Saturday, noon to 4:00 p.m.

Don't miss the big spring sale at these two sister wine shops. It's a big catered party where they open eighty to a hundred wines for your tasting pleasure. Find out more—and sign up for the newsletter—at their Web site.

Wine and Beer Tasting for the Week

SHOP	MONDAY	TUESDAY	WEDNESDAY	THURSDAY	FRIDAY	SATURDAY	SUND
Auburndale Wine and Spirits						noon–4 P.M.	
Bauer Wine and Spirits						4–6:30 P.M.	
Beacon Hill Wine and Spirits				5–7 P.M.	5–7 P.M.	noon–3 P.M.	
Best Cellars	5–8 P.M.	5–8 P.M.	5–8 P.M.	5–8 P.M.	5–8 P.M.	2–5 P.M.	2–5 P
Blanchards Wine and Spirits						2–5 P.M.	
Boston Beer Company (tour/tasting)			2 P.M. (May 1– August 31)	2 P.M.	2 and 5:30 P.M.	noon, 1 P.M., and 2 P.M.	
Brix					6–8 P.M.	6–8 P.M.	
Brookline Liquor Mart						1–5 P.M.	
Federal Wine and Spirits			5–7 P.M.				
Fine Wine Cellars						3–7 P.M.	
Gary's Liquors					4–7 P.M.	1–4 P.M.	
Gimbel's Discount Liquors				6–9 P.M.	6–9 P.M.	10 A.M.– 5 P.M.	
Gordon's Fine Wine and Liquors Main Street Watertown Street				5–8 P.M.	5–8 P.M. 5–8 P.M.	1–4 P.M.	
Harpoon Brewery (tour/tasting)	3 P.M.	3 P.M.	3 P.M.	3 P.M.	1 P.M. and 3 P.M.	1 and 3 P.M.	
(5:30 Club)		5:30–7 P.M.	5:30–7 P.M.	5:30–7 P.M.	5:30–7 P.M.		
Huntington Wine and Spirits				5:30–7 P.M.	5:30–7 P.M.		
Lower Falls Wine Company						noon–4 P.M.	
Martignetti Liquors					5–8 P.M.	5–8 P.M.	
Marty's Fine Wines and Gourmet Foods Allston Newton						noon–2 P.M. 3–5 P.M.	
Merchants Wine and Spirits				5–7 P.M. (selected)			
Reservoir Wine and Spirits				5:30–7 P.M.			
University Wine Shop (except July–August)						2:30–5:30 P.M.	
Upper Falls Liquors						noon–4 P.M.	
V. Cirace and Sons Inc.					4–7 P.M.	4–7 P.M.	
Wine Bottega					5–8 P.M.		
Wine Emporium (Tremont and Columbus)					afternoons (times vary)	afternoons (times vary)	
Wine Gallery (Brookline) (Kenmore)				5–7 P.M. 6–8 P.M.	5–7 P.M. 6–8 P.M.	3–6 P.M. 6–8 P.M.	
Wine Press						noon–6 P.M.	

Bauer Wine and Spirits

330 Newbury Street
(617) 262-0363
www.bauerwines.com
Wine tastings: generally Saturdays 4:00 to 6:30 p.m.
Beer and tequila tastings: dates and times vary, check the Web site.

Bauer wine buyer Howie Rubin made wine accessible to a whole generation of college students when he started doing wine commentary for local
alternative radio station WFNX back in the 1980s, and the education continues today. This shop prides itself on its knowledgeable staff, and customers
sometimes come here just to hang out and talk wine. They're also known for
their excellent selection of exotic beers and plenty of tequilas.

Beacon Hill Wine and Spirits

63 Charles Street
(617) 742-8571
www.beaconhillwine.com
Tastings generally Thursday and Friday, 5:00 to 7:00 p.m. and Saturday, noon
to 3:00 p.m.

In addition to the regular tastings, this wine shop has one or two bottles
open every night of the week for you to sample. The owner has a policy of
tasting every wine before he'll stock it, and he puts copious tasting notes up
on all the shelves to help you make your selection. Visit the Web site to read
tasting notes contributed by their many loyal customers.

Best Cellars

www.bestcellars.com
745 Boylston Street (Copley Square); (617) 266–2900;
1327 Beacon Street (at Harvard Street); Brookline; (617) 232–4100
Tastings generally 5:00 to 8:00 p.m.; weekends, 2:00 to 5:00 p.m.

This unique chain of wine stores categorizes its wines based on each one's dom-
inant aspect: luscious, smooth, fizzy, big, or sweet. They pour about four wines
at their tastings. The shop has over a hundred bottles at $15 and under and has
become one of the most popular wine stores in town because its owners have
made wine affordable and understandable. They occasionally do a grand tasting, so check the Web site or sign up for the e-mail newsletter for updates.

Blanchards Wine and Spirits

www.blanchardsliquor.com
741 Centre Street; Jamaica Plain; (617) 522–9300
286 American Legion Highway; Revere; (781) 289–5888
418 LaGrange Street; West Roxbury; (617) 327–1400

This liquor store chain has regular tastings as well as additional tastings throughout the week. They also feature a monthly grand tasting at one or more locations. Sign up for their newsletter to get the latest schedule and tasting notes on newly stocked products from the staff.

Brix

www.brixwineshop.com
1284 Washington Street
105 Broad Street
(617) 542–2749

This wine and liquor store is sleek and modern, filled with frosted glass and an easy-to-navigate selection. It could be mistaken for a bar (which is what it will become once the state agrees to allow wine stores to sell wines by the glass). Wines for tasting are poured into crystal stemware along a beautiful 10-foot granite tasting table, presented by one of the knowledgeable owners. It's a great local gathering place.

Brookline Liquor Mart

1354 Commonwealth Avenue
Brookline
(617) 734–7700
www.blmwine.com
Tastings Saturdays, 1:00 to 5:00 p.m.

This local treasure (despite the strip-mall name) has been in the Miller family for seventy-six years, and these folks have passed their love of the grape down through the generations. Wine tastings here are an educational affair. They open seven bottles, usually on a theme (similar grape, style, or region), but the real fun happens at the periodic blind tastings, when they cover the bottles and let the customers figure out which wine is which (they give the answers at the end). Sign up on the Web site for a weekly newsletter, which includes tasting notes for new offerings. It will also keep you up to date on the grand tastings they host three or four times a year—seven tables with seven wines at each. À votre santé, indeed!

Federal Wine and Spirits

29 State Street
(617) 367–8605
www.federalwine.com
Wine tastings: Wednesdays, 5:00 to 7:00 p.m.
Scotch tastings: check Web site for schedule.

Tastings at this Faneuil Hall–area wine shop take place in the store's wine cellar. In addition to its regular tastings, this shop hosts eclectic tastings (a recent one showcased wines that go well with moose—and even offered roast moose for tasters to try). Check the Web site for additional tasting events and scotch tastings—they specialize in single malts—in addition to the scheduled events.

Gary's Liquors

655 VFW Parkway (Route 1)
Chestnut Hill
(617) 323–1122
www.garysliquors.com
Tastings Friday, 4:00 to 7:00 p.m. and Saturday, 1:00 to 4:00 p.m.

This award-winning wine shop has a mailing list to keep customers updated on coming events, in addition to regular wine tastings.

Gordon's Fine Wines & Liquors

www.gordonswine.com
894 Main Street; Waltham; (781) 893–1900;
599 Moody Street; Waltham; (781) 894–2771
Wine tastings Thursday and Friday, 5:00 to 8:00 p.m.; Saturday, 1:00 to 4:00 p.m.
Beer tastings twice a month; call or see the Web site for dates and times.
51 Watertown Street; Watertown; (617) 926–1119
Wine tastings Friday, 5:00 to 8:00 p.m.

In addition to its frequent regular tastings, Gordon's—an award-winning wine, liquor, and beer store now owned by the fourth generation of Gordons—has grand tastings throughout the year featuring 150 wines with twenty different suppliers.

Through their Web size, they offer an e-mail service, the Daily Flash, which updates their many happy customers on sudden specials, wine dinners, and the not-to-be-missed grand tastings. There's also a *Wine Source Newsletter* with more wine news, and Gordon's boasts one of the area's only personal wine shoppers—even if you can't tell Zinfandel from Bordeaux.

Lower Falls Wine Co.

2366 Washington Street
Newton Lower Falls
(617) 332–3000
www.lowerfallswine.com

From plonk to Grand Crus, they do it all here. And Friday night brings a special event known as the Friday Night Bottle, when the shop decides at the last minute (by 3:00 p.m.) which nice bottle from its private stock it will open for tasting, posts the news on the Web site, then uncorks it for appreciative oenophiles.

Marty's Fine Wines and Gourmet Foods

193 Harvard Avenue; Allston; (617) 782–3250
Tastings Saturday, noon to 2:00 p.m.
675 Washington Street; Newton; (617) 332–1230
Tastings Saturday, 3:00 to 5:00 p.m.

A fixture on the tastings scene since it opened in 1948, and known for its outstanding selection of high-end wines, Marty's tastings feature wines from a single region. They tend to pour wines in the $20 to $60 range, so if you normally don't drink wines that good, Marty's is a great place to learn what you've been missing. Marty's boasts an exceptional gourmet foods section, so expect one heck of a cheese and snack platter during their tastings. Their wine events get very busy, so go early.

V. Cirace and Sons Inc.

173 North Street (North End)
(617) 227–3193
www.vcirace.com

The Cirace family has owned this North End shop for more than a hundred years. The current owners' grandfather was in the wholesale grocery biz, and he claims to have been the first store owner in town to be granted a liquor license when Prohibition was repealed. The grandkids upgraded the wholesale food selection to a gourmet food shop featuring Italian specialties, and the wine selection at this North End landmark runs to similar tastes. Tasting events are seasonal; call to find out what's up.

Wine Bottega
341 Hanover Street
(617) 227–6607
Tastings Friday, 5:00 to 8:00 p.m., except on religious holidays.

This tiny treasure is in Boston's North End (the city's Italian section), and it likes to plan its wine-tasting schedule in summer around the many festivals that take over this neighborhood to honor a different Catholic saint each week. If a saint is from Tuscany, they taste Tuscans. For the fisherman's festival, they taste Sicilian wines. And sometimes a guest just riffs on unknown vineyards somewhere in Italy. This shop prides itself on finding good values for its customers, and salespeople wear the title "wine geek" proudly. Do yourself a favor and drop by.

Wine Emporium
www.thewineemporiumboston.com
607 Tremont Street
474 Columbus Avenue
(617) 262–0379

This local wine store chain—with two locations, just a block apart—sometimes offers wine tastings on Friday and Saturday afternoons. There are also occasional special events (consult the Web site). Start times vary, so call ahead.

The Wine Gallery
www.wine-gallery.com
375 Boylston Street; Brookline; (617) 277–5522
Wine tastings 5:00 to 7:00 p.m. Fridays, 3:00 to 6:00 p.m. Saturdays
Beer tastings 5:00 to 7:00 p.m. Thursdays.
516 Commonwealth Avenue (Hotel Commonwealth, Kenmore Square);
(617) 266–9300
Wine tastings 5:00 to 7:00 p.m. Fridays, 3:00 to 6:00 p.m. Saturdays
Beer tastings 6:00 to 8:00 p.m. Thursdays.

This place is heaven for Boston wine lovers: a store that has a self-service wine-tasting machine that lets you select from about sixteen whites and thirty-two reds—all free. This miracle of science is called an Enomatic, but it's affectionately known as the Wine Jukebox by its owners at the Wine Gallery. (It's only at the Brookline location, by the way; those Kenmore kids would blow the poor thing out in a day.)

Massachusetts liquor laws prohibit wine stores from giving tasters more than six to eight ounces of wine in one sitting, so the folks at the Wine Gallery devised a smart method to keep track. Each wine in the jukebox is assigned a point value based on its price ($10 wines are 1 point, $20 to $30 wines are 2 points, $30 to $40 wines are 3 points, and so on). Each taster is assigned a free card with twelve credits that you use to "pay" the jukebox for each half-ounce taste. The more expensive the wine, the fewer tastes you'll get. The most anyone can get is a nice, legal six ounces.

In addition to the Jukebox, the Gallery also hosts "traditional" wine, beer, and liquor tastings. At the Brookline location, tastings are conducted in the specially designed tasting room, where you can sip samples from real glasses while you sit at the wood tasting table, which accommodates up to thirty people. The Kenmore Square location offers free valet parking—a huge bonus in downtown Boston! In addition to regularly scheduled tastings, the stores also host a variety of other free beer and wine events.

Wine Press
1024 Beacon Street
(617) 277–7020
Tastings Saturday, noon to 6:00 p.m.

This fun local wine shop presents the monthly wine specials at its tasting events, and the owner reports that there's a bottle or two open "nearly every day of the week." Nice. We're there. (But it is best to call ahead just to be certain something's been uncorked.)

BEER **TASTINGS**

Bostonians are lucky to have not one but two breweries to call our own. Both welcome visitors with open arms and icy-cold free samples, as long as you're over twenty-one and have the ID to prove it. Note that a number of the wine shops listed above also do free beer tastings; check at the same time you're calling about wine.

Harpoon Brewery

Mass Bay Brewing Company
306 Northern Avenue
(888) 427–7666, extension 522
www.harpoonbrewery.com
Tours/tastings Tuesday through Saturday, 4:00 p.m.; additional tour/tastings on Friday and Saturday, 2:00 p.m. and Saturday at noon.

Since the 1980s, the Harpoon Brewery has been creating award-winning, custom-crafted beer for the discerning beer drinker. Their seasonal beers are eagerly awaited not just in Boston, but in every lucky city that gets a batch of this liquid gold. No reservations are necessary to attend the tour/tastings; just remember to bring your ID. The tours last approximately thirty to forty-five minutes. Groups of fifteen or more can make reservations ahead, but others can't—expect to get in anytime except the last two Saturday tours, when the place is chock-full of tourists.

Harpoon also hosts the 5:30 Club, a group tour of the brewery held Tuesday through Friday from 5:30 to 7:00 p.m. Group size can range from fifteen to eighty people, but it must be scheduled in advance (can you say "office happy hour"?).

The brewery charges a nominal $1.00 per person (refundable if you cancel the tour twenty-four hours ahead) for these events. Call the private tour phone line to make 5:30 Club reservations.

The Samuel Adams Brewery

Boston Beer Company
30 Germania Street
Jamaica Plain
(617) 368–5080
Tours Thursday, 2:00 p.m.; Friday, 2:00 and 5:30 p.m.; Saturday, noon, 1:00 p.m., and 2:00 p.m.; additional tours held on Wednesday at 2:00 p.m. from May 1 through August 31.

The Catch Suggested donation is $2.00, but it goes to charity. Ante up.

We feel bad for the guy who has to dress up as Sam Adams, but the beers are pretty good (I even like the Cherry Wheat—what?), so we'll let it slide. Be sure to bring ID.

BARGAIN BEAUTY:
FREE AND CHEAP HAIR CARE, BEAUTY TREATMENT, AND MASSAGE

"Sex appeal is 50% what you've got and 50% what people think you've got."

—SOPHIA LOREN

Beauty may be skin deep, but that broke feeling you get after a trip to a high-priced salon goes right to the bone. Cheap Bastards to the rescue! You need not pay through the nose to get nicely styled, made up, and massaged—you just need to know when and where to book your appointments. Some of the top stylists on Newbury Street give their cuts away for free; pedicures and manicures can be had for a song; and you can get a great $20 massage if you're into that.

BLOWOUT **SALES:** **LOW-COST** HAIR **SALONS**

Some of the top salons in the city—salons that charge up to $200 for a cut and blow dry—actually give away their services once or twice a week. Although newly hired salon stylists have met basic training and licensing requirements, they must still be taught the salon's signature techniques and styles. And the experienced stylists need ongoing training and education. They have to practice on *someone's* hair, and if you volunteer to be a hair model, that someone could be you. You'll get your cut free or dirt cheap. If that sounds a bit risky, don't fret: The salon's senior stylists supervise trainees every step of the way, so you probably won't leave in shock. Note that you will probably be required to stay for the duration of an entire trainee class, which could take two or more hours, and that women volunteers are generally in higher demand than men. You also won't get a whole lot of say in the style—you'll get whatever is being taught that day, not what you demand. But if you're open to new things, this is definitely the way to go. Unless otherwise stated, services are free. Tip: Even if you don't see your favorite salon listed, call them directly and ask—most have training nights from time to time.

Dellaria Salon
623 Commonwealth Avenue (Kenmore Square)
(617) 262–8750
www.dellaria.com

This salon dynasty began in Boston, and they actively train their stylists at both their Kenmore Square and Newton Centre locations. Training happens in Kenmore Square on Monday nights at 5:30 p.m. (cut and blow-dry for longer hair) and 6:30 p.m. (for short-hair barbering). Get your name on the list by calling the salon; if you're called in, you get a free cut! Note that these free cuts vanish during school vacations (such as the period from mid-December to early January and spring break) because the students aren't in town.

Highlights Salon
286 Newbury Street
(617) 247–8200

This friendly salon uses lots of volunteers, so call and let them know what you're looking for. They'll match you with a stylist, who will call you to get more information about your hair. Salon training takes place on Wednesday nights at 7:00 p.m.

I Soci
8 Newbury Street, third floor
(617) 867–9484
www.isocisalon.com

I Soci is an edgy salon that holds employee training sessions every Tuesday night around 5:00 p.m., and they need volunteers for both cuts and color. But do not show up expecting a free cut; that ain't gonna happen. Call the salon if you're interested, tell them about your hair (color; short or long) and the services you want, then wait. The salon will call you back—if they need your type of hair.

James Joseph Salon
30 Newbury Street
(617) 266–7222
www.jamesjosephsalon.com

The Catch Cuts, including blow-dry, are about $10 and coloring is about $25.

Cut and color apprentice training takes place at this award-winning salon twice a week, on Tuesday and Wednesday at around 6:00 p.m. To get in, call and explain your hair to them; they will put all this info into a "model book," then call you in—if your hair matches what they need to teach sometime. There's no guarantee they'll call. But it can't hurt to get on the list.

LIQUID Hair Studios

640 Tremont Street
(617) 425–4848
www.liquidhairstudios.com

The Catch Cuts only.

This salon, one of the funkiest in town, is renowned for its edgy style and its friendly, funny, welcoming staff. In-salon training happens on Wednesday nights at 7:00 p.m. Call ahead and tell them all about your hair to get on the list.

Runway Salon

11 Newbury Street, third floor
(617) 375–0002
www.runwaysalon.com/HairModels

The Catch Cuts are $15 and up. Coloring is from $20.

Runway uses lots of hair models and schedules training appointments, usually Mondays and Tuesdays beginning around 10:00 a.m. and continuing through to late afternoon. You'll pay $15 and up for a cut, $20 or more for a color treatment. Sign up online or call the salon and voice your interest. The Web site sign-up form also lists the types of hair models they're looking for that week.

Super Cuts Studio

24 Mystic View Road
Everett
(617) 381–5102 (hotline)
www.supercuts.com

It's a bit of a haul out of central Boston, but Super Cuts holds training throughout the week, and is usually in need of lots of hair models. Just check the hotline for exact details and the week's schedule; this place takes walk-in models only, no appointments, and they don't give cuts during their lunch hour, which seems to start around 12:45 p.m.

Umi Salon
75 Newbury Street
(617) 247–0770
www.umisite.com/umisalon_modelcall.html

The Catch *Cuts are free; coloring is $45.*

In-salon training is held on Tuesday nights beginning at 5:00 p.m. at this salon, which caters to some of the city's grandest dames. There are a few ways to sign up to be a hair model—sign up on their Web site (click on "model call"), go in person to the salon on Tuesday at 4:30 p.m., or call the salon ahead of time. They'll want as much info as possible about your current hair style and what you're looking for. They'll give you a thorough description of what they are planning to do in the training session before you agree to come. Training sessions last about one to two hours.

Vidal Sassoon
14 Newbury Street
(617) 536–5496 (main number)
(617) 536–0254 (hair model line)

The Catch *Cuts are $15, and coloring is more.*

Vidal Sassoon salons hold their training workshops on Fridays. The best way to take part is to schedule a free consultation in the week before the workshop. They'll evaluate your hair, tell you about what they're working on in that week's workshop, and schedule you into a training session if it's a good match. Call the special hair model hotline to schedule your consultation.

HAIR TODAY, GONE (TO A GOOD CAUSE) TOMORROW

DeKwa Elements of Hair
132 Newbury Street, fourth floor
(617) 236–8081
www.dekwa.com

Here's a salon that offers free cuts to those who are donating to Locks of Love. DeKwa take appointments for donations to the charity during regular business hours, and they'll even ship the hair to Florida for you. They'll shape your (remaining) hair into a blunt cut for free, plus a junior stylist will also wash, style, and blow-dry it. These appointments book up far in advance, so call at least a month beforehand. Note that all of these appointments must be held with a credit card, and you'll be charged $25 if you fail to show up or cancel less than 24 hours prior.

Locks of Love
234 Southern Boulevard
West Palm Beach, FL 33405
www.locksoflove.org

Locks of Love is a nonprofit organization that provides hairpieces to financially disadvantaged children suffering from medical hair loss. Salons around the country offer free haircuts to anyone who is willing to donate their hair. The children receive the hairpieces free of charge. You must have at least 10 inches of hair to donate, from tip to tip. You can pull curly hair straight to measure the minimum 10 inches. They need hair from men and women, young and old, all colors and races. Hair may be colored or permed, but not bleached or chemically damaged. Call your favorite salon if you want to make a donation. Once they know it's for a good cause, they may be willing to offer a free or discounted cut and send the donation to the organization. Salon requirements can be found on the group's Web site.

CHEAP **IS** BEAUTIFUL: **BEAUTY** SCHOOL **DEALS** AND **DISCOUNTS**

While they're not free, a number of local beauty schools offer dramatically reduced prices on all sorts of services—haircuts, colors, manicures, pedicures, facials, and other fabulously exotic treatments that normally cost you an arm and a leg. The treatments are all performed by students after they have achieved a certain number of training hours, and their work is overseen by teachers. All these schools charge fees for student services, and some charge slightly higher fees if you're treated by instructors. The beauty of going to one of these schools is that you can book a reservation in advance and tell them what you want; in a training class at a regular salon, you get a free cut but you have to wait for an opening, and you have to take whatever style they want to try out on you.

Aesthetic Institute of Boston
47 Spring Street
West Roxbury
(617) 327–4550
www.aestheticsinstituteofboston.com

and

The Blaine School
30 West Street (Downtown Crossing)
(866) 232–2771
www.blainebeautyschools.com

The Blaine School (a division of the Empire beauty school chain) has a number of branches outside the city, one in downtown Boston, and one in Malden (they also do some skin care, manicures, and waxes). Haircuts are just $14 (sometimes just $5!), and colorings start from just $20. Amazing.

Bojack Academy of Beauty Culture
47 Spring Street
West Roxbury
(617) 323–0844
www.bojackacademy.com

This training school offers a variety of services, ranging from cuts and colors to massages, facials, and even advanced microdermabrasion (a skin-smoothing technique). All fees charged are dramatically lower than those charged in salons elsewhere in Boston—the catch is, all work is done by students. All fees are listed on the school's Web site.

Elizabeth Grady
222 Boston Avenue
Medford
(781) 391–9380

This is a little off the beaten path, but worth the effort. This fine nation-wide spa has its headquarters and training center right in our backyard, a facility that offers (at half price!) tons of world-class services. Our skin feels better already. Needless to say, reservations go very quickly, and they're not easy to get even if you know how. Test clinics run for just a few months, once each year's students have completed their coursework. Call the school directly and ask to be put on a mailing list; three months before the next clinic is about to begin, you'll get (postal) mail or an e-mail notifying you of the clinic dates. As soon as you get that, start dialing! The massage clinics run pretty consistently, about twice a week throughout the year, so those appointments at least are somewhat easier to get.

La Newton
636 Warren Street
Dorchester
(617) 427-6886

La Newton, a hair and beauty school, offers walk-in customers good manicures at an unbeatable price ($5!) Mondays through Thursdays (from 10:00 a.m. to 2:00 p.m. only). You must walk in to get the discount; no appointments are taken.

New England Hair Academy
492-500 Florence Street
Malden
(781) 324-6799

This beauty school offers cheap haircuts, color processes, and other similarly priced goodies. The academy prefers walk-ins during regular business hours, which vary with the season. Call ahead to learn more about their services and hours.

FEELING **CHEAP:** LOW-COST **MASSAGE**

These schools charge fees for their massages, but they're as little as one-*quarter* what the average folks pay at downtown hotel spas.

Cortiva Institute

103 Morse Street
Watertown
(617) 668–2000

Book a massage through the student clinic, and it costs you just $35 an hour. The massages are only available when school is in session, so call ahead for appointment hours. There's a 15-minute interview as part of the process.

Salter School

2 Florence Street
Malden
(781) 324–5454

This wellness school accepts walk-ins or appointments for Swedish-style massages from its massage therapy students on weekday mornings. Your massage shouldn't cost more than about $25, and there are also slight further discounts for seniors and military personnel.

NO-COST **MAKEOVERS**

There's nothing like a free professional makeover to leave a girl feeling like a goddess. (Guys, skip this section.) Most of the cosmetics stores in the city offer makeovers for free, though the expectation is that you'll buy something when you're done. Who cares about that? You don't *have* to buy anything. Some are a harder sell than others.

The Beauty Mark

33 Charles Street
(617) 720–1555

This quaint store is small, so they've chosen their product lines very carefully. If you're looking to sample top-of-the-line items you can't find elsewhere, this is the place. If you want a full makeup application done by a makeup artist, however, it'll cost you more—$75.

MAC

The Atrium Mall
300 Boylston Street
Chestnut Hill
(617) 244–9501
www.maccosmetics.com

The salespeople in this store absolutely love makeup, and they love playing with it on their customers, so don't be shy about asking for help. The sales pressure is low, and the quality of the service is excellent.

Sephora

800 Boylston Street (Prudential Center)
(617) 262–4200
www.sephora.com

Sephora deserves special mention; it's a makeover nirvana for Cheap Bastards. There are always hordes of professionally trained makeup artists wandering the store, showing customers how to use the dizzying array of product choices here. These folks know their stuff, and they're happy to share what they know with you. Of all the cosmetics retailers in the city, this is also the most laid-back about pushing you to buy something. They have a multitude of brands to choose from when making you over, too. The shop is open Monday through Saturday from 10:00 a.m. to 8:00 p.m. and Sunday from 11:00 a.m. to 6:00 p.m.

Shu Uemura

130 Newbury Street
(617) 247–3500

If you love the look of Madonna's crystal-flecked mink false eyelashes, this is the store that stocks them. Even if you don't, they'll let you try on makeup to your heart's content. (But if you want a full makeover, it'll cost you something beyond the cheap range. They will let you apply it toward your purchases.)

DEPARTMENT **OF** HOMELAND
CHEAPNESS: MORE **MAKEOVERS**

Most salespeople in department stores work on commission, so be aware that you're stepping into a bit of a lion's den when you ask for a makeover. If you're a regular buyer of a particular brand at a particular store, and you have a relationship with the salespeople, you'll often find that they're happy to provide a free makeover for the big night—some will even let you book an appointment. But if you don't already have a relationship, expect the very hard sell. Most of these stores host visiting "celebrity" makeup artists who schedule free makeover appointments with customers from time to time throughout the year, but, again, the assumption is that you'll buy. (Call the stores directly for a calendar of upcoming makeover events.) The following stores have extensive cosmetics departments.

Barneys New York
100 Huntington Avenue (Copley Place); (617) 385–3300

Bloomingdales
55 Boylston Street (Route 9); Chestnut Hill; (617) 630–6000

Lord & Taylor
760 Boylston Street; (617) 262–6000; www.lordandtaylor.com

Macy's
450 Washington Street (Downtown Crossing); (617) 357–3000; www.macys.com

The Mall at Chestnut Hill
199 Boylston Street; Chestnut Hill; (617) 969–5354

Neiman Marcus
100 Huntington Avenue (Copley Place); (617) 536–3660; www.neimanmarcus.com

Saks Fifth Avenue
800 Boylston Street (Prudential Center); (617) 262–8500; www.saksfifthavenue.com

SMALL CHANGE:
FREE AND CHEAP STUFF
FOR THE KIDS

"Your children and grandchildren will have their share of happiness; there's no need to work like a horse for them."

—CHINESE PROVERB

Boston is a great city for kids—it's packed with history, beaches, playgrounds, tours, and interactive museums, much of it created specifically for our littlest residents and visitors. The city's cultural institutions are also keenly aware that today's kids are tomorrow's patrons, so they provide plenty of ways for children to get exposure to the arts in a child-friendly way. Most of these activities are within walking distance from downtown Boston, or a short ride on the subway. Here is a partial list of what's out there—there are also many more activities that are administered through the Commonwealth of Massachusetts Department of Conservation and Recreation and through Boston's Parks and Recreation Department. Both organizations have searchable online databases that list all of their offerings.

AFTER-SCHOOL PROGRAMS

Boston Centers for Youth & Families (BCYF)
1483 Tremont Street
(617) 635–4920
www.cityofboston.gov/BCYF

BCYF is Boston's largest youth and human services agency, overseeing forty-six community facilities that provide a variety of activities geared to the city's young people and their families, including after-school programs, fitness programs, recreational facilities and pools, and educational programs for children, teens, and adults. You can find a complete list of community centers in Appendix C or in a searchable directory with contact information and programs on the BCYF Web site.

Some of these community centers are free to residents of the communities they serve, but most have a small annual membership fee that rarely exceeds $50 a year for an entire family. You can also download a complete listing of free or very inexpensive children's activities throughout the city sponsored in partnership with the BCYF.

Boston Community Learning Centers

Boston Public Schools
26 Court Street
(617) 635-9000
http://boston.k12.ma.us

These programs operate in twenty-five public schools throughout Boston's neighborhoods. They provide after-school sports and educational activities, as well as adult and parenting classes, with a special focus on English as a Second Language. A complete list of locations of BCLCs can be found in Appendix D.

Boys and Girls Clubs of Boston

50 Congress Street, Suite 730
(617) 994-4700
www.bgcb.org

The Boys and Girls Clubs were founded in Boston over 110 years ago, and there are now five clubs throughout the Greater Boston and Chelsea area serving children and teens. The clubs provide a wide array of after-school activities for kids ages six to eighteen. Membership fees do apply and are based on ability to pay. Most clubs charge $25.00 for the school year, September through June, with decreased fees of $5.00 for teen members, since many are paying out of their own pockets. During the summer the clubs run a summer camp program (including field trips) from 8:00 a.m. to 5:00 p.m. The cost is $150 to $200 for the summer. The Boys and Girls Clubs have no income restrictions for members and welcome all children to participate.

HOMEWORK HELP

Homework Assistance Program

Boston Public Library
(617) 859-2381
www.bpl.org/homework

Stumped on the definition of an isosceles triangle? The Boston Public Library and all of its branches offer Boston public school students free help with homework through the Homework Assistance Program (HAP). The program provides two services to students in Boston: a mentoring program serving third- through eighth-graders at every local branch, and an online service, HAP Online, serving fourth- through twelfth-graders. The One-on-One Mentoring Program places high-performing tenth-, eleventh-, and twelfth-graders in branch libraries throughout Boston. These mentors help third- through eighth-graders with homework and assist fourth- through twelfth-graders with the use of library resources. They also read with kids who are in pre-kindergarten and higher grades. The HAP Online service offers online help with tutors for students in grades four through twelve on subjects including math, science, social studies, and English. The service is provided from Monday to Thursday 3:30 to 5:30 p.m., and Saturday from 11:00 a.m. to 1:00 p.m. Contact the branch library nearest you (there's a complete list in Appendix B of this book).

ARTS, CRAFTS, DANCE, AND MUSIC

ArtBeat
212-A Massachusetts Avenue
Arlington
(781) 646–2200
www.artbeatonline.com

The Catch The course is free, but they charge for materials.

Try the ArtBeat drop-in open studio for kids' crafts projects. The hands-on art studio is open to the public every day and serves artists from four years old to adult. The instruction is free, but there is a charge for the materials you use. Depending on the medium, it could be as much as $10.

Boston Ballet
19 Clarendon Street
(617) 456–6359
www.bostonballet.com

The Catch Taking Healthy Steps has a $25 registration fee.

The Boston Ballet's free Taking Steps after-school program is a special twelve-week workshop that meets three times a week to introduce girls ages eleven through fourteen to a variety of dance and movement forms. It is held at the Roxbury Community College and the Reggie Lewis Athletic Center. Taking Healthy Steps, a weeklong program in August reserved for girls ages eleven through fourteen, helps develop basic movement awareness, leadership skills, and self-esteem. Call the ballet directly to register.

Cloud Place
647 Boylston Street (Copley Square)
(617) 262–2949
www.cloudfoundation.org

This performance and exhibit space also houses a nonprofit organization that is committed to providing opportunities for young artists to showcase their work. The group's Youth Fusion program is a year-round series of film screenings, exhibitions, workshops, and performances organized by curators to highlight the exceptional art being produced by kids right here in Boston. Check the Web site for current events and exhibitions.

Coop for Kids
Harvard Coop
1400 Massachusetts Avenue Cambridge
(617) 499–2000
www.harvard.bkstore.com

The Coop offers arts and crafts after their Story Telling events, which take place every Tuesday and Saturday. Story Telling events begin at 11:00 a.m. and run for a little under thirty minutes. After the stories, children are offered the opportunity to make crafts for free. This activity is best for kids ages two through six.

FILMS FOR THE YOUNG'UNS

AMC Boston Common
175 Tremont Street
(617) 423–3499
www.amctheatres.com/smc

This fun summer movie camp runs each Wednesday from mid-June to early August. The pre-movie activities run from 9:30 to 10:15 a.m. and include coloring contests, balloons, and special guests. Then the real fun starts: movies! They begin at 10:30 a.m. and are rated G or PG. Children are admitted on a first-come, first-served basis.

Boston Public Library Kids Cinema
Boston Public Library
700 Boylston Street
(617) 536–5400
www.bpl.org

The BPL's Kids Cinema program occurs on the first Friday of each month at the Central Branch Library in Copley Square. The program features two or three short movies, geared to short attention spans, and they begin at 10:15 a.m. The program runs about fifty to sixty minutes and is appropriate for kids ages three through seven. The showings happen in the Rabb Lecture Hall, which seats 350, but arrive early as these shows do fill up. Occasionally, feature movies are presented on Sunday at 2:00 p.m. and are more appropriate for children who are slightly older. Check the Web site for the most up-to-date information. (See Appendix B and the Film chapter for a list of other metropolitan-area libraries that host periodic films.)

Children's movies are also regularly screened at the following branch libraries throughout the city:

Charlestown
179 Main Street; (617) 242–1248; children's films on Tuesday at 10:30 a.m.

Dorchester
Lower Mills Branch, 27 Richmond Street; (617) 298–7841; children's films on Friday at 10:30 a.m. (schedule varies; consult Web site for details).

East Boston
276 Meridian Street; (617) 569–0271; children's films on Friday at 10:00 and 11:00 a.m.

Jamaica Plain
Connolly Branch, 433 Centre Street; (617) 522–1960; children's films on Wednesday at 10:30 a.m.

Mattapan
10 Hazelton Street; (617) 298–9218; children's films on Thursday at 10:30 a.m.

North End
25 Parmenter Street; (617) 227–8135; children's film on Monday at 11:00 a.m.

Roslindale
4238 Washington Street; (617) 323–2343; preschooler films on Monday at 10:30 a.m.

Roxbury
Egleston Square Branch, 2044 Columbus Avenue; (617) 445–4340; preschooler film on Monday at 11:00 a.m.; grown-up films on Thursday at noon.

Parker Hill Branch, 1497 Tremont Street; (617) 427–3820; preschooler film on Friday at 10:30 a.m.

South Boston
646 East Broadway; (617) 268–0180; children's films every other Wednesday at 10:30 a.m. and noon.

South End
685 Tremont Street; (617) 536–8241; preschooler films Mondays at 10:30 a.m.

Brookline Public Library
361 Washington Street
Brookline
(617) 730–2370
www.town.brookline.ma.us/Library/Children/programs.htm

This good library hosts the Friday Flicks, a series of movies for preschoolers, every Friday morning at 10:30 a.m.

GOING **BATS** FOR **BASEBALL:** GETTING **YOUR** SOX **ON**

It would be impossible to visit, or live in, Boston without experiencing the Boston Red Sox. If you're a New Englander (like me), you already know the heroic tale too well: for eighty-six long years this apparently cursed franchise ripped the hearts out of locals, coming close but never quite making it, while the hated Yankees ran off something like seven hundred World Series championships. Perennially depressed New Englanders figured we'd die before the curse was broken.

In 2004, though, that all changed: amazingly, Boston did win a World Series, and then in 2007 they did it *again*.

Now people in Boston actually smile in summertime—and some say it's all because of what the Sox accomplished.

Attending a game at Fenway—the oldest and (still) coolest-looking park in the majors—is the Holy Grail of a Boston visit. It used to be a legitimately cheap experience (I remember $2.00 bleacher seats in the '70s, though you were taking your chances with *that* crowd). But it isn't cheap anymore. With the team's new success have come rising ticket prices and a squeeze on available seats; now, amazingly, Fenway commands the *most* expensive ticket in baseball's least modern park. We're talking $20 to $30 for the cheapest grandstand seats, *if* you can get one; a lot higher if you have to buy through a ticket broker.

If you really want to attend a game in person on the cheap, you're down to a few options, none of them promising: 1. There are a few tickets reserved by the club and sold by the box office on game day, but those draw long lines for a limited shot at the goods. 2. Show up and the park and buy from a scalper on game day. Are you nuts? Figure $150 apiece for *that* privilege. Or, 3. Score some from a friend who works with the team or works for a company that reserves season tickets for VIP clients. Yeah. Fat chance.

But don't despair. I've put together a Sox-on-the-cheap itinerary just for you that combines many elements of the Red Sox experience that gets you entrée to Red Sox nation without paying through the nose. It involves a clever three-part strategy of touring the park before the game, suiting up at a discount . . . then catching the contest at the de facto fan headquarters of the team (a nearby bar, of course).

And don't be ashamed. Lots of locals do what I'm about to describe.

Fenway Tours

Depart from The Souvenir Store
19 Yawkey Way
(617) 226–6666
tours@redsox.com

Next best thing to catching a game live? Touring the ballpark before the game, then watching in a bar nearby. And Fenway's got you covered both ways. Tours of the park depart from the Souvenir Shop (right on Yawkey Way, across from service gate D) on the hour from 9:00 a.m. to 4:00 p.m. (if there's a daytime game, there are no tours), and cost only $12 per person for adults and $10 for kids—a lot cheaper than game tickets. And you don't get to see jockstraps hanging in lockers in the bleachers. Note that during the off-season the tours continue, but don't touch the field; they're a little cheaper, come with historical presentations, and take place in climate-controlled suites rather than down on the diamond, which must be protected.

Game On!

82 Lansdowne Street
(617) 351–7001

Ah, the stories this bar could tell. This sports pub, right across the street (literally) from Fenway's Green Monster—and if you don't know what that is, you're living in the wrong town—is ground zero for Sox activity on game days. Outside it looks like a Harvard Square bookstore or cafe, except for the Sox fans milling about enjoying pre-game banter about pitching matchups. Inside, though, it's a sports bar all the way, with what seem like a million TVs broadcasting every pitch in high-def. Celebs and even actual Red Sox players (ones on the disabled list) sometimes wander in; home runs over the left field wall could roll right in the door.

To get you started, here are some critical fashion tips on *not* appearing to be a newbie at this. First, do *not* under any circumstances allow your girl (or yourself, if you are a girl) to wear a pink Red Sox hat; locals will go bananas. Do *not* say anything nice (nothing!) about New York. Do *not* mangle Japanese pitchers' names; keep it simple—Dice-K, Okie. Do *not* pronounce your r's. Do not question Big Papi. And do *not* call Kevin Youkilis by his first or last name, ever; it's "Youuuuuuuuuuuuk." Only.

Total cost of enjoying a game at the bar? One beer, my friend. One beer.

The Souvenir Store
19 Yawkey Way

Everybody who's anybody drops by The Souvenir Store, run by Arthur D'Angelo. Henry co-ran it until passing away in the 1980s), pre-game. Angelo has stories aplenty to tell: he hung out with Hall of Famer Ted Williams while the cantankerous outfielder patrolled left field at Fenway. And the best part? You can drop a load suiting up in full gear with a regulation hat, Daisuke Matsuzaka uniform, and a pennant to wave—or just browse for an hour, buy a fridge magnet or bumper sticker for a loved one, and call it good.

BOATLOADS **OF** FUN: **WATER** SPORTS

Community Boating Inc.
21 David Mugar Way
(617) 523–1038
www.community-boating.org/jr_classes.php

The Catch Junior Program membership is $1.00, and kids must be able to swim 75 yards.

For more than sixty years, Community Boating has been teaching people how to sail, kayak, and windsurf on the gentle waters of the Charles River. Community Boating headquarters is located in a historic boathouse to the east of the Hatch Shell on the Esplanade. For $1.00, kids ages ten through eighteen can take part in the Junior Program, which runs from mid-June through late August, Monday through Friday from 9:00 a.m. to 3:00 p.m. Participants must have parental permission. Classes in all water sports are offered in a variety of skill levels.

Courageous Sailing Center
1 First Avenue (Charlestown Navy Yard)
Charlestown
(617) 242–3821
www.courageoussailing.org

The Catch Sign up by the first week of April to get in. Spots fill quickly.

For more than two decades, Courageous Sailing has taught kids eight to eighteen years old how to sail. Classes are free and are held in Charlestown, Jamaica Plain, and Dorchester on a first-come, first-served basis. The sessions are eight weeks long, with classes held in the morning and afternoon.

G-Row Boston
600 Pleasant Street
Watertown
(617) 923–7564
www.growboston.org

Started by Olympic rower Holly Metcalf, this rowing program is free to girls who are in the seventh through twelfth grades in the Boston public schools. The program helps girls learn a new sport, develop self-confidence, and learn the importance of teamwork and competition. There is an after-school program that runs from September through May and meets three afternoons per week. Registration begins in September and again in November. There's also a weeklong summer camp program, also for seventh- through twelfth-grade girls, that meets every day for one week from 9:00 a.m. to 2:00 p.m. Registration takes place near the end of the school year. All classes take place at the Community Rowing Boathouse, located on Nonantum Road on the Newton/Brighton line, and G-Row provides transportation from local subway stops for team members.

Piers Park Sailing Program
95 Marginal Street
East Boston
(617) 561–6677
www.piersparksailing.org

This program offers free sailing lessons throughout the year for Boston kids ages ten through seventeen. To participate, teens must have basic swimming skills and a health/immunization record. PPSP is also wheelchair accessible for kids with physical challenges. Programs run after school in the spring, all summer, and after school in early fall. In addition to sailing instruction, each summer program includes a full-day sailing field trip to some of the beautiful islands in Boston Harbor.

PARKS AND PLAYGROUNDS

Boston Common Frog Pond
Boston Common
(617) 635–2120
www.bostoncommonfrogpond.org

The Frog Pond is a privately funded facility that is jointly operated by the Parks Department and the private foundation created to build it. During the winter months, it's a skating rink; in the summer months, it's a wading pool and fountain. There's a warming hut and refreshment stand next to the pond, and it's one of the most popular spots in the city when the temperature dips. The skating rink is open from mid-November to mid-March and is free for children thirteen and under. (Skate rental is $8.00, $5.00 for kids under thirteen.) For children older than thirteen, admission is $4.00. It's open Monday from 10:00 a.m. to 5:00 p.m., Sunday through Thursday from 10:00 a.m. to 9:00 p.m., and Friday and Saturday from 10:00 a.m. to 10:00 p.m. There's no charge for use of the wading pool in the summer months.

Christopher Columbus Waterfront Park
Commercial Street (next to Long Wharf)
(617) 635–4505
www.bostonharborwalk.com

This is Boston's first waterfront park, and it features a magnificent view of the harbor and the sailboats moored along the nearby wharves. The park has grassy open space, a wisteria-covered trellis, spray showers for kids to play in (bring towels), a play lot, and a rose garden. It's a great relaxing place to sit down and cool off after a day of trotting the kids around town.

Feast of the East Festival
East Arlington Business District
Massachusetts Avenue
East Arlington
(781) 643–4600
www.feastoftheeast.com

This annual festival, organized by the Arlington Chamber of Commerce, happens in early June and offers free entertainment to children—pony rides, face painting, cotton candy and popcorn, clowns, and balloons. Come to hear the free musical entertainment and to enjoy free arts and crafts.

GREENS **KEEPERS:**
FREE KIDS' **GREEN** SPACES

Boston Parks and Recreation Department
1010 Massachusetts Avenue, third floor
(617) 635–4505
www.cityofboston.gov/parks

The Parks and Recreation Department administers and/or maintains dozens of playgrounds, tot lots, gardens, parks, cemeteries, and playing fields throughout metropolitan Boston. Their Web site provides a complete searchable list, as well as links to ongoing activities sponsored by the department.

Massachusetts Department of Conservation and Recreation
251 Causeway Street, Suite 600
(617) 626–1250
www.mass.gov/dcr

The DCR is the state agency that administers many of the public spaces, state parks, and recreational facilities throughout the Commonwealth of Massachusetts. These facilities include ice-skating rinks, tennis courts, public pools, beaches, and playgrounds. The Web site features a searchable, comprehensive, well-organized list of all the public recreation facilities and parks throughout the metro area and Massachusetts, including the Esplanade and the Paul Dudley White Bike Path. The site also includes an updated calendar of current events at DCR facilities, which includes the Hatch Memorial Band Shell on the Esplanade, as well as other popular outdoor event locations.

Memorial Drive Sundays
Cambridge
(617) 626–1250
www.mass.gov/dcr/parks/metroboston/charlesR-activities.htm

Memorial Drive from Eliot Bridge to Western Avenue is closed on Sunday from 11:00 a.m. to 7:00 p.m., beginning the last Sunday of April and ending the second Sunday of November. The road becomes a family park where you and the kids can walk, bike, and skate without worrying about traffic. Vendors, music, and skating lessons are often available along the route, and there are plenty of benches and grassy areas between Memorial Drive and the Charles River, which flows next to the road for the length of the closed area.

Minuteman Bike Path
www.minutemanbikeway.org

This 11-mile trail, which begins at Alewife Station in Cambridge and ends at Depot Park on South Street in Bedford, literally passes through New England's colonial heritage. In towns like Lexington, Arlington, and Bedford, the trail passes locations where our forebears fought for independence. The Minuteman Path, administered by a variety of local bike-oriented volunteer organizations, including MassBike, is one of the first and best bike path conversions in the country. It met with stiff community resistance when first proposed, but now it's a very popular weekend family destination and, as such, can get very crowded. It's mostly flat, so it's perfect for young bicyclists or in-line skaters. Markers pointing out areas of historic or natural significance add a nice educational element. It's also a popular bike commuter route, since it ends at a major subway station. The path is open from 5:00 a.m. to 9:00 p.m. every day. (In winter, it becomes a popular cross-country ski path.)

Miriam & Sidney Stoneman Playground
On the Charles River Esplanade, between Fairfield Street and Massachusetts Avenue (Back Bay). From Copley Square, follow Fairfield Street to the river.
(617) 227–0365
www.esplanadeassociation.org

This beautiful playground along the banks of the Charles River is owned by the state Department of Conservation and Recreation and was built with funds raised by the Esplanade Association. The play space has two areas. One is for kids under three and features climbing structures, slides, baby swings, and a toy car. Older kids can climb on the challenging jungle gym, which has a cool fire pole, monkey bars, swinging tire, and more. The playground is open daily from dawn to dusk. On Sunday afternoons during the summer, the volunteers with the Esplanade Association host a variety of fun events for kids, including model sailboat racing, fishing lessons, and puppet shows. Check out the Web site for event details and times.

A **FREE** INDOOR **PLAY** SPACE

Play Space at Atrium Mall
300 Boylston Street Chestnut Hill
(617) 527–1400

This play space in a suburban shopping mall is free, although constant parental supervision is required. There are climbing structures for the kids, a seating area (with big-screen TV!) for parents, and funhouse-like mirrors on the walls, and the floor is padded with soft mats. The play area is located on the fourth floor, but keep in mind that the restrooms are located way down on the first floor. It's open during regular mall hours Monday through Saturday 10:00 a.m. to 9:30 p.m. and Sunday 11:00 a.m. to 6:00 p.m. Tip: The place gets more crowded with young schoolkids after school; if you have an infant, come in the morning.

FREE AND **CHEAP** **MUSEUMS** AND **HISTORIC** SITES

Boston Children's Museum
300 Congress Street
(617) 426–6500
www.bostonkids.org

The Catch $1.00 admission on Friday from 5:00 to 9:00 p.m.; admission is $8.00 to $10.00 per person at other times. Children under sixteen must be supervised by an adult at all times.

For more than ninety years, this museum has featured terrific interactive and educational exhibits that keep the kids occupied and enthralled. Exhibits include a section celebrating Boston's ethnic diversity, a science workshop, a turtle-viewing area, and historical toys. There are also ongoing special events, and everything at this award-winning museum is hands-on. Admission is about ten bucks on most days, but thanks to sponsorship from the department store chain Target, it's just $1.00 per person on Friday nights. Go then (but you won't be alone).

Castle Island and Fort Independence

William Day Boulevard
South Boston
(617) 727–5290
www.bostonharborwalk.org

This outdoor space is historic and eclectic and can provide more than enough activities to keep your family occupied all day. Part of the Harborwalk system of walking trails throughout Boston, Castle Island is a peninsula that juts into Boston Harbor, providing spectacular views of the airport, harbor shipping activity, and the Harbor Islands. On one end of Castle Island is an enclosed lagoon that boasts a beautiful beach. The walking path that surrounds the lagoon is great for cycling, walking, and in-line skating. Castle Island is also home to Fort Independence, a stone armory that dates back to 1851. It's open during summer, when walking tours are free on Saturday and Sunday between Memorial Day weekend and Labor Day weekend, from noon to 3:30 p.m. The tours last about thirty minutes. The fort and the island are on the State and National Registers of Historic Places, and Fort Independence is a National Historic Landmark. There's a clam shack near the large parking lot (the lot fills up early in the summer), and a place to rent little sailboats to use in the lagoon if that's your thing. Picnic tables and grills are located throughout the area, and the entire place is swarming with families on nice summer days.

Faneuil Hall

State Street across from City Hall
(617) 523–1300
www.faneuilhallmarketplace.com

This shopping and dining paradise is also a bonanza for kids—entertainers of all stripes fill the walkways and courtyards throughout the day to make you laugh, sing, or marvel at their magic. Several musicians, storytellers, acrobats, and clowns are usually strolling around on any given summer weekend day. Check the Web site to see who is performing, but it's best to simply show up and see who's around. Just walk toward the big, clapping crowd.

John Fitzgerald Kennedy National Historic Site

83 Beals Street
Brookline
(617) 566–7937
www.nps.gov/jofi

This is the renovated birthplace and first home of President John F. Kennedy. Each May through mid-September, it's open Wednesday through Sunday 10:00 a.m. to 4:30 p.m., with guided tours occurring every thirty minutes until 3:30 p.m., after which a sort of informal open house takes place until closing. The home, where JFK was born in 1917, was purchased back by the family after his 1963 assassination. His mother, Rose Kennedy, painstakingly decorated the home and chose the mementos and photographs that commemorate the president's life. Student learning and activity materials are available. National Park Service rangers also lead tours in the neighborhood to point out places that played an important role in JFK's childhood.

Massachusetts State House

Beacon Street at Park Street
(617) 727–3676
www.sec.state.ma.us/trs/trsgen/genidx.htm

Designed by renowned architect Charles Bulfinch and completed in 1798, the impressive Massachusetts State House (overlooking Boston Common) is a fascinating walk through one of the earliest houses of democracy in the country. The State House is open to the public Monday through Friday year round from 10:00 a.m. until 4:00 p.m., and free tours are given throughout the day. Tours take thirty to forty-five minutes, and guides dispense fascinating facts, like this one: the ladybug is the official state bug of Massachusetts. Who knew?

Museum of Afro-American History

46 Joy Street (Beacon Hill)
(617) 725–0022
www.afroammuseum.org

The Catch Donations accepted. No parking on site.

This not-for-profit cultural museum celebrates the contributions of African Americans. It's open Monday through Saturday 10:00 a.m. to 4:00 p.m. and is free. Learn about black film stars, scientists, politicians, movers and shakers, and more. Special events and lectures are also available. Check the Web site for updated info.

Museum of Science

O'Brien Highway (Science Park)
(617) 723–2500
(617) 589–0267 (observatory hotline)
www.mos.org

One of the best science museums in the United States (maybe the world), Boston's very own Museum of Science charges a fee to get in, and it's not cheap. Fortunately for families, it also offers several participatory events that are free to all. The first, located in the lobby of the museum's Charles Hayden Planetarium, is called Welcome to the Universe. Its goal is to put into perspective the vast size of our universe and solar system. The exhibit includes the Community Solar System Trail, an interactive treasure hunt for bronze "planet" models that have been placed around the city at appropriate relative distances from the "sun" model in the Hayden Planetarium. Before you visit the Universe exhibit, go to the MoS Web site, and print out the **Community Solar System Passport** (www.mos.org/automedia/media/pdf/1893_passport.pdf). It includes directions to locations throughout the metro-Boston area where you can find each "planet." Take a rubbing of each planet to complete the passport. Then, mail the passport to the museum, and your child will get a special certificate commemorating his or her planet-finding prowess. Planets are located as far away as the Riverside T station in Newton. All planets are accessible by public transportation.

The museum lets all comers visit the Gillian Observatory and its Meade LX200 telescope for free on Friday nights from 8:30 to 10:00 p.m. The observatory is located on the top level of the museum's parking garage (parking is not free). Call the observatory hotline to find out what constellations are visible on a given night. Museum employees will be on hand to help you enjoy the stars.

USS *Constitution* and Museum

Charlestown Navy Yard, Charlestown
(617) 426–1812
www.ussconstitutionmuseum.org

This museum/ship, the oldest commissioned ship in the U.S. Navy, has free admission and offers a number of free child-oriented programs. Kids can explore the life of a sailor, discuss piracy, and look at nautical art. Tours are available. The museum is open May 1 through October 15 from 9:00 a.m. to 6:00 p.m. and October 16 through April 30 from 10:00 a.m. to 5:00 p.m.

TOY STORES:
A GREAT PLACE TO HANG OUT

These stores are destinations in and of themselves—packed with the latest in fun toys and teeming with other kids. And while I think it's borderline cruel to take kids to a toy store if you're not going to buy them a toy, these stores make it worth your while to stop in. Each one has a fun space for kids to enjoy themselves, but don't be surprised if you hear that familiar, plaintive cry—"Pleeeeeeez!"

The Construction Site
200 Moody Street
Waltham
(781) 899–7900
www.constructiontoys.com

Build it and they will come. This store has just about every building block or tool ever made for kids. Play spaces around the store are equipped with various types of building toys and blocks to help your child discover the budding architect within.

Curious George Goes to Wadsworth
1 JFK Street
Cambridge
(617) 498–0062
www.curiousg.com

This great bookstore features artisan toys. Although the store is centered around the theme of the beloved monkey, there are hundreds of other books and products that kids can peruse.

Henry Bear's Park
www.henrybear.com
361 Huron Avenue; Cambridge; (617) 547–8424
19 Harvard Street; Brookline Village; (617) 264–2422
685 Massachusetts Avenue; Arlington; (781) 646–9400

This store has repeatedly been named the best toy store in the Boston area by a variety of local publications. It has an amazing array of toys and a friendly, attentive staff. Kids can drive trains across the big train table, play house in the kitchen play space, and play with Legos and Duplos on the building-block table. Parental supervision is required.

Home Depot Kids' Workshops
www.homedepotclinics.com
5 Allstate Road; South Bay Plaza; (617) 442–6110
75 Mystic Avenue; Somerville; (617) 623–0001
1 Mystic View Road; Everett; (617) 389–2323
615 Arsenal Street; Watertown; (617) 926–0299
1100 Revere Beach Parkway; Chelsea; (617) 889–4258
1213 VFW Parkway; West Roxbury; (617) 327–5000
Hours may vary due to unforeseen circumstances, so call ahead.

The Catch For kids ages five to twelve. Children must be accompanied by an adult.

Give a kid a dollhouse, and she'll play for a day. Teach her to build her own, and one day she just might build you a new dining room set. Home Depot workshops help kids complete a small construction project—like a birdhouse or a picture frame. These workshops are taught at every Home Depot in the country and are designed to teach children ages five through twelve do-it-yourself skills and tool safety. (Plus, nothing beats the feeling of building something yourself.) Prefabricated kits help make the projects easy (or at least easier), and every kid receives the coveted orange Home Depot associate's apron and an achievement pin. Projects include art easels, leaf presses, and the like. The workshops are held the first Saturday of each month between 9:00 a.m. and noon.

Magic Beans
312 Harvard Street Brookline
(617) 264–2326
www.mbeans.com

This great upscale kids' store features a fenced-off play space called Play-scape in the back; it's perfect for babies who are crawling or just learning to walk. There's also a restroom close by the area—which can be key for on-the-fly diaper changing. Magic Beans holds story hours for kids at the shop, though the times vary—call the store ahead for the latest details, or check their Web site. Also remember that Playscape sometimes shuts down, such as in December (when it becomes an ad hoc gift-wrapping area).

Stella Bella Toys

1360 Cambridge Street
Cambridge (Inman Square)
(617) 491–6290

and

1967 Massachusetts Avenue
Cambridge (Porter Square)
(617) 864–6290

This is a great place for new moms and little tykes. It has a play space with a huge, colorful mural as the backdrop and lots of great books and games. At the Inman Square location, a New Parent Coffee Hour is held Friday mornings at 10:30 a.m., an event that allows parents to socialize while their babies play with (or chew on) toys for sale at the store. The store also offers toddler and infant play groups on Tuesday mornings and kids' music classes on Saturdays and Mondays. There are fewer events at the newer Porter Square location.

STORYTELLING HOURS

The public library system in the metro-Boston area has made an enormous commitment to ensuring that children develop a love of reading as early as possible. That's why nearly every branch of the public libraries in Boston, Cambridge, Newton, Dedham, Needham, Milton, and other surrounding communities host frequent story hours for children from toddlers up to school age. For a complete listing of branches, and Web sites that list story hours, see Appendix B.

In addition, most bookstores in the area run some sort of children's story hour (in the hope you'll buy the books your kid enjoyed so much). Here's a partial list of shops.

Barefoot Books

1771 Massachusetts Avenue
Cambridge
(617) 349–1610
www.barefootbooks.com

This home-grown kids' bookstore/publisher is so good that the FAO Schwarz toy store in New York City has a section dedicated to its creations! Check the store's Web site for story-time events; each Friday and Saturday morning there's a regular story hour (usually beginning at 10:30 a.m.), and occasionally musical performances in-shop on Sundays as well.

Barnes and Noble Bookstores

Prudential Center, 800 Boylston Street, Suite 179; (617) 247–6959
325 Harvard Street; Brookline; (617) 232–0594
170 Boylston Street; Chestnut Hill; (617) 965–7621
www.bn.com

These bookstores offer free story hours (appropriate for two- through six-year-olds), and the story times come with other fun activities geared to further expanding kids' creativity. Call the store closest to you for updated schedules and times of story hours.

Coop for Kids

Harvard Coop
1400 Massachusetts Avenue Cambridge
(617) 499–2000
www.harvard.bkstore.com

Story-time events happen on Tuesday at 11:00 a.m. and run for a little under thirty minutes.

Newtonville Books

296 Walnut Street
Newton
(617) 244–6619
www.newtonvillebooks.com

There are no formal story hours here, but there are monthly readings and signings by young adult and children's book authors. Some of these events are free. Some charge for admittance. For others, buying the book will get two people in free.

PLAY **TIME:**
CHILDREN'S **THEATER** PROGRAMS

City Stage Co. of Boston
539 Tremont Street (classes at various locations)
(617) 542–2291
www.citystage.org

This theater company offers several good free after-school theater-arts programs for children. One is geared for kids nine to twelve years old, after
school on Mondays and Wednesdays at 4:00 p.m. at 50 West Brookline Street
in the South End's lovely Blackstone Square; there's also a more intensive
Saturday program for teens, held in a different location on Copley Square.
Both programs encourage kids to write and perform their own material. Call
to register.

Dorchester Nazarene Compassionate Center Youth in Action
Theatre Arts Program Second Church of Dorchester
44 Moultrie Street (Codman Square)
Dorchester
(617) 288–2289, extension 210

The Catch There is a one-time application fee.

This program hosts an after-school theater-arts program that teaches kids
ages fifteen to seventeen about scriptwriting and staging theatrical productions. The program also includes an educational component that teaches the
history of theater arts. Admission takes place throughout the school year.
Most sessions take place on Fridays after school and on weekends. Hours
vary.

Huntington Theatre Company
264 Huntington Avenue
(617) 273–1558
www.huntingtontheatre.org

One of the best theater companies in the city, Boston University's Huntington
Theatre is also one of the most dedicated to community outreach and education—and that includes of young ones. The company offers comprehensive
after-school programs during the school year. For younger kids, ages eleven to

fifteen, acting classes provide a comprehensive introduction to theater; teens and more experienced thespians can take a second-level class. There are also Scene Study and Playwriting workshops overseen by theater professionals. All programs meet once a week, usually from 4:00 to 6:00 p.m., during the school year (day of week varies by semester and program). Inquire about current costs, as well as the theater company's scholarship program, which generally involves nothing more than a kid-written essay to the company's education director; this can dramatically slash the cost of the classes. And here's the best part: After completing any one of these programs, kids get a special Huntington Student Club card that entitles them to two free tickets to every Huntington Theatre production each year until they turn twenty-one!

Parking Allowed: Arts in the Parks

Boston is a city of parks, and since 1997 the mayor's office has sponsored a celebration of the arts, known as **ParkARTS,** that makes full use of those glorious green spaces. The program features more than eighty free, participatory, performing and visual arts programs in parks and common spaces throughout the city all summer long. The performances and offerings include theater (Shakespeare in local parks; stages for small local theater groups to showcase their talents), musical performances, Monday night movies (family-friendly flicks screened in a different neighborhood park each week), and hands-on arts and crafts workshops during the summer.

Since 1998 the Parks Department has also worked with Boston's Institute of Contemporary Art (ICA) to present contemporary works of art in Boston's open spaces through the ICA's Vita Brevis program. ParkARTS is responsible for almost half of the programs offered throughout the park system, and they are all free and open to the public. For more information on events coming to a park near you, check out the schedule on the Parks Department Web site at www.cityofboston.gov/parks/parkarts.

CHEAP CHIC:
LOW-COST CLOTHING AND HOUSEHOLD GOODS

"One man's trash is another man's treasure."

—ANONYMOUS

In a city as affluent as Boston, there are some real treasures hiding in our thrift stores—some are so good you feel like you're stealing. It's not unusual to find couture from last year on the racks next to beat-up sweatshirts and scratched lamps.

Nothing this good comes easy, though. You will pay with shoe leather, elbows in the ribs from other aggressive shoppers, and, possibly, a headache from time spent sifting through the haystack to find the proverbial needle. Also note that some of our thrift stores sell such high-end stuff that although items are marked way, way down, they're still far from what you'd call cheap. It's all about value: What would you pay for last season's Versace? (If "nothing" is still your preferred price point, and you're in need of some household goods, there's no better place to look than curbside on trash day. If you hit the right part of town, you could potentially furnish your home with high-quality stuff in need of just a little fluffing and buffing. But we didn't tell you to do that. Not us.)

FREE **STYLE:** THRIFT, **CONSIGNMENT,** AND **SECONDHAND** SHOPS

This is by no means a comprehensive list of every thrift, consignment, or secondhand store in the Boston area, but these are widely regarded as having the best selection, the best turnover of product, and the best prices.

Boomerang's
716 Centre Street
Jamaica Plain
(617) 524–5120
www.aac.org/boomerangs

Boomerangs is the Boston AIDS Action Committee's award-winning resale store, stocking new and used clothes for men, women, and children. It'll be tough to find many items over $10, unless you want a new men's suit—which would cost you about $20. A portion of the sales go to support the AAC's outreach to people living with AIDS.

Children's Orchard
807 Boylston Street Brookline
(617) 277–3006
www.childrensorchard.com/component/option,com_store/store_num,75/
action,home

This store is the most central Children's Orchard franchise store in Massachusetts, and if you're looking for kids' toys, furniture, books, or accessories—name it—you can find it here. The shop features gently used children's items. If you don't see what you want the first time you visit, come back in a week, as merchandise turns over frequently.

(You could also call the company's customer service line, at 1–800–999–KIDS; they might be able to track the item down.)

Christ Church Thrift Shop
17 Farwell Place Cambridge
(617) 492–3335
www.cccambridge.org/programs_shop.php

The Catch September through June, open Tuesday, Wednesday, Thursday, and Saturday from 10:00 a.m. to 4:00 p.m. Summer, call ahead for opening hours.

The Church Lady has never looked this chic. Started in Christ Church back in the 1960s, the Thrift Shop now occupies three large rooms in a building behind the church, and proceeds fund the 240-year-old church's preservation. The rooms are packed with what the Thrift Store likes to call "experienced" clothing: pre-read books, tested knickknacks, small home goods, and the like. You might also find some designer dresses, costume jewelry, and fine men's suits, shirts, and sweaters. The Thrift Shop is a favorite with the college crowd—and Cheap Bastards, too. Note that this shop is open four days a week most of the year, and often closed in summertime; call for hours at that time.

The Closet
175 Newbury Street
(617) 536–1919

This store falls into the category of "you get what you pay for." The items are a bit north of your basic "thrift" or "secondhand" store price point, and they no longer sell furniture, but the quality and selection are so high that some shoppers never tell their friends they buy their couture here. The word is out anyway, though: The Closet is one of the most popular, well-stocked secondhand stores on all of Newbury Street. Clothing sold here is usually not older than two years, or else it's clearly vintage. Generally it's open from 10:00 a.m. until 5:30 p.m.

Garment District
200 Broadway
Cambridge
(617) 876–5230
www.garment-district.com

Take a deep breath and put on elbow pads. At the Garment District, which bills itself as an "alternative department store" (cool!), there's a tremendous variety of jeans, fun costumes, wigs, vintage, accessories, housewares, jewelry, and makeup on its second floor. But everybody knows about it. Save the second floor for later—first hit the ground floor, known as "Dollar-a-Pound," where all clothing in the warehouse-sized space is $1.50 a pound (not one dollar)—there's every style of clothing here for young and old. Some of it is ripped and some of it's perfect, some is stained and some is clean as a whistle. Take your chances. (Toys and household items are a dollar a pound.) On Friday, all the Dollar-a-Pound stuff is just 75 cents a pound. Wear a mouth guard on these days; the competition can be fierce among even-cheaper-than-you locals.

Karma Designer Consignment Boutique
26 Prince Street
(617) 723–8338

Enter this store and be transfixed. Gorgeous high-end consignment items—Versace, Chanel, even some new items—await. Nothing here is exactly cheap, but it's super-cheap compared with the original ticket price you would have paid when these little gems were new. Besides, they're new to you, right? The store's usually open from about noon until 7 p.m., sometimes even later—amazing, in Boston.

Morgan Memorial Goodwill Inc.

www.goodwillmass.org
1010 Harrison Avenue; (617) 541–1270
520 Massachusetts Avenue (Central Square); Cambridge; (617) 868–6330
230 Elm Street; Somerville; (617) 628–3618
470 West Broadway; South Boston; (617) 307–6367

Shop in the stores that first started the secondhand craze. From vintage and retro to designer brands and popular household items, you'll find it all—and you'll be funding a good cause—at these Boston Goodwill branches. Think these prices couldn't get any cheaper? Wrong! The Harrison Avenue location even has an outlet section. (The outlet center is closed Sundays, but otherwise all locations are open daily.)

Oona's

1210 Massachusetts Avenue
Cambridge
(617) 491–2654

Looking for just the right item to wear to that '70s disco party? Halloween? A fancy cocktail party? Tiny Oona's is legendary for its costumes, crazy vintage items (like garish fake furs), leather coats, and peacoats. It's the place to go for vintage and retro clothing. You could spend an entire afternoon playing dress-up with all the wigs and gloves they have in stock. Usually open 11:00 a.m. until about 7:00 p.m.

Poor Little Rich Girl

416 Highland Avenue
Somerville
(617) 684–0157
www.poorlittlerichgirlstore.com

The Catch No men's clothing.

There's barely room to move at Poor Little Rich Girl, but everywhere you look is a designer label no more than two or three years old (unless it's clearly vintage) and in perfect condition. Want a suede jacket for under $50? A Saks brocade cocktail dress for an impossible $40? This might be the place. The staff is super picky about what they take in on consignment, so you'll be sure to find good quality. Check the discount racks in the front of the store, too. Only catch? Girls only: no clothes for guys here, dudes. Usually open 11:00 a.m. until 7:00 p.m.

Savers
1600 VFW Parkway
West Roxbury
(617) 323–8231
www.savers.com

Savers is a chain of thrift stores across the country, and they get shipments frequently from their nonprofit partners. They stock designer and vintage clothing, home decor, books, toys, electronics—it's like the Wal-Mart of thrift stores. Go early and go often, as they replenish their stock several times a week.

Second Time Around
www.secondtimearound.net
176 Newbury Street; (617) 247–3504
219 Newbury Street; (617) 266–1113
82 Charles Street; (617) 227–0049
8 Eliot Street; Cambridge; (617) 491–7185
1169 Walnut Street; Newton; (617) 964–4481
300 Boylston Street; Chestnut Hill (Atrium Mall third floor); (617) 928–0100

For more than thirty-five years, Second Time Around has been selling barely used designer and couture items. If you set up an account on their Web site, you can even search their stock virtually and find out which store is hiding a perfect Chanel cocktail dress or pair of Blahnik pumps.

Urban Renewals
122 Brighton Avenue
Allston
(617) 783–8387

The Catch Cash only.

It's big, it's hugely popular with the college kids, and it's in "Rock City"—as Allstonians like to call their town. With all that going for it, how can you help but find the perfect shirt, dress, shoes, necklace, chair—and more—at rock-bottom prices? It gets packed here on the weekends, so head over on a weeknight. It's open from very early (usually from 8:00 a.m.) until 6:00 p.m.

Worshipping at the Original Altar of Cheap

If you have anything even approaching attention deficit disorder, you'll want to avoid the chain known as **Filene's Basement** (497 Boylston Street; (617) 424–5520; www.filenesbasement.com). This mammoth place, which for a hundred years has sold overstock and out-of-season apparel and accessories for men and women from brand-name retailers and designers, invented the term "chaos," and it is not for the faint of heart. Luckily for Cheap Bastards, its founders also invented the term "automatic markdown." The longer an item is on the shop floor, the less it costs—the reduced price is already printed right on the price tag, right next to the date on which that price will take effect. It's like eBay, except in slower motion.

The Basement started as a basement (literally) in a now-deceased Boston department store near here, but hard times forced the parent to close; the Basement, though, survived and it's now an East Coast mall chain. It piles merchandise in what look like boxes in the aisles, and hangs (some) designer clothing, dresses, and lingerie on racks. Every August, the Basement becomes a lace and satin scrum when the store holds its world-famous bridal gown sale (imagine a thousand brides trying to grab a $3,000 dress marked down to $300, and you get a pretty good mental picture).

TROLLING **FOR** TRASHY **TREASURE**

Bostonians are big consumers of stuff. When it's time to upgrade that stuff, many of them can't be bothered to go through the hassle of selling their old stuff in consignment stores or through an online auction site. For them, the most effort they're willing to put into getting rid of all their stuff is dragging it down to the curb on trash day. That's where you come in. If you are open to the idea of picking through someone else's "trash"—and I use the term loosely—you are in for a treat. It's not only furniture that you'll find out there, but lamps, filing cabinets, rugs, housewares, televisions, even computers. It may or may not operate correctly and possess all its knobs/levers/

drawers, but it's there for the taking. There are some common-sense rules you'll want to follow, though, if you want to dumpster-dive the streets.

GOLDEN RULES OF TRASH DAY ETIQUETTE

1. Only "shop" the best neighborhoods. The general rule of thumb about trash picking is this: The more expensive the real estate, the higher the quality of the trash. The hot spots are Back Bay, Beacon Hill, South End, the waterfront of the North End, and Cambridge near Harvard. From mid-May to early June, the best stuff can be found near any college or university in greater Boston—Commonwealth Avenue around Kenmore Square near Boston University, Beacon Street in Chestnut Hill near Boston College, Harvard Square, and Harvard Business School graduate housing near Western Avenue—as students clear out and head home.

2. Get there early. Trash haulers come early in the morning of the specified trash day. Boston rules stipulate that you can't put anything out on a curb any earlier than 5:00 p.m. on the day before. So: Begin your hunt around 7:00 p.m. the night before the scheduled trash pickup. That's when most people have come home from work, and they're likely to lug the big items down to the curb before they settle down for dinner.

Rarely will people put the good stuff out on the morning of trash day—the trucks come too early, and who wants to lug furniture out of the house before they've even had a cup of coffee?

3. Bring a hand truck. If you don't mind being clearly identified as a trash picker, bring a hand truck, or a small rolling grocery cart (the ones that you can pull behind you on two wheels). When you see something good, it won't be there for long, so you'll want to cart it away immediately.

4. Be polite. Don't open up trash bags looking for stuff (or, if you do, tie them back up again). Some trash pickers think nothing of opening up bags, strewing the contents hither and yon, and just walking away. These people are slime in the trash-picking world; don't emulate them.

5. Expect fierce competition. There are hordes of individuals trolling the street along with you, and they've been doing it for longer than you have (sometimes out of necessity). There's no hierarchy among trash pickers, but if you find yourself in a standoff with an obvious veteran of the wars, it's probably best to back down—and live to trash-pick another day.

6. Be discreet. Wait until the person putting out the trash has gone back inside before pouncing. People really don't want to see their former items being hauled off by people who are clearly going to reuse them right at the moment of dispensement. It destroys the illusion that the item is simply disappearing into the Big Dump in the Sky. I've seen people haul stuff back *inside* if they think there's a feeding frenzy brewing—if it's that valuable, they figure they'll keep it and put in on eBay. Discretion is the better part of trash-picking valor. Um. Yeah.

TRASH-HAULING SCHEDULE
City of Boston Public Works Department
Sanitation Division
Boston City Hall, Room 714
(617) 635–7575
www.cityofboston.gov/myneighborhood

Boston's trash-hauling schedule is a little complicated. Neighborhoods are divided up for trash hauling in various ways, and sometimes the same street has one, two, or three collection days, while a neighbor down the same street might have anywhere from one to three pickup days—on different days! To be safe, use the city of Boston's convenient search engine to plug in your specific street addresses and find out exactly when the trash pickup is scheduled for that street.

CHEAP CHECKUPS:
LOW- AND NO-COST HEALTH
AND MEDICAL CARE

"The first wealth is health."

—RALPH WALDO EMERSON

Boston has got to be the undisputed medical capital of the free world (or at least North America), with more quality hospitals than most cities twice its size. As the cost of care continues to skyrocket, it's comforting to know that dozens of hospitals and clinics in town offer free and reduced-cost care. Factor in the medical schools here, and this becomes a great place to get sick. Not that there is a good place to get sick. Heck. You know what we mean.

CLINICAL **TRIALS** AND **RESEARCH**

Boston has one of the most active medical research communities in the country; boatloads of grant money flow into town to fuel the world-class researchers, fellows, university science departments, and private pharma firms here. That means clinical trials are conducted at almost every hospital in town: good news for under-the-weather cheapies. If you meet the requirements for a particular clinical trial, you can get treatment for free, plus follow-up care and guaranteed lickety-split attention to any complications that might arise from a medication. Some of the trials even offer stipends for participation. Many hospitals conduct psychiatric clinical trials and research, as well.

There are always risks associated with clinical trials, of course, so be sure to balance your need for care with the potential risks of becoming a human guinea pig. Consult the Center for Information & Study on Clinical Research Participation (online at www.ciscrp.org) for a comprehensive overview of exactly what being in a clinical trial entails—including the risks.

Beth Israel Deaconness Medical Center
300 Brookline Avenue
(617) 667–7000
www.bidmc.harvard.edu

Though you'd hardly guess from the name, Beth Israel is actually a teaching hospital operated by Harvard's medical school. To access a list of its clinical trials, go to the home page (see above) and type "clinical trial" into the search box at the top of the page; in response, it will display links to information about all current clinical trials available for enrollment, both on-site and also sometimes off-site. Trials are available in all clinical areas.

Boston Clinical Trials and Medical Research, Inc.
18 Shepard Street Brighton
(617) 202–6322
www.bostontrials.com/forpatients1.htm

This local firm coordinates trials of various medications for a wide variety of ailments for various sponsors, including hospitals and pharmaceutical companies.

Boston Medical Center
One Boston Medical Center Place (Massachusetts Avenue at Harrison Avenue)
(800) 841–4325 (hotline)
www.bmc.org/patients/healthconnection.html

Call the Health Connection hotline to find out about any available clinical trials. The hotline is operated from 8:30 a.m. to 5:00 p.m. weekdays (you can leave a message during other hours, and they'll call you back). Trials are available in all clinical areas.

Boston Shriners Hospital
51 Blossom Street (at Cambridge Street)
(617) 722–3000
www.shrinershq.org/Hospitals/Boston

This hospital conducts clinical trials and research relating to the treatment of burns and pain management in children. Call the hospital directly for information about current trials.

Caritas Christi Hospitals
www.caritaschristi.org

This clinical trials database lists all trials for the Caritas Christi hospitals in Massachusetts. Boston Caritas hospitals include Caritas St. Elizabeth's Medical Center (at 736 Cambridge Street) and Caritas Carney Hospital (at 2100 Dorchester Avenue in Dorchester). Trials are available in all clinical areas. Click on "Clinical Trials & Research" on the left-hand side of the organization's Boston page to get started.

Children's Hospital Boston
300 Longwood Avenue
(617) 355–6000
www.childrenshospital.org/clinicalservices.cfm

Boston's children's hospital is one of the leading pediatric hospitals in the nation. The hospital conducts clinical trials in all areas related to infant health, children's health, teenage health, and even sometimes young adults. Go to the clinical services home page (see above) to get started.

CRNet
http://crnet.mgh.harvard.edu

This great Web site serves as a clearinghouse for all the clinical trials currently being run at Massachusetts General Hospital (along Cambridge Street near Charles Street), Brigham and Women's Hospital (75 Francis Street in the Longwood area), Spaulding Rehabilitation Hospital (125 Nashua Street in the West End), and McLean Hospital (psychiatric hospital at 115 Mill Street in Belmont). Trials are available in all clinical areas, and they're easy to view and search on this very user-friendly interface.

Dana Farber Cancer Institute
44 Binney Street
(866) 408–DFCI (3324)
www.dana-farber.org/res/clinical
www.cancercare.harvard.edu/cli/find.asp

This hospital conducts numerous clinical trials on new cancer treatments and drugs, as well as psychiatric trials relating to the impact of cancer on patients and their families.

Massachusetts Eye and Ear Infirmary
243 Charles Street
(617) 523–7900
www.meei.harvard.edu/research/trialstudies.php

The Massachusetts Eye and Ear Infirmary conducts clinical trials relating to conditions and diseases of the eye, ear, nose, and throat. Visit the Web page listed above for details. (Tip: "Otolaryngology" means trials and research related to the ear, hearing, and related structures in the head and neck. Don't feel bad. We had to look it up, too.)

Mount Auburn Hospital

330 Mount Auburn Street Cambridge
(617) 499–5774 (clinical trial center line)
(617) 492–3500 (main hospital switchboard)
www.mtauburn.caregroup.org/body.cfm?id=37

This hospital, on lovely Mount Auburn Street in Cambridge, is another teaching hospital of the Harvard Medical School. It too conducts clinical trials in all clinical areas. Call the hotline for a complete listing of current trials.

New England Baptist Hospital

125 Parker Hill Avenue (off Huntington Avenue)
Roxbury
(617) 754–5800; (617) 754–5616 (clinical research line)
www.nebh.org/ResearchPrograms/5/default.aspx

This Roxbury hospital conducts clinical trials and research on diseases and conditions of the musculoskeletal systems. Check the Web site for updates on trials.

Tufts Medical Center

750 Washington Street (at Kneeland Street)
(617) 636–5000
www.tuftsmedicalcenter.org/Research/default

Tufts Medical Center and the affiliated Floating Hospital for Children conduct trials in all clinical areas. This is the home page with links to research areas.

CLINICAL **TRIAL** DATABASES

Several national online databases keep track of all clinical trials and studies in the country or specialize in a particular medical area.

AIDS Clinical Trials Information Service
http://aidsinfo.nih.gov

This site provides information on federally and privately sponsored clinical trials for people with AIDS and HIV infection. Click on "Search for clinical trials" on the right-hand side of the top of the home page (under the heading Clinical Trials) to go directly to a search engine for trials nationwide.

Center Watch
www.centerwatch.com

This site is an open resource claiming to list more than 40,000 active industry- and government-sponsored clinical trials, as well as new drug therapies in research and those recently approved by the FDA.

Coalition of Cancer Cooperative Groups
www.cancertrialshelp.org

This database lists current clinical trials relating to cancer.

EmergingMed
www.emergingmed.com
(877) 601–8601

This database of cancer-related clinical trials connects participants directly with the doctors who are conducting the trials.

National Cancer Institute
(800) 4–CANCER
www.cancer.gov/clinicaltrials

This site provides a nationwide listing of cancer-related clinical trials, plus a search engine with access to more than 6,000 trials nationwide.

U.S. National Institutes of Health
www.clinicaltrials.gov

This huge database is the granddaddy of clinical trials: it lists trials in all clinical areas, all over the world; when we spot-checked, there were 65,000 total! Surely a few (or more) were in Boston, right? Right: 1,600 at that moment.

CLINICS **AND** HOSPITALS **OFFERING** LOW-COST **CARE**

Technically speaking, all medical care in Boston is potentially free. That's because every hospital in the state is required by law to provide emergency medical care regardless of ability to pay, and some hospitals (such as Boston Medical Center, which was founded as a public hospital) give away hundreds of millions of dollars' worth of free care each year. Of course, somebody *is* ultimately paying for that care—anyone who has medical insurance, which helps reimburse hospitals for their freebies. For that reason, as well as the extremely long waiting times one finds in emergency rooms (and the impact it would have on people with genuine emergencies), avoid the E.R. as a cheap-care stop . . . unless you are faced with a true emergency, of course.

There are also dozens of low-cost insurance plans available to Bostonians who fall within certain income, demographic, or family parameters. More details on plans administered through the city of Boston and its partners, like CareNet and CenterCare (available at local community centers), are available at the Boston Public Health Commission's Web site (www.bphc.org/howto/access_adult care.asp) or through the Mayor's Health Line at (617) 534–5050.

Information on state and federal insurance programs (like MassHealth, the state's Medicaid insurance program) are available through the Commonwealth of Massachusetts Department of Health and Human Services, at www.mass.gov or by calling the Health Access and Resource line at (800) 531–2229.

HOSPITALS
Boston Medical Center
One Boston Medical Center Place (Massachusetts Avenue at Harrison Avenue)
(617) 638–8000
www.bmc.org

The BMC is the result of the merger of its predecessor hospital, the Boston City Hospital (the first public hospital in Boston), with Boston University School of Medicine. Despite the merger, the BMC has maintained its commitment to serving low- and middle-income families and underserved communities and is still considered by many as Boston's "safety net" hospital because it gives away more free care than any other hospital in the city. The BMC administers HealthNet, a managed care organization, in cooperation with fifteen community health centers throughout Boston.

Boston Shriners Hospital
51 Blossom Street
(617) 722–3000
www.shrinershq.org/Hospitals/Boston

This hospital is one of about two dozen around the country that offer free care for children under eighteen. This one specializes in burn care and rehabilitation.

BOSTON COMMUNITY HEALTH CENTERS

Boston is home to more than two dozen community health centers. In fact, the first such health center in the country opened in Dorchester in 1965. These health centers provide low-cost care geared to the needs of a neighborhood; staff deliver primary care, mental health, pediatrics, obstetrics and gynecology, dental care, and social services. (But it's not the place to go for a true emergency—go to the hospital in that case.)

Allston/Brighton
Joseph M. Smith Community Health Center
287 Western Avenue; Allston; (617) 783–0500
www.josephsmith.org

St. Elizabeth's Health Care at Brighton Marine
77 Warren Street; Brighton; (617) 562–5200
www.caritas-semc.org

Boston
Fenway Community Health Center
7 Haviland Street; (617) 267–0900; www.fenwayhealth.org
(Note: this facility is scheduled to relocate to a new building a few blocks west at 1340 Boylston Street [near Fenway Park] in 2009. Call ahead to check on the status.)

MGH Back Bay Healthcare Center
388 Commonwealth Avenue; (617) 267–7171;
www.mgh.harvard.edu/primarycareweb/primary_backbay.htm

North End Community Health Center
332 Hanover Street; (617) 643–8000; www.mgh.harvard.edu/northend

Sidney Borum Jr. Health Center
130 Boylston Street; (617) 457–8140; www.jri.org

Charlestown
MGH Charlestown Healthcare Center
73 High Street; Charlestown; (617) 724–8135; www.massgeneral.org/ctweb/index.htm

Chinatown
South Cove Community Health Center
885 Washington Street; (617) 482–7555; www.scchc.org

Dorchester
Bowdoin Street Community Health Center
230 Bowdoin Street; Dorchester; (617) 754–0100; www.bowdoinstreethealth.org

Codman Square Health Center
637 Washington Street; Dorchester; (617) 825–9660; www.codman.org

Dorchester House Multi-Service Center
1353 Dorchester Avenue; Dorchester; (617) 288–3230; www.dorchesterhouse.org

Geiger Gibson Community Health Center
250 Mount Vernon Street; Dorchester; (617) 288–1140; www.massleague.org/MACHCs/HHS.htm

Harvard Street Neighborhood Health Center
632 Blue Hill Avenue; Dorchester; (617) 825–3400; www.harvardstreet.org

Neponset Health Center
398 Neponset Avenue; Dorchester; (617) 282–3200; www.massleague.org/MACHCs/HHS.htm

Upham's Corner Health Center
www.uphamscornerhealthctr.com
415 Columbia Road; Dorchester (primary care and mental health); (617) 287–8000
636 Columbia Road; Dorchester (dental and eye care); (617) 825–9839
500 Columbia Road; Dorchester (adolescent and infant care); (617) 287–0786

East Boston
East Boston Neighborhood Health Center
10 Gove Street; East Boston; (617) 569–5800; www.ebnhc.org

Jamaica Plain
Brookside Community Health Center
3297 Washington Street; Jamaica Plain; (617) 522–4700;
www.brighamandwomens.org/primarycare/offices/brookside.aspx

Martha Eliot Health Center
75 Bickford Street; Jamaica Plain; (617) 971–2100; www.childrenshospital
.org/clinicalservices/Site2274/mainpageS2274P0.html

Southern Jamaica Plain Health Center
640 Centre Street; Jamaica Plain; (617) 278–0710; www.brighamandwomens
.org/primarycare/offices/sjphc.aspx

Mattapan
Mattapan Community Health Center
1425 Blue Hill Avenue; Mattapan; (617) 296–0061; www.mattapanchc.org

Roslindale
Greater Roslindale Medical & Dental Center
4199 Washington Street; Roslindale; (617) 323–4440; www.roslindale.org

Roxbury
Dimock Community Health Center
55 Dimock Street; Roxbury; (617) 442–8800; www.dimock.org

Roxbury Comprehensive Community Health Center
435 Warren Street; Roxbury; (617) 442–7400

Whittier Street Health Center
1125 Tremont Street; Roxbury; (617) 427–1000; www.wshc.org

South Boston
Harbor Family Health Center
37 Devine Way; South Boston; (617) 269–0312; www.massleague.org/
MACHCs/HHS.htm

South Boston Community Health Center
409 West Broadway; South Boston; (617) 269–7500; www.sbchc.org

South End
South End Community Health Center
1601 Washington Street; (617) 425–2000; www.sechc.org

LOW-COST **STD** CLINICS

In addition to the clinics listed above, many of which offer free, confidential testing for sexually transmitted diseases, there are also low-cost clinics. All clinics operate on a first-come, first-served basis, so go early, bring a book, and be prepared to wait.

Before you go, though, check out the Massachusetts Department of Public Health's excellent Web guide to STD clinics. Begin at the state's home page (www.mass.gov), then type in "STD Clinical Services" in the search box and click on the top result. This primer is a good overview of what to expect at a clinic regarding confidentiality.

Boston Medical Center
One Boston Medical Center Place (at Harrison and Massachusetts Avenues, South End)
(617) 414–4290
Hours: Monday and Tuesday, 8:00 a.m. to 3:00 p.m.; Wednesday, 1:00 to 7:00 p.m.; Thursday, 1:00 to 3:00 p.m.; Friday, 8:00 to 11:00 p.m.

Massachusetts General Hospital Chelsea Health Center
151 Everett Avenue
(617) 887–4600 or (617) 726–2748
www.mgh.harvard.edu/id/clinical_practice/std_clinic
Hours: Tuesday, 1:30 to 3:30 p.m.; Thursday, 3:00 to 6:00 p.m.

Massachusetts General Hospital GID Clinic

55 Fruit Street (off Cambridge Street, near Charles Street)
Cox Building, fifth floor
(617) 726–2748
www.mgh.harvard.edu/id/clinical_practice/std_clinic/
Hours: Monday and Wednesday, 8:30 to 11:00 a.m. and 1:00 to 3:00 p.m.;
Tuesday and Thursday, 8:30 to 11:00 a.m.; Friday 8:00 to 11:00 a.m. Also
Monday 5:00 to 7:00 p.m. by appointment only.

Planned Parenthood Express Center

Davis Square Plaza
260 Elm Street
Somerville
(617) 616–1600
www.plannedparenthood.org
Hours: Monday, 11:00 a.m. to 7:00 p.m.; Tuesday, 8:00 a.m. to 4:00 p.m.;
Wednesday to Friday, 11:00 a.m. to 7:00 p.m.; Saturday, 10:00 a.m. to 5:00
p.m.

The center offers walk-in screenings during regular business hours for all
sexually transmitted diseases, or you can call to make an appointment.

Planned Parenthood Greater Boston Center

1055 Commonwealth Avenue
(617) 616–1600
www.plannedparenthood.org
Hours: Monday, 8:30 a.m. to 7:00 p.m.; Tuesday, 7:30 a.m. to 7:00 p.m.;
Wednesday, 7:30 a.m. to 5:00 p.m.; Thursday, 7:30 a.m. to 7:00 p.m.; Friday,
7:30 a.m. to 5:30 p.m.; Saturday, 7:30 a.m. to 2:00 p.m.

The center offers STD testing and HIV testing by appointment. It also runs a
Sexual Health Counseling & Referral Hotline from 9:00 a.m. until 6:00 p.m.
(until 8:00 p.m. some days) which is free, anonymous, and confidential. Call
(800) 258–4448 and choose option 3.

MEDICAL **INSURANCE**

MassHealth
Commonwealth of Massachusetts Executive
Office of Health and Human Services
One Ashburton Place, eleventh floor
(800) 841–2900 (MassHealth information)
www.mass.gov

MassHealth is the program in the Massachusetts Department of Health and
Human Services that provides free and reduced-cost health insurance coverage, through private providers, Medicaid, and other sources. There are a
number of different plans depending on your circumstances. Coverage type
is based on your age, health, and family and employment circumstances. If
you are not eligible under those criteria, you may qualify based on income
alone—many of these programs are geared to people who are living within
150 to 200 percent of the federal poverty level. Call the information line for
more details about the specific programs that may suit your needs.

EXERCISING YOUR RIGHT TO CHEAPNESS: **FREE FITNESS, FUN, AND GAMES**

"The word aerobics came about when the gym instructors got together and said, 'If we're going to charge $10 an hour, we can't call it jumping up and down.'"

—RITA RUDNER

It happens every April. After five months of nearly continuous bad weather, the air temperature rises, trees begin to bud, and working late no longer seems like a healthy option; Bostonians burst from their homes and offices to soak up as much of the glorious daylight as they can (because they know summer will be short), and they head straight for the beaches, parks, and playgrounds of the city.

Boston's founding fathers recognized just how important it would be for Bostonians (and their dogs) to enjoy green spaces. They established Boston Common way back in 1634, and local politicians have been adding to the city's public spaces ever since. As a result, the city is literally surrounded by playgrounds, skating rinks, tennis courts, ball fields, gardens, and beaches, all created for the most important job of all: having fun.

Even in the depth of winter, there are lots of places to recreate until the weather turns warmer. (This may be a baseball town, but in winter just about every guy from New England wants to strap on skates and play some rec-league hockey.) Boston has a vast infrastructure of community centers that provide affordable fitness and recreation opportunities year round. Most of it is free, or else so inexpensive that there's no excuse to hibernate during the bleak season.

LOTS **OF** PARKING: **USING** THE **BEST** CITY **PARKS**

City of Boston Parks and Recreation Department
(617) 635–4505
www.cityofboston.gov/parks

Commonwealth of Massachusetts Department of Conservation and Recreation
(617) 626–1250
www.mass.gov/dcr

These two organizations control nearly all the public spaces in the city of Boston, including playgrounds, skating rinks, pools, tennis courts, tot lots, and ball fields.

The city Parks Department hosts ParkARTS, a summer-long program that brings arts, music, theater, festivals, and other interactive activities to parks throughout metropolitan Boston. For a complete schedule of ParkARTS events, visit www.cityofboston.gov/parks/parkarts. All events are free.

In addition to its parks and recreational facilities, the Department of Conservation and Recreation also oversees local state parks and wildlife refuges, and helps to administer the lovely, oft-overlooked Boston Harbor Islands. The Web sites of both organizations have online databases of all their properties and facilities, and both allow you to narrow your search to specific areas, neighborhoods, or facility types. Many of the parks listed below are overseen by one of these two organizations.

Blue Hills Reservation
695 Hillside Street
Milton
(617) 698–1802 (headquarters)
www.mass.gov/dcr/parks/metroboston/blue.htm

Named for the hills that dominate the interior of this wilderness park, the Blue Hills Reservation is just minutes from downtown Boston (head due south). The reservation hosts hiking and biking trails, an educational museum, historic Native American artifacts, several ponds, ball fields, fishing, camping, an observatory, horseback riding—there's even a ski hill. Reservations are required for some activities, like camping or using the ball fields, so call ahead.

Boston Nature Center and Wildlife Sanctuary
500 Walk Hill Street
Mattapan
(617) 983–8500
www.massaudubon.org/Nature_Connection/Sanctuaries/Boston/index.php
Hours (Nature Center): Monday through Friday, 9:00 a.m. to 5:00 p.m.; Saturday, Sunday, and Monday holidays, 10:00 a.m. to 4:00 p.m.
Hours (trails): Open every day, dawn to dusk.

The Catch There is a $2.00 suggested donation for non-Mass Audubon members. No pets are allowed on the site.

This sixty-seven-acre sanctuary, run jointly by the Massachusetts Audubon Society and the city of Boston, is located in the heart of the city, on the grounds of the former Boston State Hospital. Two miles of wheelchair-

accessible trails and boardwalks traverse meadows and wetlands that coyotes, pheasants, and many species of migratory birds now call home. The
George Robert White Environmental Conservation Center hosts a variety of
educational programs designed to teach children and adults the impact that
humans have on nature. The sanctuary also includes the Clark-Cooper Community Gardens, one of Boston's oldest and largest community gardens.

Charles River Reservation
Along the Charles River from Boston University Bridge to Brighton
www.mass.gov/dcr/parks/charlesriver

This park is simply one of Boston's very finest natural resources. Its 20
miles of pedestrian/bicycle trails are interspersed by recreational facilities,
baseball fields, opportunities for boating and canoeing, and more. It's also a
great place to walk or in-line skate, and the wonderful Hatch Shell concert
venue is on the reservation, as well.

The Emerald Necklace
Conservancy headquarters: 891 Centre Street, Jamaica Plain
(617) 522–2700
www.emeraldnecklace.org

In 1896 the city of Boston christened an interconnected chain of parks and
gardens, known as the Emerald Necklace, that form a chain of green roughly
delineating the perimeter of the city. Each park within the necklace was
designed by renowned landscape architect Frederick Law Olmsted (the same
dude who designed Central Park in New York). The Emerald Necklace is now
listed in the National Register of Historic Places. Here are some of the beautiful parks that make up this local treasure.

Arnold Arboretum; 125 Arborway; Jamaica Plain; (617) 524–1718; www
.arboretum.harvard.edu; www.emeraldnecklace.org/arboretu.htm

The Arnold Arboretum was created from funds generated by the Arnold
estate when it was bequeathed to Harvard University in 1872. Today, this
265-acre park, owned by Harvard University but leased for 1,000 years to
the city of Boston for use as a public park, is a riot of colors, ponds, forests,
and hidden treats, like the Larz Anderson Bonsai Collection, which includes
bonsai trees dating back to the mid-1700s. As the oldest arboretum in the
country, the Arnold Arboretum contains trees and shrubs from around the

world, with special emphasis on plants native to Asia and New England. Lilac Day happens every Mother's Day, and it is the only day that picnicking is allowed in the Arboretum. The Hunnewell Building houses the Arboretum's permanent collection, library, and archives. Restrooms are available here as well. Best of all? It's free! (Donations are accepted, of course.)

Back Bay Fens; Along Boylston Street in the Fenway area

The Fens still retains remnants of its origins as a freshwater marsh (so it doesn't always smell good), and it's a place to avoid at night due to low lighting, low foot traffic, and the potential for crime. But during the day, it's one of the most beautiful parks in the city and home to the Kelleher Rose Garden, ball fields, and the city's oldest remaining original Victory Garden (where families grew fresh fruits and vegetables during the rationing of World War II, in case you're too young to have heard stories about that). Trails meander along the ponds and marshes that dot the area.

Boston Common; Located between Park, Beacon, Boylston, Charles, and Tremont Streets

Boston Public Garden; Located between Arlington, Beacon, Charles, and Boylston Streets

America's oldest public park and one of its most impressive, the Boston Common was first used in 1634 as a grazing ground for cattle for the young city's residents. It later became a military training ground, but today its forty-eight acres are filled with monuments, music performances, picnics, and outdoor activities. It's amazing that a large city can have such a huge public green space right smack in the center—unlike, say, New York's Central Park, which isn't so central if you work on Wall Street). Also unlike Central Park, this one has few trees: it's mostly an open grassy space, interspersed with a few ponds and gardens.

Among other events (and impromptu political demonstrations), the Common hosts the annual Shakespeare on the Common series as well as fund-raising events nearly every weekend from Memorial Day to Columbus Day. The Public Garden, which was the first botanical garden in the United States, is located right across Charles Street to the west; it's free. Here, famous swan boats glide across a twenty-four-acre lagoon, and meticulously tended rose gardens spring to life each spring. In fact, gardeners plant an ever-changing rotation of seasonal flowering plants throughout the park. It's a great spot for wedding photos, reading, picnicking, relaxing on a sunny bench—and, above all, people-watching.

Franklin Park; Walnut Street; Jamaica Plain; (617) 635–4505

At over five hundred acres, Franklin Park is the largest park in the Emerald Necklace. Olmsted designed this as a "country park" similar to New York's Central Park. Distinct areas within the park include a zoo, golf course, stadium, playing fields, and plenty of wooded areas laced with trails, picnic areas, tennis courts, ponds, streams, and historic ruins. You just might visit J.P. for the first time ever; it's worth it.

Jamaica Park; 507 Jamaicaway; Jamaica Plain; (617) 522–6258

The main attraction of this park is Jamaica Pond, a sixty-acre kettle hole formed by an ancient glacier. Natural springs feed this 90-foot-deep pond, which is the largest naturally occurring body of water in Boston. An ice-cutting industry once flourished here, but today fishing (for trout, which is stocked by the city, as well as naturally occurring pickerel, bass, hornpout, salmon, and perch), rowing, sailing, and walking/jogging are the primary activities.

Olmsted Park; Pond Avenue; Brookline

This park on the Boston-Brookline line, originally named Leverett Park, was renamed in the 1900s to honor the designer of the necklace, and has woodlands, meadows, and three ponds. There are plenty of spots where you can sit down and contemplate. Footbridges and pedestrian paths are located around Wards Pond, at the center of the park, and a bike/pedestrian path system on the Brookline side from Jamaica Pond to Boylston Street (Route 9) has also been completed.

Riverway Park; Along Muddy River (from Landmark Center to Route 9)

This narrow little park in the Fenway area is hidden away behind a thick bank of trees along the Muddy River. Even though you're next to a busy roadway, the well-groomed trail, footbridges, and stand of beech trees lining the river make you feel like you're a thousand miles away from civilization.

The Esplanade

South side of Charles River (from Museum of Science to Boston University Bridge)
The Esplanade Association
10 Derne Street (administrative offices)
(617) 227–0365

Created in stages beginning in 1910, the Esplanade is a 3-mile-long ribbon along the Charles River filled with green spaces, gardens, forests, fountains, lagoons, the performances stage known as the Hatch Memorial Band Shell, a boathouse, docks, playgrounds, and memorials to those who helped bring this lovely oasis to fruition. It's simply a great place to read, sunbathe, sail toy sailboats, or listen to a concert. During the summer months there is a free concert nearly every weekend day, including the world-famous Fourth of July Concert by the Boston Pops. The concert and the accompanying fireworks display are televised internationally. (For more information on this spectacular show, see pages 13–14 in the Music chapter.) For a complete schedule of Hatch Shell concerts, check the DCR's online events guide at www.mass.gov/dcr/hatch_events.htm.

FISHED **IN:**
LOW-COST **ISLAND** EXCURSIONS

Boston Harbor Islands

(617) 223–8666
www.bostonislands.org

The Catch Ferry *(operates in summer only) costs $14.00 per adult, $10.00 seniors, $8.00 children ages three to eleven; family of four $42.00. Campsites (maximum four campers) cost $8.00 to $10.00 each per night, plus transaction fees, for Massachusetts residents. No loud music or alcohol are allowed at these campsites.*

Boston may not be at the top of your list as a camping destination for the family, what with all the noise, traffic, and concrete. But turn your eyes east and behold the beautiful Boston Harbor Islands: thirty islands of dramatically varying sizes and types located just off the city's coastline, many with picnic or camping facilities at little or no cost. That's good, because the ferry ride is a little pricey.

Catch the $14.00 ferry from Long Wharf to Georges Island first, from where ferries (ranging from free to $3.00 per person) shuttle you to the other islands. On three of the islands—Grape, Bumpkin, and Lovells—camping is available, but you must have an advance reservation, available online through ReserveAmerica.com (phone number 877–422–6762) or by calling the state at 617–223–8666. The islands each have ten to twenty individual campsites and one group campsite.

Note that pets and bikes are only permitted on the walkways of Deer and Nut Islands, and that only two of the islands (Georges and Spectacle) are really suitable for those in wheelchairs. Insiders' tip: Spectacle Island features free Sunday afternoon jazz concerts in summer! (There's also a cafe.)

Stonybrook Reservation
Turtle Pond Parkway
West Roxbury, Hyde Park
(617) 698–1802

This peaceful 476-acre woodland area is filled with trails for hiking and biking, ponds teeming with fish, soccer and baseball fields, tennis courts, picnic areas, an ice-skating rink, and a pool. Here you can also find the John F. Thompson Center, New England's first recreational facility designed specifically to accommodate visitors with physical impairments. You can make reservations for the center by calling (617) 361–6161.

RECREATION **NATION:**
FREE **RECREATION** CENTERS

Boston Centers for Youth & Families (BCYF)
(617) 635–4920
www.cityofboston.gov/BCYF

BCYF is Boston's largest youth and human services agency, overseeing nearly fifty community facilities that provide a variety of activities geared to the city's young people and their families, including after-school programs, fitness programs, recreational facilities and pools, and educational programs for children, teens, and adults. See Appendix C for a complete listing of BCYF locations, or you can find a searchable directory with contact information and programs on the organization's Web site. Some of these community centers are free to residents of the communities they serve, but most have a small annual membership fee, which rarely exceeds $50 a year for an entire family.

INLINE **SKATING** EVENTS

Inline Club of Boston
P.O. Box 426185
Cambridge, MA 02142
www.sk8net.com
membership@sk8net.com

The Catch Helmet and wrist guards are required to participate in group skates.

The ICB has been teaching Bostonians how to inline skate since 1992. Their weekly group skates are a great way to learn the best routes with the best surfaces, pick up some good urban skating skills, and meet like-minded athletes. Novice skaters can join the Midweek on the Minuteman (MOM) skates Wednesday at 6:30 p.m. on the public Minuteman Trail out in Arlington; check the Web site for maps. (Yes, there's limited parking by the trailside.) Intermediate skaters head for the group skate that meets Sunday mornings at 10:30 a.m. at JFK Park (corner of Memorial Drive and North Harvard Street, just off Harvard Square) for an easy skate tour. Advanced skaters meet at the Hatch Shell on the Esplanade on Tuesday nights at 7:30 p.m. for a 12-mile advanced urban skate tour. Advanced skaters interested in racing should contact the club directly; the ICB is happy to give instructor referrals to newbies.

The club also hosts an annual three-day skating event in early August, SkateBoston, but it costs $55 to $85 to participate in those events.

For more information about SkateBoston, visit www.skate-boston.com.

BIKE **PATHS**

Biking is really popular in Boston, thanks to the relatively flat terrain and the commitment to bike paths made by local pols. But, in true Boston tradition, some of the paths aren't so well designed; many cross dangerous intersections; and they're not always in great condition. Also they inevitably get very crowded on the weekends. Despite all that, they're definitely a nice alternative to fighting Boston traffic (and drivers). Here are some of the best paths.

Dr. Paul Dudley White Bike Path
Along the Charles River, through Boston, Cambridge, Newton, Watertown, and Waltham
www.mass.gov/dcr/parks/metroboston/maps/bikepaths_dudley.gif

This 17-mile paved and gravel trail begins at the Museum of Science in Boston, follows the Esplanade, then Charles River Park, and officially ends in Watertown Square. New extensions are adding to the trail, and with a little hunting for the next leg (since some parts of it aren't well marked), it's possible to follow the path all the way to Waltham and beyond. It's a very popular bike commuter route during the week, and packed with walkers, in-line skaters, and strollers on the weekends. In the summer, charity "walk-a-thons" take over the Esplanade section of the path at least one day each weekend, so you'd want to avoid that (unless you're feeling charitable).

Lower Neponset River Trail
(617) 727–5290
www.mass.gov/dcr/parks/metroboston/lnrt.htm

The Lower Neponset River Trail, a former railroad bed along the shore of said river, is like taking a ride through the industrial history of the area. The 2.4-mile path links the Neponset area to the larger network of DCR trails, stretching from the historic Port Norfolk neighborhood in Dorchester through Pope John Paul II Park; across Granite Avenue and through the Neponset Marshes; and on through the Lower Mills area, where it crosses several railroad bridges and passes beside converted mills. It ends at Central Avenue in Milton. Busy roads also bring the trail from Port Norfolk to the Harborwalk Trail along Boston's shoreline, which travels past the JFK Museum and up to Castle Island; intrepid riders with a local map can navigate to the Harborwalk and turn this ride into a round-trip route of 20 scenic miles or more.

Minuteman Bikeway
From Alewife MBTA station to Bedford
www.minutemanbikeway.org

This 11-mile asphalt path, administered by a variety of local biking organizations, has become a major thoroughfare for bike commuters living in communities west of the city into the Cambridge area. The path, formerly a rail bed with a very gradual uphill grade as you proceed west, is very well maintained. And the scenery—marshes, forests, gardens, and ponds—is breathtaking in places. But the path attracts hundreds of families and young bicyclists on the weekends, so it's best to avoid it if you're an advanced rider with a need for speed. It's perfect for in-line skating, though. In the winter this trail is not plowed, so it makes for a superb and scenic ex-urban cross-country skiing trail. The bike path is open year-round, from 5:00 a.m. until 9:00 p.m.

Mystic River Bike Path
Mystic River Reservation
Medford, Somerville, Everett
(617) 727–5380
www.mass.gov/dcr/parks/metroboston/mystic.htm

The Mystic River bike path can be a little tricky to follow, as it sometimes involves confusing road crossings and dead ends onto major highways, but a map provided by the DCR can help you find your way. You can access the paths in Somerville near the Assembly Square Mall and Route 28, and ride them along the Mystic River to Medford. You can download the map at the DCR Web site listed above. The bike path is open year-round from dawn to dusk.

Pierre Lallement Bike Path
Southwest Corridor Park
From Melnea Cass Boulevard to Forest Hills
(617) 727–0057
www.mass.gov/dcr/parks/metroboston/southwestCorr.htm

Named for the Parisian who is credited with patenting the first design for a bicycle (and who lived out his final years in Roxbury), the Southwest Corridor Park is a 4.7-mile, fifty-two-acre linear park stretching from Back Bay to Forest Hills. It winds through the South End, Back Bay, Roxbury, and Jamaica Plain, mostly cruising alongside Amtrak and MBTA Orange Line tracks. Along the way, there are eleven tot lot areas, two spray pools, seven basketball courts, five tennis courts, two street hockey rinks, two amphitheaters, and about 6 miles of biking, jogging, and walking paths.

HITTING **THE** WATER: **BOATING**

Community Boating
At the Charles River across Storrow Drive from the Charles Street pedestrian overpass
(617) 523–1038
www.community-boating.org

The Catch Adult learn-to-sail packages start at around $80 per person.

Community Boating, housed in the historic boathouse along the banks of the Charles River, teaches thousands of people to learn to sail every year. Kids can learn for just $1.00 (see page [X-REF] in the Kids chapter of this book for details), and adults can purchase thirty-day learn-to-sail packages for less than a hundred bucks; a sixty-day boating pass doesn't cost much more. There are also kayaks available for rent.

Public Garden Swan Boats
(617) 522–1966
www.swanboats.com/new/welcome.shtml
Hours: Mid-April to mid-June, 10:00 a.m. to 4:00 p.m.; mid-June to Labor Day, 10:00 a.m. to 5:00 p.m.; Labor Day to late September, noon to 4:00 p.m. on weekdays and 10:00 a.m. to 4:00 p.m. on weekends.

The Catch Tickets are $2.75 for adults, $1.50 for children (ages two to fifteen), and $2.00 for seniors.

You know it's spring when you see the Swan Boats gliding silently along the waters of the big lagoon in the Boston Public Garden. Immortalized in the children's book Make Way for Ducklings, the Swan Boats were launched by the Paget family in 1877, and a fourth generation of Pagets still runs the attraction today. And they're cheap! A wooden likeness of a giant swan hides the driver/pedalers at the backs of these beautiful boats, and it takes about fifteen minutes to pedal passengers around the entire lagoon. It's a must-do adventure that children just love: the squeals-per-dollar ratio (SPD?) here has got to be just about the highest in the city.

THINGS **GOING** SWIMMINGLY:
FREE CITY **POOLS**

Many of the city's recreation centers have pools available for their members, but free public pools administered by the DCR are also located throughout the metropolitan area, keeping Bostonians cool when the summer heat ramps up. The pools are usually open from mid-June until Labor Day weekend, 10:00 a.m. to 6:00 p.m., although the DCR sometimes opens them earlier in the year and keeps them open a couple of extra hours at night if we get a heat wave. For a full listing of opening dates, visit www.mass.gov/dcr/recreate/pools.htm.

Brighton
Artesani Playground Wading Pool, 1255 Soldiers Field Road; (617) 626–4973
Brighton-Allston Swimming and Wading Pool, North Beacon Street; (617) 254–2965
Reilly Memorial Swimming Pool, 355 Chestnut Hill Avenue, Cleveland Circle; (617) 277–7822 or (617) 698–1802

Cambridge
McCrehan Memorial Swimming and Wading Pool, 359 Rindge Avenue; (617) 354–9154 or (617) 576–2081
Veterans Memorial Swimming and Wading Pool (Magazine Beach), 719 Memorial Drive; (617) 354–9381

Hyde Park
Moynihan Wading Pool, 920 Truman Parkway
Olsen Swimming and Wading Pool, 95 Turtle Pond Parkway; (617) 364–9524 or (617) 333–7403

Jamaica Plain
Johnson Playground Spray Deck, corner of Lamartine and Green Streets, Southwest Corridor Park
Stony Brook Spray Deck, corner of Lamartine and Boylston Streets, Southwest Corridor Park

Mattapan
Ryan Wading Pool, 350 River Street

Roxbury
Cass Memorial Swimming Pool, Washington Street; (617) 445–0062
Mission Hill Spray Deck, behind Boston Police Headquarters, Southwest Corridor Park

Somerville
Dilboy Memorial Swimming and Wading Pool, Alewife Brook Parkway; (617) 623–9321
Latta Brothers Memorial Swimming and Wading Pool, McGrath Highway; (617) 666–9236

Watertown
Dealtry Memorial Swimming and Wading Pool, Pleasant Street; (617) 923–0073

REACHING **THE** BEACH

The idea of swimming in or near Boston Harbor has been a touchy subject ever since the harbor was determined to be one of the country's most polluted in the late 1980s. But a lot has happened since then. Although the water isn't yet pristine, it's getting there, and the beaches are beautiful despite the fact that they're usually right next to prominent reminders that you're still in a city (the airport, the interstate, the natural gas tanks).

Remember that extended bouts of hot weather or days of rain can still dramatically affect water quality, so it's best to call the DCR's water quality hotline (617–626–4972) before you hit a beach in either case. Most of these beaches open on Memorial Day weekend and close right after Labor Day, and lifeguard service usually begins in mid-June (unless hot summer weather arrives unusually early). For more info on water quality, check the DCR Web page on the subject at www.mass.gov/dcr/waterquality.htm.

EAST BOSTON
Constitution Beach
799 Bennington Street

This half-mile-long, deep stretch of sand overlooking Logan Airport underwent a major renovation in the 1990s and now has upgraded amenities, plus a new pedestrian overpass that gets visitors safely over the MBTA tracks running next to it.

You'll find parking, recreational fields for softball, seasonal skating and basketball, a bathhouse, boating, a large playground, a picnic area, tennis and handball courts, shade shelters, and foot showers. To get here, take the Blue Line to the Orient Heights stop.

SOUTH BOSTON
Carson Beach
William J. Day Boulevard

This popular beach offers some of the most stunning views of the harbor anywhere in town. There's (some) free parking, plus public restrooms, shaded shelters, a cafe, the renovated Edward J. McCormack Bathhouse, and a walkway along the water running from Castle Island to the John F. Kennedy Library. Take the Red Line to the JFK/UMass stop.

L Street Beach and M Street Beach
Pleasant Bay/Castle Island
William J. Day Boulevard

The L and M Street Beaches are located along busy Day Boulevard, but they're separated from the road by a grassy strip of parkland with benches and shade trees that helps give you the feeling of being in the middle of nowhere. Pleasant Bay is completely enclosed by a causeway that extends from Day Boulevard to Castle Island, so the beach along Pleasant Bay is clean and the water is warm. It also abuts Castle Island, and from here you can look out into Boston Harbor. Castle Island also has plenty of free parking, picnic facilities, a beautiful boardwalk, a snack bar, and a pre–Civil War stone garrison (Fort Independence) from which you can take tours during the summer months. It's one of the most popular beaches in the area.

To get here, take a #9 or #11 bus from the South Station T stop to City Point, then stroll along the boardwalk until you find your spot in the sun.

DORCHESTER
Savin Hill Beach
Playstead Road
Malibu Beach
Morrissey Boulevard

These two adjacent beaches feature new sand, boardwalks, lighting, promenades, and bathhouses—though they're surrounded on both sides by very busy roads, so it can be a little noisy. There's a small parking lot holding about fifty cars. The beaches are accessible by taking the Red Line of the T to the Savin Hill station.

Tenean Beach
108 Tenean Street

Tucked away in the shadow of Interstate 93, Tenean Beach abuts an industrial area and the neighborhood of Port Norfolk. Still, it's a remarkably quiet and peaceful beach with great views of downtown Boston. There's a new playground, bathhouses, picnic shelters, new water fountains, bike areas, and shade shelters.

Getting here by public transportation is tough—the closest stop is North Quincy station, on the Red Line, and then it's a long walk along very busy roads. Fortunately, there's parking for up to about 150 cars, and this hidden little beach usually doesn't get *that* crowded.

QUINCY
Wollaston Beach
Quincy Shore Drive

Wollaston Beach, at more than 1.5 miles long, is the largest Boston Harbor beach. It looks south toward Hull and into the Atlantic Ocean, rather than at the harbor, so you get the feeling of being miles away from the city—like, say, in Maine. A continuous walkway, seawall, concession stands, outdoor showers, and enclosed changing areas are located along the beach. There's plenty of beachside parking, but this beach still gets packed in the summer, so if you're driving, arrive early! You can also get there by public transit by taking the Wollaston Beach/Ashmont Bus #217 from the T station at Wollaston (Red Line), or simply walking along Beach Street from Wollaston station.

REVERE
Revere Beach
Revere Beach Boulevard
www.mass.gov/dcr/parks/metroboston/revere.htm

Revere Beach is the oldest public beach in America (designated as such in 1896). The beach is miles long, with a bandstand, shade shelters, and a bathhouse; the beach sand is gorgeous; and the views out over the Atlantic Ocean are excellent. But it's not exactly Cape Cod: just across Revere Beach Boulevard, on the inland side, you'll find a host of kitschy souvenir stores, plus world-famous Kelly's Roast Beef (makers of huge roast beef sandwiches), dive bars, restaurants, and tricked-out cars cruising the boulevard attempting to impress . . . who?? Anyway, throngs of locals turn up here on hot days, thanks to the easy accessibility on public transportation; it's more Coney Island or Old Orchard than a truly relaxing family beach experience. To get here, take the Blue Line to the Revere Beach or Wonderland station.

FREE EXPRESSION:
BOSTON'S BEST LIBRARIES

*"Books are the treasured wealth
of the world and the fit inheritance
of generations and nations."*

—HENRY DAVID THOREAU

Boston practically invented the concept of the free municipal library. The first large library in the country to be funded by the public was our very own, built originally in 1854 with 16,000 volumes (the "new" Boston Public Library building was built in Copley Square in 1895). It was also the first library in the U.S. that allowed the public to borrow materials and take them home; home of the first children's library; and it's still a treasure trove of history today. The main BPL houses the personal books and papers collection of President John Adams. The Central branch in Copley Square is home to world-famous murals by John Singer Sargent and Pierre Puvis de Chavannes, as well as an exhaustive collection of rare books and manuscripts such as first-edition folios by Shakespeare and original scores from Mozart. There are also loads of CDs and DVDs, Internet access, and hundreds of annual readings, performances, lectures, and films—all completely free. (A complete listing of branches, as well as a listing of locations and branches of the public library systems for all the cities and towns immediately surrounding Boston, can be found in Appendix B of this book.)

In addition to its public library system, the city's long-standing history as an academic powerhouse has fostered the growth of a wonderful selection of cultural, ethnic, research, and historical libraries, many of which are open to the public.

RESEARCH LIBRARIES

HARVARD UNIVERSITY LIBRARIES

There are many fine universities in Boston with many fine libraries, but for sheer depth, historical significance, and public access, you can't beat those of Harvard University. Harvard's library began thanks to the bequest of a Charlestown minister named John Harvard; upon his death in 1638, half his estate and his entire private library of 400 books (a lot, in those days) were given to the fledgling college, which had been formed by a vote of the Great and General Court of the Massachusetts Bay Colony two years earlier. Nearly 400 years later, that small collection has grown into a phenomenal repository of knowledge and history. There are more than ninety libraries on or near school grounds (for the full list, visit http://lib.harvard.edu/libraries), but only a few allow public access. Those that do allow such access are worth at least one visit. Most require you to show one or more forms of picture ID, and none will allow you to check out materials. That's okay; go anyway. Check each library's hours and admittance policies before venturing out.

These libraries also hold frequent events and exhibitions, including displays of materials rarely seen by non-librarians (in other words, the rest of us). For a complete listing of happenings at Harvard's libraries, visit www .hcl.harvard.edu/info/exhibitions.

Andover-Harvard Theological Library

45 Francis Avenue; Cambridge; (617) 495–5788; www.hds.harvard.edu/ library

Arnold Arboretum/Horticulture Library

125 Arborway; Jamaica Plain; (617) 522–1086; www.arboretum.harvard .edu/library/library.html

Arthur and Elizabeth Schlesinger Library
on the History of Women in America

3 James Street; Cambridge; (617) 495–8647; www.radcliffe.edu/ schlesinger_library.aspx

Blue Hill Meteorological Observatory Library

Pierce Hall, 29 Oxford Street (third floor); Cambridge; (617) 495–2836; http://library.seas.harvard.edu

Davis Center for Russian and Eurasian Studies Library

Inside Fung Library, Knafel Building, 1737 Cambridge Street (concourse level); Cambridge; (617) 495–4037; www.daviscenter.fas.harvard.edu

Houghton Library

Harvard Yard; Cambridge; (617) 495–2441; www.hcl.harvard.edu/libraries/ houghton

John G. Wolbach Library (Harvard-Smithsonian Center
for Astrophysics Library)

60 Garden Street; Cambridge; (617) 495–7289; www.cfa.harvard.edu/library

John K. Fairbank Center for Chinese Studies Library

Inside Fung Library, Knafel Building, 1737 Cambridge Street (concourse level); Cambridge; (617) 495–5753; www.fas.harvard.edu/~fairbank/library/library.html

Library at Minda de Gunzburg Center for European Studies

27 Kirkland Street; Cambridge; (617) 495–4303; www.ces.fas.harvard.edu/about/library.html

Ukrainian Research Institute Reference Library

34 Kirkland Street; Cambridge; (617) 495–4053; www.huri.harvard.edu/library.html

Massachusetts Historical Society Library

1154 Boylston Street
(617) 536–1608
www.masshist.org/library
Hours: Monday to Friday, 9:00 a.m. to 4:45 p.m.; Saturday, 9:00 a.m. to 4:00 p.m. Reading room only, open Thursdays until 7:00 p.m.

The Catch Photo ID required.

This 200-year-old library hold a vast collection of manuscripts, books, pamphlets, newspapers, maps, works of art, photographs, and artifacts that track the evolution of early American history and carry serious historical weight. Special collections include letters between Abigail and President John Adams; the pen that Abraham Lincoln used to sign the Emancipation Proclamation (wow!); and casts of Lincoln's face and hands. The library welcomes researchers, but since the book stacks are closed to all but library staff, you'll need to fill out call slips for any books you want to view. You'll also have to fill out a registration form and present a current form of photo ID to get in. All materials must be used in the reading room. You need an appointment with the curator if you'd like to see the artifacts—and, again, the library welcomes requests from those with a genuine research interest.

New England Historic Genealogical Society Research Library

101 Newbury Street
(617) 536–5740
www.newenglandancestors.org/about_library.asp
Hours: Tuesday, Thursday, Friday, and Saturday, 9:00 a.m. to 5:00 p.m.;
Wednesday, 9:00 a.m. to 9:00 p.m.

The Catch Membership is $75, but day passes cost just $15.

Looking for your royal roots? This comprehensive research library offers a glimpse into the family tree of nearly everyone who lives in New England. Its collection includes more than 200,000 books, periodicals, and microform materials, as well as over one million manuscripts. (The book holdings alone include nearly every published New England genealogy, local history, and related periodical.) You're sure to find your family nom somewhere in the catacombs. The best news is that, while membership is a little steep, it's only fifteen bucks to visit for a full day—which ought to be enough to get anyone started on some serious digging.

PRIVATE LIBRARIES

Boston Athenæum

10½ Beacon Street
(617) 227–0270, extension 279 (tour bookings)
www.bostonathenaeum.org
Hours: Monday through Friday, 9:00 a.m. to 5:00 p.m.; Saturday, 9:00 a.m. to 4:00 p.m.

The Athenæum, a National Historic Landmark, is the heart and soul of Boston's literary and artistic history and a destination in and of itself if you're a writer or reader. Founded in 1807 by fourteen Boston literati, it became the repository of the private libraries of George Washington and Henry Knox, plus the private papers of hundreds of notable authors. The library houses rare manuscripts and books, while its art collection was the genesis for Boston's superb Museum of Fine Arts (which vacated the Athenæum for its own building in 1876). Membership is required ($230 per person) to visit the library, but the public is welcome to visit the first-floor art gallery for free during regular business hours. If you do, make sure to take the free half-hour Art and Architecture tour, which gives you a glimpse into the rest of this historic building; it departs from the front desk on Tuesday and Thursday at 3:00 p.m. and is led by docents.

Congregational Library
14 Beacon Street (second floor)
(617) 523–0470
www.14beacon.org
Hours: Monday through Friday, 9:00 a.m. to 5:00 p.m., except Wednesdays until 6:00 p.m.

The Congregational Library houses an extensive closed-stack collection of printed church histories, town histories, sermons, annual reports of religious and charitable associations, Boston city directories, and contemporary religious studies material. Books may be borrowed in person or by mail. Members of the public may borrow books for up to four weeks as long as you provide a valid address.

The French Library and Cultural Center/Alliance Française
53 Marlborough Street
(617) 912–0400
www.frenchlib.org
Hours: Monday, Tuesday, and Thursday, 10:00 a.m. to 6:00 p.m.; Wednesday, 10:00 a.m. to 8:00 p.m.; Friday, library closed (cultural center open); and Saturday, 10:00 a.m. to 5:00 p.m.

The French Library and Cultural Center is located in two adjacent, historic mansions on Marlborough Street, and its mahogany-paneled periodical room is as pleasant a place for quiet reading and contemplation as you're likely to find in the city—regardless of the language. Members of the public may use the library for free and can browse its thousands of French-language books, newspapers, magazines, films, videos, and CDs. To borrow, however, you must be a member. A membership isn't cheap ($70), but it does buy you reduced-price admission to cultural programs, film series, special events (like a show-stopping Bastille Day party, which takes over a block of Marlborough Street each July), and borrowing privileges.

Goethe-Institut Boston

170 Beacon Street
(617) 262–6050
Hours: Monday through Thursday, 9:00 a.m. to 1:00 p.m. and 2:00 to 5:30
p.m.; Friday, 9:00 a.m. to 1:00 p.m. and 2:00 to 4:30 p.m. Closed holidays.

This institute-slash-library, dedicated to all things German, has a reading
room with a magnificent view of the Charles River and is open to the public
at all times (although it only lends materials to educational organizations).
Its library collection includes German books, newspapers, periodicals, and
DVDs. It also hosts a variety of free events throughout the year such as parties, lectures, films, and visual arts.

The Mary Baker Eddy Library for the Betterment of Humanity

200 Massachusetts Avenue
(617) 450–7000
www.marybakereddylibrary.org
Exhibit and shop hours: Tuesday through Sunday, 10:00 a.m. to 4:00 p.m.
Reference Room hours: Tuesday through Saturday, 10:00 a.m. to 4:00 p.m.
Research Room hours: Tuesday through Friday, 10:00 a.m. to 4:00 p.m.; first
Saturday of each month by appointment only.

The Catch *Most spaces free, but $6.00 per adult (discounts for students
and seniors) to enter Mapparium or Quest Gallery. Membership ($25) required
to borrow books.*

You might be drawn to the Christian Science Church area at the corner of
Huntington and Massachusetts Avenues for its mammoth reflecting pool, a
peaceful yet powerful landmark in the Symphony Hall section of Boston.
But the Mary Baker Eddy Library, which houses two collections open to the
public, is also interesting. At its core are works relating to the life, work,
and ideas of Eddy, who was the founder of the Church of Christ, Scientist
(not to be confused with Scientology). She was also a women's rights activist and founder of the Christian Science Monitor newspaper. The library's
materials include collections emphasizing American history, women, religion, the history of science, and the relationship of science and religion. You
can research and read the holdings in both the Reference and the Research
Rooms for free, but to borrow you need a membership, which costs $25.
Access to the Mapparium, a 30-foot stained-glass globe built in 1935 that
you view from the inside, costs $6.00.

Scandinavian Library

206 Waltham Street
West Newton
(617) 965–0621
www.scandinavianlibrary.org
Hours: Saturday, 11:00 a.m. to 3:00 p.m.

This library, founded in 1994, holds more than 6,000 books by Nordic authors or about the Nordic countries (Sweden, Norway, Denmark, Finland, and Iceland) and their cultures. The library keeps subscriptions to newspapers from these countries, as well as Scandinavian-language CDs, audio books, and videos; there's also a well-stocked travel, business, and Nordic organization reference area. Check its calendar to learn about ongoing events, parties, and other activities of interest to Scandinavians and those with an interest in the region.

Social Law Library

John Adams Courthouse
One Pemberton Square, Suite 4100
(617) 226–1500
www.sociallaw.com

Founded in 1804, this excellent resource for lawyers and those interested in the law is the oldest law library in the country. Although located in the Massachusetts Supreme Judicial Court courthouse, the library is largely funded through private sources and offers access to a vast collection of historic and contemporary legal documents for both the public and practicing lawyers. Public access is allowed (but borrowing is reserved for members). The library also hosts a variety of events and lectures open to the public; some require an RSVP, which can be completed right on the library's Web site.

SUPER-SIZING **YOUR** LIBRARY **CARD:** THE **POWER** OF **INTER-LIBRARY** LOAN

There are dozens of libraries throughout the metropolitan Boston area, including public, university, and private collections. Thanks to an active consortium program, you may already have free access to many of them with the library card you possess (if you live here already). Nearly every library in this area is a member of one or another, and there are even some members in neighboring states; holding a card in a consortium member library will get you borrowing privileges at most, but not all, member locations. Many have private and specialized research facilities, too, that are not open to the public. Visit each consortium's Web site for specific details on which libraries will honor your consortium membership for an inter-library loan.

The Boston Library Consortium
www.blc.org

This consortium includes Boston College, the Boston Public Library, Boston University, Brandeis University, Brown University, the Marine Biological Laboratory & Woods Hole Oceanographic Institution, the Massachusetts Institute of Technology, Northeastern University, the State Library of Massachusetts, Tufts University, the University of Connecticut, the University of Massachusetts–Amherst, the University of Massachusetts–Boston, the University of Massachusetts–Dartmouth, the University of Massachusetts–Lowell, the University of Massachusetts Medical Center, the University of New Hampshire, Wellesley College, and Williams College.

Fenway Library Consortium
www.fenwaylibraries.org

This is a consortium of the Brookline Public Library and the libraries of Emerson College, Emmanuel College, the Cardinal Cushing Library, Hebrew College, Lesley University, the Massachusetts College of Art, the Massachusetts College of Pharmacy & Health Sciences, the Museum of Fine Arts, the New England Conservatory of Music, Roxbury Community College, Simmons College, Suffolk University, the University of Massachusetts–Boston, and the Wentworth Institute of Technology.

Minuteman Library Network
www.mln.lib.ma.us

This consortium includes the public libraries of Acton, Arlington, Bedford, Belmont, Brookline, Cambridge, Concord, Dedham, Dover, Framingham, Franklin, Holliston, Lexington, Lincoln, Maynard, Medfield, Medford, Medway, Millis, Natick, Needham, Newton, Norwood, Somerville, Stow, Sudbury,

Waltham, Watertown, Wayland, Wellesley, Weston, Westwood, Winchester, and Woburn, plus the libraries of Dean College, Framingham State College, Lasell College, MassBay Community College, Mount Ida College, and Newbury College.

Old Colony Library Network
www.ocln.org

This consortium takes in public libraries of Abington, Avon, Braintree/Thayer, Brockton, Canton, Cohasett, Duxbury, Hanover, Hingham, Holbrook, Hull, Marshfield, Massasoit Community College, Milton, Norwell, Plymouth, Quincy, Randolph, Rockland, Sandwich, Scituate, Sharon, Stoughton, Walpole, Weymouth, and Whitman.

Professional Arts Consortium/ProArts
www.proarts.org

This arts-library consortium includes the holdings of the libraries of the Berklee College of Music, the Boston Architectural College, the Boston Conservatory, Emerson College, the Massachusetts College of Art and Design, and the School of the Museum of Fine Arts.

FREE PRESS:
GETTING THE NEWS WITHOUT SPENDING A DIME

"Most of us probably feel we couldn't be free without newspapers, and that is the real reason we want the newspapers to be free."

—EDWARD R. MURROW, 1958

With so many newspapers giving away their content for free on the Internet these days, the idea of shelling out money for the daily news is so last year. Sometimes, though, holding a paper in your hands is a welcome change of pace. And in Boston, you can find all the news—local, regional, entertainment, specialty, and national—you need for free at the corner of nearly every major intersection in the city. Just hunt down a news box—the metal thing that looks like a filing cabinet with windows.

FREE **AND** EASY **NEWSPAPERS**

COMMUNITY WEEKLIES

Free community-based weeklies flourish in Boston, and that's no surprise. The city is made up of clearly defined neighborhoods, the needs of each one as unique as the mix of people there. A local weekly might cover condo conversion hearings and crime, but it will also contain impassioned editorials about the importance of curbing your dog and notes on high school sports. Not to mention such pressing topics as preservation of the inalienable right to save an on-street parking spot with your lawn chair if you've shoveled it out after a snowstorm. (I'm not kidding.) Most of these papers are mailed directly to all homes in the neighborhood (whether you want them or not); they're also readily available at local stores. They show that even residents of a sophisticated metropolis like ours are really just myopic, self-interested villagers at heart—but they also contain news, opinions, and classified ads you won't find anywhere else, not even online.

Back Bay Sun
(617) 523–9490
www.backbaysun.com

This weekly is distributed to all homes in Back Bay and is available in Back Bay shops.

Beacon Hill Times
(617) 523-9490
www.beaconhilltimes.com

A weekly distributed to all homes in Beacon Hill and available in local stores.

Boston Courant
(617) 267-2700

This weekly paper covers all things dealing with the Back Bay, South End, Beacon Hill, and Fenway neighborhoods. Distributed through news boxes and free home delivery.

Bulletin Newspapers
(617) 325-1500
www.bulletinnewspapers.com

These small local weeklies—West Roxbury Bulletin, Roslindale Bulletin, Hyde Park Bulletin, Jamaica Plain Bulletin, Allston/Brighton Bulletin, and Boston People's Voice—are distributed through local stores in each of the neighborhoods they cover.

Charlestown Patriot-Bridge
(617) 241-8500
www.charlestownbridge.com

Covering the town of Charlestown and the Navy Yard. Delivered free to all neighborhood homes, but it costs 25 cents in the local stores.

East Boston Times
(617) 567-9600
www.eastietimes.com

Delivered weekly to homes and available in local stores.

Everett Independent
(617) 567-9600
www.everettindependent.com

Delivered weekly to homes and available in local stores.

Jamaica Plain Gazette
(617) 524–2626
www.jamaicaplaingazette.com

Available every two weeks in stores throughout the neighborhood.

Lynn Journal
(617) 567–9600
www.lynnjournal.com

Delivered weekly to homes and available in local stores.

Mattapan Reporter
(617) 436–1222
www.mattapanreporter.com

Delivered monthly to all households in the 02126 zip code. Also available in local stores.

Mission Hill Gazette
(617) 524–2626
www.missionhillgazette.com

Available monthly in stores throughout the neighborhood.

South End News
(617) 266–6670
www.southendnews.com

Weekly news and entertainment paper distributed through convenience stores and libraries exclusively in the South End.

SPECIALIZED AND ALTERNATIVE WEEKLIES
Bay Windows
(617) 536–0770
www.baywindows.com

This newspaper, distributed weekly throughout the state, is the largest gay and lesbian publication in New England. It covers national, state, and regional news from a gay and lesbian perspective. It's available in news boxes, bookstores, and convenience stores throughout the state, but especially in downtown Boston. Visit the Web site for a complete listing of distribution locations.

Boston Haitian Reporter
www.bostonhaitian.com
(617) 436–1222

This monthly, which focuses on local and national news of interest to Bostonians of Haitian descent or Haitian immigrants, is distributed to stores and health and community centers serving Haitian communities in Brockton, Milton, Dorchester, Roslindale, Mattapan, Hyde Park, Cambridge, and Somerville.

Boston Metro
(617) 210–7905
http://boston.metro.us

If you took any bus or subway recently, you probably sat on top of one of these free papers. This ubiquitous little tabloid, available in news boxes absolutely everywhere, is one in a chain of regional weekday papers that distill the previous day's events into the written version of a sound bite. The news is a combination of stories from national and international wire services as well as local and national *Metro* reporters. The *Metro* is tops at what it does, which is keeping the commuter population busy in between stops on their chosen form of public transportation.

The *Boston Parents' Paper*
(617) 522–1515
http://boston.parenthood.com

Geared to today's moneyed parents, this local edition of a national parents' newspaper has articles about parenting, extensive lists of parent resources—and plenty of advertisements to show you where to buy it all. That's why it's free and available wherever parents go: doctors' offices, toy stores, bookstores, and supermarkets.

The *Boston Phoenix*
(617) 536–5390
www.thephoenix.com
Stuff@Night
www.stuffatnight.com

The *Phoenix,* a full-color tabloid, is more than fifty years old, and the undisputed granddaddy of local alternative newsweeklies. After a brief foray as a paid publication, it's free and available in news boxes all over the city. The paper has won a number of journalism awards, including a Pulitzer Prize for Classical Music Criticism, and it continues to break news with its crack investigative reporters. But it's probably best known for lively coverage of Boston arts, nightlife, and music, as well as a provocative personals section (do all these people really love "long walks on the beach"?). The paper's success has helped its owner, Stephen Mindich, build a media empire that includes radio station WFNX; offshoots in Maine and Rhode Island; and another freebie, *Stuff@Night,* that focuses more on nightlife.

Boston's Weekly Dig
(617) 426–8942
www.weeklydig.com

If you don't need a weekly dose of angst and snark, skip the Dig. This hip, edgy magazine, covering entertainment, pop culture, and local news, is authoritative, funny, and geared to a young audience. It's written with all the ennui and world-weariness its young editorial staff can muster up; they regularly give glimpses into a side of the city that high-powered professionals with steady paychecks rarely see. Pick it up if you're young, youngish, or want to feel young for a few minutes. The listings section includes many excellent ways for college-age Cheap Bastards to make their monthly allowance stretch as far as possible. You'll find it in news boxes throughout the city.

The *Improper Bostonian*
(617) 859–1400
www.improper.com

While the cover of the bimonthly *Improper* is all about superlatives (Boston's Best [fill in the blank]!), smart, funny writing rules the rest of the publication. It's a witty, urbane, and helpful magazine to have when you're looking for something to see, hear, eat, date, or buy in the city of Boston. It's available in news boxes throughout the metro area.

READING NON-FREE NEWSPAPERS FOR FREE

To read the news for free, use a few tricks. First, go online. Almost all Boston's papers are free online if you're willing to register, including the *Boston Herald* and the *Boston Globe*—which costs money if you buy it on the street. (Some premium content, mostly columnists, is available only to paid subscribers, however.) While the business logic of this arrangement eludes me, I'm more than happy to take advantage of it.

If you don't have Internet access but need your daily news fix, there's a way to get it for free. The Boston Public Library and its branches (listed in Appendix B) receive hundreds of local, regional, national, and international newspapers and magazines, which are available for you to read free. You won't be allowed to remove any of the periodicals from the library branch, but don't despair. Head to the Main Branch in Copley Square, and with a free library card you may check out newspapers for use in the beautiful Newspaper Room, located on the first floor in the McKim Library, the library's historic original wing.

If you want magazines, head to the Periodical Desk on the second floor of the McKim Library, where you will also need a library card. You can't take magazines out of the building, but you can read them in the grand reading room, Bates Hall. Built with a grant in 1852 from Joshua Bates, a self-educated senior partner at the banking firm Baring Brothers and Company, Bates Hall is a soaring but peaceful space with vaulted ceilings and fifteen arched and grilled windows that let in tons of natural light. It is the perfect place to sit and catch up on world events. You'd never guess that the bustle of Copley Square is just on the other side of those gracious windows.

Finally, while heading home from work after 5:00 p.m., keep your eyes peeled—especially outside major subway and bus terminals—for *Boston Herald* vendors handing out that day's paper for free!

BORN FREE: PICKING UP A PET ON THE CHEAP

"'Cause I'm as free as a bird, now."

—LYNYRD SKYNYRD

Sometimes it feels as though there are more dogs in the city of Boston than there are people. While purebred pets can be extremely expensive ($1,000 or more), there are plenty who can be adopted for less—as in free. Well, most adoptions aren't free, especially for puppies and kittens, because most adoption agencies spay or neuter and vaccinate the animals before you can take them home. But it's low-cost, and high-benefit.

THE **ADOPTION** OPTION

Free pets are rare in Boston, but they are out there. The best way to locate a free pet is to go through bulletin board postings at a veterinarian's office, or check out reputable Web site listings. Remember that free adoptions posted on bulletin boards (either paper or online) rarely include a medical report from a veterinarian.

Many agencies also post on bulletin boards, but they'll charge you a fee to complete an adoption. So make sure you know exactly from whom you're adopting to avoid any surprises. If you adopt from a different state, you'll often be liable for shipping; in addition, you won't have any chance to inspect the pet's condition before it arrives, and there's little recourse once it does if it's sick or injured.

Here are some reputable places to find a new companion.

Animal Rescue League of Boston
10 Chandler Street
(617) 426–9170
www.arlboston.org

The Catch *Adoption fees start at $25 to $155. You must be twenty-one or older, with Massachusetts ID with current address, to adopt.*

To adopt through ARL, you must have proof of home ownership or a landlord's contact info (to ensure there are no pet policies that will interfere with your adoption), plus up-to-date vet records for your own pets (if you have any). Then you must complete an application and go through an interview with ARL personnel. Your adoption fee includes the costs of health screening, initial vaccinations, spaying or neutering, veterinary care for the first two weeks (which can run up to $300) if the animal develops any shelter-related illnesses, a rabies vaccination, microchip ID and registration, heartworm test and preventative medications for dogs, a feline leukemia test for cats, deworming, a tag and collar, and a leash or carrier.

The center is open Tuesday through Thursday from 1:00 to 7:00 p.m. and Friday through Saturday from 1:00 to 4:00 p.m.

Boston Animal Control

26 Mahler Road, Roslindale (pet adoption location)
(617) 635–1800 or (617) 635–1913
www.cityofboston.gov/animalcontrol/default.asp
Adoption hours Tuesday to Saturday 10:30 a.m. to 3:30 p.m., Wednesday to 7:00 p.m.

The Catch Adoption fees are $25 to $125. You must be twenty-one to adopt.

This office is the central adoption point for the Boston Animal Control department, which is responsible for enforcing animal laws in the city of Boston. The adoption fee includes neutering/spaying, rabies vaccination, distemper vaccination, implantation of a microchip ID for dogs, deworming, and physical examination. Puppies and kittens adopted under the age of four months can return to the shelter for the remainder of their puppy and kitten shots, as well as heartworm tests and either their first heartworm pill (for dogs over six months of age) or a feline leukemia test (for cats). Check the Adoption Center Web site (see above) and click on "Adopt a Pet" to get started; Timmy the terrier, Snoopy the beagle, and other cuties await.

Craigslist Boston

http://boston.craigslist.org/pet

The Catch You can also find tons of pet-related toys, products, and furniture posted here at low or no cost. Look under the "Pets" forum or in the "Free" section of the "For Sale" area.

Bostonians are constantly moving to new apartments that won't take their cats. Or they're getting unwelcome results from doggie pregnancy tests. And where do they go to pass on their pals to new homes? Often, they turn to Craigslist. Always use discretion and your best judgment when using this site—it's best to ask for some references (like a vet's name) before arranging a meeting.

Massachusetts Society for the Prevention of Cruelty to Animals

Animal Care and Adoption Center
350 South Huntington Avenue
(617) 522–5055
www.mspca.org
Adoption center hours: Tuesday and Thursday, 2:00 to 7:00 p.m., Wednesday, Friday, Saturday, and Sunday, 1:00 to 5:00 p.m.

To adopt, you'll need a form of picture ID, something that shows your current address, and your landlord's name and contact info if you rent your home. If you own your own home, they'll ask to see verification, either through a tax, water, or mortgage bill. If you have other animals in the household, please bring information about your veterinarian (the clinic name and phone number are fine) to ensure everyone is up to date on vaccinations. Adoption fees vary by pet: dogs are most expensive (about $155), followed by cats (about $100), rabbits, and other animals. These fees include full exams, spaying/neutering, vaccinations, heartworm tests and preventatives, flea/tick preventatives, ID tags, leashes, and implantation of a microchip IDs and registration where appropriate.

PETCO Stores

www.petco.com
119 First Street; Cambridge; (617) 868–3474
Hours: Monday through Saturday, 9:00 a.m. to 9:00 p.m.; Sunday, 10:00 a.m. to 8:00 p.m.
304 Western Avenue; Brighton; (617) 254–8800
Hours: Monday through Saturday, 9:00 a.m. to 9:30 p.m.; Sunday, 10:00 a.m. to 8:00 p.m.

PETCO locations hold adoption events throughout the year. Local adoption agencies bring pets or photos of pets, and adoption agency personnel are on hand to answer questions and schedule adoption interviews.

Saint Meow's

(617) 767–6294

www.saintmeows.com

The Catch Fee of $100 per cat, or $225 for a pair of kittens.

Saint Meow's cat adoption service holds clinics on Thursday nights from 6:00 to 8:00 p.m. at the First Church of Somerville (89 College Avenue) in Davis Square; the church entrance is located on Francesca Street. Adoptions through Saint Meow's include a vet exam, spay/neuter surgery, rabies vaccine, feline leukemia and FIV blood test, deworming, full grooming, nail-trimming demonstration, and a discount coupon booklet. There are fees of $100 per cat, $180 for two adult cats, or $225 for a pair of kittens. You must bring a driver's license, proof of residence, be twenty-one years old or older, and have a job.

RESCUE ME:
THE CHEAP WAY TO ADOPT A DOG

Dog rescue organizations help place dogs, often purebreds, that are either abandoned by their owners or returned to breeders for a variety of reasons: medical issues, changing family circumstances, or a poor pet/family dynamic. Adopting a rescue dog is an excellent way to adopt a quality purebred dog for a fraction of the cost of going through a breeder.

The American Kennel Club (www.akc.org/breeds/rescue.cfm) has links to hundreds of breed-specific rescue groups throughout the United States. There is usually a fee (which varies according to the popularity of the breed) if you go through one of these organizations. You might have a long wait for especially popular breeds. Several other Internet sites list pets available through pet rescue programs. They include: www.petfinder.org, www.petark .com, www.adoptapet.com, and www.pets911.com.

LOW-COST **PET** CARE

Alliance for Animals Metro Action Clinic
232 Silver Street
South Boston
(617) 268–7800
www.afaboston.org/clinic.htm

The Catch This clinic requires prepayment by credit card.

This clinic offers low-cost spaying, neutering, and vaccinations. It's open seven days a week from 9:00 a.m. to 5:00 p.m. A complete list of fees is available on their Web site.

Animal Rescue League Spay Waggin' Program
10 Chandler Street
(617) 426–9170 or (617) 426–3028 or (877) 590–7729
www.arlboston.org

The Spay Waggin' is a low-cost mobile spay/neuter program created by the Animal Rescue League to help clients in financial need. While they require no proof of financial need, they ask that those with adequate resources have the surgery performed at their local veterinarian. The Waggin' doesn't accept appointments but they do save you big bucks on operations that normally cost in the $200 to $350 range. Here it costs just $65 to $80 for a spay or neuter, $19 for a feline leukemia test.

Everything is done on a first-come, first-served basis. The Spay Waggin' arrives at all surgery sites at around 9:30 a.m., but clients often start lining up as early as 7:00 a.m. You should expect to stay until at least 10:30 a.m. to fill out paperwork. Only pet owners may drop off pets for services—you'll need to sign a legal consent form and answer any questions the veterinarian may have. Call the ARL for a list of Waggin' surgery sites and times.

Massachusetts Society for the Prevention of Cruelty to Animals/Massachusetts Veterinary Medical Association Spay/Neuter Assistance Program (SNAP)
Animal Care and Adoption Center
350 South Huntington Avenue
(617) 541–5007 (helpline)
www.mspca.org

The Catch You must apply to participate in this low-income program.

This jointly administered program gives reduced-cost spay and neuter operations for low-income pet owners. By obtaining a discount certificate, you can take your pet to more than 200 veterinary hospitals or clinics throughout Massachusetts and pay a reduced charge for services.

You will be notified as to your eligibility for the Spay/Neuter Assistance Program within two weeks of the time your application is received. Applications are available online at the MSCPA Web site listed above.

Merwin Memorial Free Clinic
542 Cambridge Street
Allston
(617) 782–5420

This low-cost clinic is run by volunteer veterinarians and is open Monday through Saturday from noon to 3:00 p.m. Their only service is animal vaccines, and they cost around $30, more or less depending on the age and type of animal and the type of vaccine. (They will also take whatever you can pay, if you're really hard up.) This is a walk-in clinic, thus the "clients" (as in the *animals*, not you) are seen on a first-come, first-served basis.

STOP (Stop the Overpopulation of Pets) Mobile Clinic
(617) 571–7151
www.thestopclinic.com

The Catch Spaying/neutering is $70 to $80.

This organization uses a 21-foot-long custom mobile van to travel throughout the Boston suburbs performing spaying/neutering for cats. Clients drop off their cats in the morning for neutering surgery and vaccinations, then pick them up the same evening. Check the Web site for current STOP visit locations and times. Feline leukemia testing is also available at a discount.

UNLEASHED **IN** THE **EAST!**
FREE-RANGE **DOG** PARKS

For dog owners, one of the drawbacks to city living is a dearth of places for Fido to do what he does best—no, not *that*. I mean run. And run and run. After years of skirmishes between city dog control officers and renegade owners who let their dogs go off-leash (contra to state and local rules, which require all dogs to be leashed at all times unless they're inside your house or on your private property), city officials have now begun to designate special parks where dogs can roam free. When you visit these, *always* clean up after your dog, and do not let your dog off-leash unless it is voice-trained to heel. Also, remember that all dogs in the city of Boston must be registered with the Boston Animal Control Office (www.cityof boston.gov/animalcontrol). Wouldn't want to give your doggie a rap sheet, would you?

Boston Common
Center of Boston
(617) 635–5348 (animal control)

For years, animal control officers ticketed anyone who let their dogs roam off-leash in Boston's biggest green space. But a form of détente has settled in since a pilot off-leash program was tested here and found to be successful. Currently, owners may officially release the hounds from 6:00 to 9:00 a.m. and from 4:00 to 8:00 p.m. daily (but check the signs posted at the park, in case these hours change). Remember that the park is usually crawling, in good weather, with walkers, bikers, and squirrels, so don't even think about unleashing your dog unless it's very well voice-trained. Or your next morning papers could be the ones served up by lawyers.

Cambridge Dog Park
Auburn Street at Hawthorne Street

Charlesgate Dog Run
Massachusetts Avenue at Beacon Street

The dog run is very small, but it's fenced in.

Danehy Park
99 Sherman Street at Garden and New Streets
North Cambridge
(617) 349–4800

This fifty-acre park is on a former landfill. There is an unfenced leash-free area located within this park.

Fort Washington Park
Waverly Street between Erie and Putnam Streets
Cambridge
(617) 349–4800

Peters Park Dog Run
1277 Washington Street at East Berkeley Street
www.peterspark.org

This beautiful park is tended by a very active community group, Friends of Peters Park, and it's open until 10:00 p.m. daily. It has its very own dedicated "Dog Recreation Space." Take that, doggie dissers. Check the Web site for rules and regulations.

Exploring Boston

FREEDOM TRAIL:
WALKING BOSTON FOR FREE

"It is good to collect things;
it is better to take walks."

—ANATOLE FRANCE

Boston is one of the most walkable cities in the nation, hands (feet?) down. It's also one of the most historic. The combination of those two factors means Boston has an embarrassment of riches when it comes to free walking tours. Many highlight the proud history of this city, which is tied inextricably with the history of the country. Other tours focus on the art and architecture of local churches, gardens, libraries—even the breweries. The miles of (sometimes hidden) shoreline and rich naval heritage (that goes back, like, to King George) provide water lovers with the opportunity to test their sea legs on free boat tours. In fact, you could spend a month taking tours of Boston and never spend a penny. Summertime offers the best selection of walking tour options, but many tours run in the winter months as well.

Make sure to wear comfortable shoes, and bring an umbrella, because as Mark Twain famously observed, "If you don't like the weather in New England, wait a minute. It will change."

FREE HISTORIC WALKING TOURS

Many of Boston's historic sites are administered by the National Park Service. There are two NPS visitor centers in the greater Boston area, both located at historic sites: one at the Old State House, another at Charlestown Navy Yard. Office hours are given below with each attraction. All the NPS tours listed here are free, but the NPS also administers several local historic sites that charge a small admission price for tours—which can add up quickly if you're traveling with the family.

Note that an "America the Beautiful" National Park Service Park Pass costs $80 a year ($10 for seniors), but it gets you and your family into any national park in the United States where an admission fee is charged, including all the NPS sites in Boston that charge a fee. If you'll be visiting other national parks in the United States during the same year—out West, in Maine, wherever—it's a good purchase.

Boston African American National Historic Site

Museum of Afro-American History
46 Joy Street (Beacon Hill)
(617) 725–0022 (museum information)
(617) 742–5415 (National Park Service tours)
www.afroammuseum.org
www.nps.gov/boaf
Museum open Monday through Saturday, 10:00 a.m. to 4:00 p.m., year-round. Guided tours year-round by appointment; scheduled tours run Memorial Day to Labor Day at 10:00 a.m., noon, and 2:00 p.m.

The Catch Museum suggests $5.00 donation.

This historic site is actually a collection of fifteen sites that are part of the rich history of black America's fight for freedom, much of which occurred here in Boston. This tour, also called the Black Heritage Trail, leaves from the Shaw Memorial, which commemorates Robert Gould Shaw and the African-American Massachusetts 54th Regiment, the only all-black regiment in the Civil War. It's located across from the State House on Beacon Street on the edge of the Boston Common. The tour ends at the Museum of Afro-American History. There are also tours of the museum, a short educational video, and interpretive exhibits. This area is called Beacon Hill for a reason, so be prepared to do some hill climbing.

Boston National Historic Park

NPS Downtown Visitor Center (across from Old State House)
15 State Street (at Washington Street)
(617) 242–5642
www.nps.gov/bost/planyourvisit/guidedtours.htm
Visitor Center hours: daily, 9:00 a.m. to 5:00 p.m.
Tours: mid-June to August, daily at 10:00 a.m., 11:00 a.m., and 2:00 p.m.; mid-April to mid-June and September to November, weekdays at 2:00 p.m. and weekends at 10:00 a.m., 11:00 a.m., and 2:00 p.m.

The Catch Tours take place weather permitting; call ahead in bad weather. Tours are first-come, first-served, limited to thirty participants each.

The Boston National Historic Park is composed of six different sites administered by the NPS, all of which are part of the world-famous Freedom Trail, a fifteen-site self-guided tour throughout Boston and Charlestown. The buildings and locations along the trail paint a vivid portrait of the crucial role that Boston and her patriots played in the American Revolution. Free ranger-led tours begin at the Visitor Center and visit six sites (from the Old South Meeting House to the Old North Church); they take about ninety minutes. The Visitor Center also has maps and educational material about the Freedom Trail for those wishing to walk the whole thing in a self-guided tour. You won't really need a map, though. There's a thick red stripe painted on the sidewalk that guides visitors around to all the sites.

Boston Women's Heritage Trail

(617) 522–2872
www.bwht.org/tour.html

Self-guided tours are usually too much like work (even when they're free), but the Boston Women's Heritage Trail is worth the effort of DIY. It's also the only tour in Boston highlighting the long history of contribution and accomplishment by the city's great women. A Web site allows you to download a variety of tours, each highlighting a different aspect of women's history or a different geographic region: women artists, activists, educators, abolitionists, and so forth. Maps are also included. Some of the tours were researched and designed by Boston schoolchildren and their teachers.

FREE AND CHEAP HISTORIC SITES

Many of the sites listed below are located along the Freedom Trail (which is noted in the descriptions). The National Park Service tour does not go to all the Freedom Trail sites, nor does it go inside the historic buildings and sites that it visits, even though many offer free tours. If you plan on trying to incorporate any of these additional tours into your day on the Freedom Trail, you'll want to allow a minimum of five hours to complete the whole thing.

Bunker Hill Monument and Museum

Monument Square
Charlestown
(617) 242–5689
www.nps.gov/bost/historyculture/bhm.htm
Monument and lodge open daily year-round, 9:00 a.m. to 5:00 p.m. (last entry 4:30 p.m.). Memorial Day to Labor Day, interpretive talks on the hour (except holidays).

It says something about Boston that one of its most notable and visible public monuments commemorates a Revolutionary War battle . . . that it lost. (The fact that the colonists kicked serious British butt in the process seems reason enough to celebrate, so we do.) This granite monument, erected in its present form in 1842, is 221 feet tall (that's 294 steps!) to the top and marks the site of the first major battle of the American Revolution. You can climb it for free any day of the year. The monument, and the interpretive center/ museum nearby, are stops on the Freedom Trail; amazingly, the museum, too, is free! You'll find the expected dioramas (dioramae?), educational exhibits, and artifacts like a Colonial-era powder horn.

Faneuil Hall
State Street (across from City Hall)
(617) 242–5642
www.nps.gov/bost/historyculture/fh.htm
Informational talks daily on the half-hour, 9:30 a.m. to 5:00 p.m. (except when Great Hall is closed); guided walks and tours daily, spring through late fall.

Wealthy merchant Peter Faneuil built his hall in 1742 and gave it to Boston as a gift; it has served as an open-forum meeting hall and marketplace ever since. Called the "Cradle of Liberty," it was the site of the November 1773 discussions between John Hancock and other Bostonians about a certain pesky tea tax—and we all know how that turned out. Talks are still held in the second-floor Great Hall meeting space, except when the city occasionally closes the hall to public access for events or meetings.

King's Chapel
Corner of Tremont and School Streets
(617) 227–2155
www.kings-chapel.org
Memorial Day to Labor Day, Monday through Saturday, 10:00 a.m. to 4:00 p.m. (closed on Tuesday and Wednesday, 11:30 a.m. to 1:30 p.m., for noon-time services), Sunday 1:30 to 4:00 p.m.; rest of the year, Saturday, 10:00 a.m. to 4:00 p.m. and Sunday, 1:30 to 4:00 p.m.

The Catch Voluntary donations are accepted. Self-guided tours are $1.00.

America's first architect, Peter Harrison, designed this small church, which was completed in 1754 (the church's predecessor, an Anglican church made of wood, occupied this spot from 1686 until this one was built). The magnificent interior is considered the finest example of Georgian church architecture in North America. A bell cast by Paul Revere still rings before every service. The church is a stop on the Freedom Trail. The "tour" is a talk given frequently to visitors throughout the day. During Fourth of July week, special "Tory Stories" (love that) from the chapel's history are told on the half-hour.

Massachusetts State House
Corner of Park and Beacon Streets
(617) 727–3676
www.sec.state.ma.us/trs/trsgen/genidx.htm
Tours given weekdays year-round, 10:00 a.m. to 4:00 p.m. (not on holidays).

The Catch Reservations required for conducted tours.

The Massachusetts State House, another stop on the Freedom Trail, is the oldest building on Beacon Hill and is famous for its enormous golden dome. You can't miss it if you're in Boston Common: look north. Built in 1798 and designed by noted local architect Charles Bulfinch, the State House is the seat of government for the Commonwealth as well as the home of the Massachusetts Senate and House of Representatives. Free tours of the building last between thirty and forty-five minutes and include an overview of the history and architecture of the building. (Tours that highlight the legislative process can also be arranged in advance.) Caution: During spring, school class trips take over the place; to avoid becoming entangled in the hordes of youngsters, try to take a tour after 3:00 p.m.

Old North Church
193 Salem Street
(617) 523–6676
www.oldnorth.com
June to October, tours daily 9:00 a.m. to 6:00 p.m.; March to May, tours daily 9:00 a.m. to 5:00 p.m.; November to February, tours daily 10:00 a.m. to 4:00 p.m.

The Catch Call ahead for reservations for larger groups. Donations are appreciated.

Built in 1723, the Old North is the oldest church building in Boston and continues to serve as an Episcopal church. It's especially famous for one historical moment: On April 18, 1775, Robert Newman, the sexton of the church, hung two lanterns from its steeple to warn Paul Revere and others of British troop movements. Paul Revere's famous "midnight ride" began when he saw that signal. Tours are geared mostly to school groups, but they'll take big people, too. The location is one of the most popular along the Freedom Trail, so make sure to hit it early in the day.

Old South Meeting House

310 Washington Street (at Milk Street)
(617) 482–6439
www.nps.gov/bost/historyculture/osmh.htm
www.oldsouthmeetinghouse.org
April to October, open daily 9:30 a.m. to 5:00 p.m.; rest of the year, open 10:00 a.m. to 4:00 p.m.

The Catch *Admission $5.00 for adults, $4.00 for seniors and students, $1.00 for children ages six to eighteen. Children under age six are admitted free. Guided tours $3.00 extra.*

Angry about the British tea tax, 5,000 colonials gathered on December 16, 1773, at the this meeting house to figure out a way to make their displeasure known to King George. Someone suggested tossing all the tea into the ocean—people seemed to like that idea. The rest is history. Now a National Historic Landmark, the meeting house continues to host regular discussions and lectures on events that shape our world just as it did more than two centuries ago. In addition to educational tours, the Meeting House hosts regular free and paid events, including readings, concerts, and lectures. Note that groups taking guided tours require a small extra charge, but you can do a self-guided tour for no extra fee. Also, while the attraction is open year-round, from November to March there are no guided tours.

Old State House

206 Washington Street (at State Street)
(617) 720–1713
www.bostonhistory.org
Open daily year-round, 9:00 to 5:00 p.m., except to 6:00 p.m. in July and August and to 4:00 p.m. in January.

The Catch *Admission is $5.00 for adults, $4.00 seniors, $1.00 children under eighteen. Audio guides $1.00. Senior Bostonians and Boston public school children enter for free.*

The Old State House was built in 1713, making it the city's oldest public building. It began its life as the seat of the royal government in the New World, then became one of the most historically significant places in Boston during the rebellion. The Boston Massacre happened near here; colonials debated the Stamp Act within its walls; and it was the location of the first public reading in Massachusetts of the Declaration of Independence. Today, this is a museum of Boston history with changing exhibits on different aspects of the city's past. Guided and self-guided tours are available to groups for a small extra charge. Soloists can self-tour with just an admission ticket.

Park Street Church
Park Street at Tremont Street
(617) 523–3383
www.parkstreet.org
Tours mid-June to mid-August, Tuesday to Friday 9:00 a.m. to 4:00 p.m. and Saturday 9:00 a.m. to 3:00 p.m.

This church is the place where William Lloyd Garrison gave the first abolitionist speech and where the song "America" was first sung. A free tour of the 200-year-old church lasts about fifteen minutes and includes a short video.

Symphony Hall
301 Massachusetts Avenue
(617) 638–9890
Tours during orchestra season only, October through early May (but no tours during last two to three weeks of December), Wednesdays at 4:30 p.m. and first Saturdays of each month at 2:00 p.m.

This free tour takes visitors throughout all nooks and crannies of the stately home of the Boston Symphony Orchestra and tells the symphony's colorful history. The tour takes one hour and begins at the Massachusetts Avenue entrance.

FREE AND CHEAP HISTORIC HOME TOURS

Cooper-Frost-Austin House
21 Linnaean Street
Cambridge
(617) 227–3956
www.spnea.org/visit/homes/cooper.htm
Three tours annually (check Web site for each year's dates).

The Catch Admission $4.00; free to Historic New England members and residents of Cambridge.

The oldest still-standing house in Cambridge, the Cooper-Frost-Austin House was built in 1690 by Samuel Cooper. Although it was expanded and updated through the years, many pieces of the original frame and original finishes survive today. They only open the house to visitors a few days each year—in 2008, just for three days. Two of the days cost $4.00 per person to visit, but one day (August 9) was free! Check the house's Web site for each year's tour dates and fees.

Frederick Law Olmsted National Historic Site
99 Warren Street
Brookline
(617) 566–1689
www.nps.gov/frla/index.htm

The Catch Call the National Park Service or visit the Olmsted Web site for more information.

The man responsible for the landscape design of Central Park, the White House Lawn, the Emerald Necklace, and thousands of other world-famous green spaces throughout the country made his home, named Fairsted, and office here in the bucolic fields of Brookline, beginning in 1883. It is free to visit both Fairsted and Olmsted's office, in which there are over one million design documents relating to some of his most notable projects.

John Fitzgerald Kennedy National Historic Site

83 Beals Street
Brookline
(617) 566–7937
www.nps.gov/jofi
Open spring through fall (check Web site for dates). Guided tours Wednesday through Sunday every thirty minutes from 10:00 a.m. to 3:00 p.m.; self-guided tours Wednesday through Sunday from 3:30 to 4:30 p.m. (first and second floor). No self-guided tours mid-May through September.

The Catch Admission is $3.00 per adult; children age seventeen and under and any National Park Service Park Pass holders enter for free.

The JFK National Historic Site, the birthplace and first home of President John Fitzgerald Kennedy, was restored by his mother, Rose Kennedy, to the condition it was in when the president was a young child (the family moved when he was four). The site, administered by the Park Service, holds frequent educational workshops for children and older students throughout the summer.

Longfellow National Historic Park

105 Brattle Street
Cambridge
(617) 876–4491
www.nps.gov/long
Open spring through fall (check Web site for dates). House tours June through October from Wednesday through Sunday at 10:30 a.m., 11:30 a.m., 1:00 p.m., 2:00 p.m., 3:00 p.m., and 4:00 p.m. The grounds are open daily from dawn to dusk.

The Catch House admission is $3.00 per adult; children age fifteen and under and any National Park Service Park Pass holders enter for free.

This place is a little-known historical gem just a few blocks off Harvard Square. Even before Henry Wadsworth Longfellow moved into this stately mansion in 1843, it had hosted General George Washington between July 1775 and April 1776 while he was planning the Siege of Boston to drive the British out of the colonies. The house has an impressive collection of historical artifacts chronicling the families that have lived here and its many famous visitors, including Julia Ward Howe, Nathaniel Hawthorne, and Ralph Waldo Emerson. The grounds also feature expansive (not expensive) gardens, which anyone can visit for free.

Otis House Museum

141 Cambridge Street
(617) 227–3957, extension 256
www.spnea.org/visit/homes/otis.htm
Tours year-round Wednesday through Sunday on the half-hour, 11:00 a.m. to
4:30 p.m.

The Catch Admission $8.00 per person ($24.00 maximum per family, but
Boston residents enter for free.

Want to see how the other half lived a couple of centuries ago? A visit to
the Otis House is like stepping back in time to witness the elegant lifestyle
of Boston's ruling class after the American Revolution. Built in 1796, the
house belonged to Harrison Gray Otis, who developed Beacon Hill and was
both a U.S. representative and a mayor of Boston. The house was designed
by Charles Bulfinch, one of the most noted architects of his time. The admission price is steep—but all Boston residents enter for free!

The Paul Revere House and the Pierce/Hichborn House

19 North Square
(617) 523–2338
www.paulreverehouse.org
Revere House open daily mid-April through October, from 9:30 a.m. to 5:15
p.m.; November through mid-April, 9:30 a.m. to 4:15 p.m. (but closed Mondays January through March).
Pierce/Hichborn House open daily by guided tour only; call for hours.

The Catch Admission $3.00 adults, $2.50 seniors and college students, and
$1.00 kids age five to seventeen. Call for daily Hichborn House tour schedules
and hours.

The home of Paul Revere was built in 1680 and it's a very popular stop on
the Freedom Trail; you won't be alone on this cutesy, cobblestoned alley.
While there are no formal tours here, there are plenty of helpful and knowledgeable staff members scattered throughout this three-story, colonial-style
house and courtyard to answer any questions you might have about the
city's fave patriot, silversmith, horse-rider, alarm-sounder.

Your admission ticket also gets you into the Pierce/Hichborn House next
door, an early Georgian-style home built around 1711 that was once owned
by Revere's cousin. It's one of the most authentically preserved examples of
this type of architecture in the city, and is filled with original period furniture and decorations. Because of its small size, it is shown by guided tour

only. (Hours at the Pierce/Hichborn House change frequently, so call ahead to reserve a tour.)

Pierce House
24 Oakton Avenue
Dorchester
(617) 227–3956 or (617) 288–6041
www.spnea.org/visit/homes/pierce.htm

The Catch Admission $5.00.

The Pierce House, built in 1683, is one of the few First Period (in other words, 17th-century) houses left standing in Boston. The house was occupied by ten generations of the Pierce family, and it offers a unique glimpse into the evolution of building styles and techniques as well as the lifestyle of one family over more than three centuries. It's only open at *very* limited times (could be for just two days and three hours each day). The $5.00 ticket is a bargain considered that it's usually closed to the public. Group tours can be booked from early summer through mid-October, however.

WATER **YOU** LOOKING **AT?** TOURING BOSTON'S SHORELINE **AND** HARBOR

Boston Harbor Islands
(617) 223–8666
www.BostonharborIslands.com
Ferry operates approximately early June to Labor Day.

The Catch Ferry $14.00 per adult ($10.00 seniors, $8.00 children) to George's Island from Long Wharf (off Commercial Street); ferries to other islands, free to $3.00.

The dozens of islands just off the Boston coast offer a wonderful mix of walking trails, historic buildings and forts, camping, and unique features (like a giant lighthouse). It will cost you to get to George's Island, but once you're there, free shuttles will take you to a variety of other islands. The National Park Service and the Massachusetts Department of Conservation and Recreation offer tours on some of these islands, and host Family Fun Days on weekends from July 1 to Labor Day. Fun Day events include Civil War reenactment encampments, underwater animal "show and tell," music, and more. For a current schedule, visit the Boston Harbor Islands Web site.

I've covered the islands much more extensively, including camping options and events, on page 173.

Boston Natural Areas Network
(617) 542–7696
www.bostonnatural.org/actcanoeing.htm

The Catch Reservations required.

Canoe for free? In someone else's canoe? With a guide?? Yes! Boston Natural Areas Network staff and volunteers will take you out along the Neponset River (in Mattapan); to Belle Isle Inlet and its marsh (in East Boston); or along the Charles River in Hyde Park and Roxbury to enjoy the hidden beauty and wildlife of riverine Boston. The trips run from April through October. Canoes are provided, or you can bring your own; the trips last two to three hours. The catch? None. But you do have to make an advance reservation, because these trips are scheduled and popular. BNAN's newsletter and Web site list canoe trips (click the "Calendar" online in the summer months).

Charlestown Navy Yard
National Park Service Visitor Center (access on Warren Street off Chelsea Street, near Gate 1)
Charlestown
(617) 242–5601
www.nps.gov/bost/historyculture/cny.htm
Visitor Center: open daily 9:00 a.m. to 5:00 p.m. Guided tour times vary.

A ranger-guided, forty-five-minute walking tour explores the Navy Yard's nearly 200-year history by taking visitors past such sites as the Chain Forge, where die-lock anchor chain was first manufactured; the Ropewalk, a quarter-mile-long building designed by famed architect Alexander Parris; and Dry Dock 1, one of the first dry docks in the nation. There are signs that help you take a self-guided tour as well. Guided tour times vary, so call ahead for the schedule. The visitor center is in Building 5.

Deer Island Wastewater Treatment Plant

Deer Island
Winthrop
(617) 660–7607
www.mwra.com/03sewer/html/sewdi_access.htm
Tours on first Tuesday of every month, April to early November, starting at 9:30 a.m.; additional tours sometimes on Fridays (call ahead).

The Catch Advance reservation required. Picture ID required at tour. Tours suspended whenever national security level reaches "orange" or higher.

Touring a wastewater treatment facility might not seem like a fun way to spend the day, but if you're into engineering or environmental science, it might be. This treatment facility treats the waste of forty-three Boston-area communities; its centerpieces are the 140-foot-high, three-million-gallon egg-shaped digester tanks that are a focal point of any harbor view. The tour takes two hours.

Not into "wasting" your time? Deer Island also has sixty acres of grounds and miles of trails and walkways (with treatment-plant views, of course). This is a surprisingly popular tour, and openings are usually booked several months in advance, so call ahead—you might need to fill out a security-clearance form, and the check takes a few weeks to clear you for entry. Be sure to wear comfortable shoes and clothing, and be ready for bad weather since a portion of the tour takes place outside.

Fort Independence

Castle Island
South Boston
(617) 727–5290
www.mass.gov/dcr/parks/metroboston/castle.htm
Tour times and open hours vary; call ahead.

The Catch Tours run weather-permitting.

Fort Independence, atop Castle Island (joined to South Boston by a causeway), began in 1634 as a simple wooden fortification with three cannons built to protect and monitor the mouth of Boston Harbor. Since then, the fort has been built and rebuilt, and today it is a granite and earthwork fort that tells a rich history of revolution and civil war. It's even said that events at this fort inspired Edgar Allan Poe, who served there briefly, to write "The Cask of Amontillado"—one of his best stories. Tours are conducted by the

Castle Island Association in the summer months on an irregular basis (call ahead to inquire), and there are also interpretive signs for self-guided tours. The association has traditionally hosted Halloween-season "Haunted Fort" events during the last weekend of October, if you have kids who enjoy having the bejeezus scared out of them.

Harborwalk
(617) 482–1722
www.bostonharborwalk.com
www.tbha.org/events.htm (current calendar)

The Harborwalk is a walking path that closely follows the shore of Boston Harbor from the North End all the way to the Kennedy Library in Dorchester. The walkway, the result of a massive urban renewal project spanning more than a decade, has reclaimed sections of the waterfront that had long been impassable to pedestrians. Today, the Boston Harbor Association offers free walking tours (sometimes even cruises) that highlight the art and history of this unique public resource. For current events, check the calendar at the BHA Web site (see above). You will actually do the city and its waterfront a service by going on one of these tours; the BHA collects comments from tour visitors to incorporate into future proposals for Harborwalk improvements.

USS *Cassin*
Young Pier 1, Charlestown Navy Yard
Charlestown
(617) 242–5601
www.nps.gov/bost/historyculture/usscassinyoung.htm
December through March, guided tours only, weather permitting, 11:00 a.m., 2:00 p.m. and 3:00 p.m.; April through November, tours on the hour daily.

This World War II destroyer was decommissioned in the 1950s and now stands in stark contrast to the USS *Constitution* docked nearby. You can self-tour the ship's deck during summer, but the forty-five-minute guided tours take you into parts of the ship (above and below decks) not usually open to the public.

USS *Constitution*
Pier 1
Charlestown Navy Yard
Charlestown

(617) 242–5670
www.ussconstitution.navy.mil
April to October, ship open Tuesday through Sunday, 10:00 a.m. to sunset;
November to March, Thursday through Sunday, 10:00 a.m. to 3:50 p.m. Open
most federal holidays. Museum open slightly longer hours.

The USS *Constitution* is the oldest commissioned warship in the world.
Launched in 1797, she got her nickname "Old Ironsides" during the War of
1812 when cannonballs fired at her bounced off her sides, which are made
of three layers of hardwood harvested from all over the United States. The
naval officers assigned to the ship give tours on the half-hour, with the last
tours leaving around 3:30 p.m. The tours, and the museum, are completely
free although they do accept donations.

All visitors are required to go through a screening process, so get there a
half-hour earlier. (Anything that isn't allowed on an airplane is also banned
from the *Constitution*: guns, mace, and any sharp objects, such as razors,
knives, pocket knives, Swiss army knives, scissors, and letter openers.) Your
backpacks, bags, purses, and wallets *will* be inspected.

FREE AND CHEAP
ART AND ARCHITECTURE TOURS

Boston Athenæum
10½ Beacon Street
(617) 227–0270
www.bostonathenaeum.org
Open Monday through Friday, 9:00 a.m. to 5:00 p.m.; Saturday, 9:00 a.m. to
4:00 p.m. Tours Tuesday and Thursday at 3:00 p.m.

The Boston Athenæum is the heart of Boston's literary scene. Although the
fine arts museum now holds much of the Athenæum's art, this building still
contains many sculptures, paintings, and other priceless works that make
the lovely old library feel like an art museum in its own right. The great (and
free) half-hour Art and Architecture tour will give you an up-close look at
these rare treasures. It takes place two times per week.

Boston Public Library

700 Boylston Street (Copley Square)
(617) 536–5400 (extension 2216 for tour information)
www.bpl.org/guides/tours.htm
Tours Monday at 2:30 p.m., Tuesday at 6:00 p.m., Thursday at 6:00 p.m.,
Friday and Saturday at 11:00 a.m., and also (October through March only)
Sunday at 2:00 p.m.

This Art and Architecture tour of Boston's main library, led by library volunteers, highlights the architecture of Charles Follen McKim and Philip Johnson, the two men who conceptualized the two vastly different wings of the first large public library in the United States. The tour also showcases sculptures, murals, and paintings within the library. The tour takes about an hour and begins in the foyer of the Dartmouth Street entrance of the McKim building (the older building).

John Joseph Moakley U.S. Courthouse

One Courthouse Way (near Fan Pier in South Boston)
John Adams Courthouse
One Pemberton Square (near the State House)
(617) 748–9639
www.discoveringjustice.org/programs/tours.shtml
Tours year-round Tuesday through Friday, 9:30 a.m. to 4:00 p.m. by appointment only.

The Catch Appointment required. You must bring two forms of identification, one with a photo, to the tour.

The Moakley Courthouse, one of the most recent additions to the Boston skyline, is noted for its unique curved walls of glass and its clean modern lines. (It also has a great view of the city.) The John Adams Courthouse, built between 1886 and 1894, houses the Commonwealth's Supreme Judicial Court. It was recently renovated to expand its facilities and to restore existing spaces and artwork.

Free tours of both locations focus on the court houses' architecture and the art housed within, which at the Moakley includes a series of paintings by Ellsworth. Visitors spend time in a typical courtroom, and some may attend an actual court session in progress. The Moakley has a great public cafeteria with windows looking out onto the city skyline and the harbor below.

Trinity Church Copley Square

(617) 536–0944

www.trinitychurchboston.org/art/tours.php

Free tours each Sunday immediately following 11:15 a.m. church service (approximately 12:15); Tuesday through Saturday, guided tours at various times (check Web site calendar) costing $6.00 per person; self-guided tours anytime Monday to Saturday 9:30 a.m. to 5:00 p.m. and Sunday 1:00 to 5:00 p.m., also $6.00 per person.

The Catch Any tour except guided Sunday tour costs $6.00 per person.

The imposing Romanesque spires of Trinity Church dominate Copley Square and promise untold architectural treasures within. The church doesn't disappoint. Completed in 1877, this award-winning architectural marvel has had plenty of renovations. The tour after the Sunday service meets at the Eagle lectern at the front of the church and encompasses the art and architecture that have made this place famous, including the Eugene Oudinot stained-glass windows. Visit the Web site for an updated list of other tour times and free events (each month's schedule is different).

OH-SO-BOSTON **TOURS** ON **THE** CHEAP

Boston Globe

135 Morrissey Boulevard

(617) 929–2653

www.boston.com

Tours Monday and Thursday at 10:00 a.m., 11:15 a.m., and 1:15 p.m., plus one Wednesday per month (same times).

The Catch Advance reservations required. Children must be nine or older.

Take a tour of the Fourth Estate! The *Boston Globe* offers tours of its facilities as well as the giant printing presses that pump out over half a million newspapers a day. The tour lasts about one hour.

Harpoon Brewery

Mass Bay Brewing Company
306 Northern Avenue
(888) HARPOON (extension 522 to schedule private tours)
www.harpoonbrewery.com
Tours Tuesday through Saturday at 4:00 p.m.; additional tours on Friday and
Saturday at 2:00 p.m. and Saturday at noon.

The Catch *Bring ID if you want to sample beer. Must be twenty-one or
older.*

Tours of this Boston brewery include tastings at the end and last thirty to
forty-five minutes. Groups of fifteen or more can make reservations. The
brewery charges $1.00 per person for certain events.

The Samuel Adams Brewery

Boston Beer Company
30 Germania Street
Jamaica Plain
(617) 368–5080
Thursday, 2:00 p.m.; Friday, 2:00 and 5:30 p.m.; Saturday, noon, 1:00 p.m.,
and 2:00 p.m.; additional tours held on Wednesday at 2:00 p.m. from May 1
through August 31.

The Catch *Suggested donation $2.00. Bring ID if you want to taste beer.*

This tour shows you the inner workings of the brewery that put Boston beer
makers on the international map. You must be twenty-one or older to taste
beer at the end of the tour.

TAKING A FREE RIDE:
TRAVELING CHEAPLY
IN BOSTON

"So, come on and take a free ride."

—EDGAR WINTER GROUP

Despite what you may have heard in the transit-trip-from-hell folk song "Charley on the MTA" (Kingston Trio fans? anyone?), most people do return from excursions on Boston public transportation. Boston's subway system is the oldest in the nation (built in 1898), though the Massachusetts Bay Transportation Authority claims to be constantly improving the system. Um, we're not so sure about that. But it is extensive. You can get to most cities and towns in eastern Massachusetts using a combination of bus, subway, commuter rail lines, and a light rail system. Link them together and you can get all the way west to Fitchburg or south to Rhode Island. There are also a number of cheap ways to get out of town (why would you want to do that? Oh yeah: winter) and to and from the city's airport.

Of course, you could always walk. That's free.

FLEET **FEET**

In Boston the cheapest, most enjoyable mode of transportation is still your own feet—or, if you're in a wheelchair, wheels. Walking or wheeling around Boston is easy and cheap because the city is mostly flat and compact. You can get from one end to the other in a couple of hours. Excellent detailed maps can be downloaded for free from Google, Yahoo, and other Web sites. Maps and other tourist information can also be found at the **Boston Common Visitor Center,** on Boston Common along Tremont Street (across from Temple Place). It's open Monday through Saturday from 8:30 a.m. to 5:00 p.m. and Sunday from 10:00 a.m. to 6:00 p.m. Call the center directly at (617) 536–4100.

The homegrown BikeMap (about $12.00 laminated or $6.00 unlaminated; available at bicycle and sporting goods stores or online at www.bike maps.com) is especially good because it's waterproof, durable, updated frequently, and has lots of detail (including attractions). Its designers have highlighted the least trafficked and most scenic routes throughout the city, which makes the map ideal for walkers as well as cyclists.

Massachusetts Bay Transportation Authority (MBTA)

(617) 222–5000

www.mbta.com

The Catch Fares vary; at press time, single rides in-town $1.70 to $2.00 on subway, $1.25 to $1.50 on bus.

The MBTA, or the T as it's universally known in Boston, oversees operation of all the subways, buses, commuter boats, and trains in and around the city of Boston (the boats and commuter rail are operated by contractors). The network is extensive and relatively cheap, though it can be very confusing. Fares vary depending on distance of travel; there are various daily, weekly, and monthly passes that cut your price dramatically, but prices vary. Also, the entire system is in the process of being upgraded to the slightly confusing **Charlie Cards** system. These debit cards are supposed to speed up the turnstile action; the only problem is, the price of a ride is different if you buy a single fare on the spot (a Charlie Ticket) or already have a card (a Charlie Card). And the two look basically the same. The touch-screens don't explain it very well. Neither do hand-written signs posted at the stations. Let's hope they get the kinks worked out soon. (Fortunately the MBTA web site is excellent and clear. See, for instance, www.mbta.com/schedules_and_ maps/subway/lines: just click on the color of your line for exact fares and maps.)

The subway's color-coded system is based on the concept of "Inbound" versus "Outbound." Inbound means a subway train is heading into the downtown area or central point (Park Street station for the Red and Green Lines, Downtown Crossing for the Orange Line, Government Center for the Blue Line). A commuter rail departs from North Station, Back Bay Station, and South Station and will get you to points as far away as Newburyport; Providence, Rhode Island; or Fitchburg. Check the Web site first for any questions about fares, routes, or maps.

If you get lost or confused when attempting to use the MBTA system, don't despair. Even those of us who grew up here get screwed up and turned around regularly, and end up asking tourists for directions or tips on how to use the Charlie Card machines. (Yeah, that works out well. But anyway.)

One caveat: In a throwback to its Puritanical roots, Boston's transit begins running at 5:30 a.m. but shuts down around 12:30 to 1:00 a.m. If you're a night owl, plan on using a cab.

GETTING **OUT** OF **BOSTON**

Logan Airport
www.mbta.com

Getting to Boston Logan International Airport by public transportation is insanely cheap—and increasingly convenient with the addition of the Silver Line bus, which goes directly to each airport terminal at Logan from South Station (on the Red Line) for as little as $1.70. Or you can take the Blue Line (same price) to the Airport T stop, from which a free MBTA shuttle bus will take you directly to your terminal. The water shuttles are a little more pricey (starting at $6.00), but they go from Long Wharf (near the Aquarium) directly to the airport docks, where the shuttle bus will drop you off at your destination. Of course, leave extra time.

The only drawback is that most of the bus and subway system doesn't start running until about 5:30 a.m. and stops running around 12:30 a.m., so if your plane is late, or you've got a really early flight, you could be out of luck on this option.

Auto Driveaway Company
480 Neponset Street, #2-B, Canton (local branch)
(781) 828–4070 or (800) 562–1558
www.autodriveaway.com

The Catch *Cash deposit of $350 required. Trunk is off-limits. Must fill gas tank before dropoff. You are expected to average 400 driving miles or more per day.*

This service is a great way to drive yourself to your desired destination for just the price of the gas (which varies wildly with market conditions, but we digress). This national auto delivery service will match you to a car that needs to be driven to a pre-determined city, and all you have to do is keep the rubber side down, pay for gas, and arrive in the predetermined number of days. It's free, but there are some conditions. All drivers must be twenty-three years old with a valid driver's license, and all drivers must provide a motor vehicle driver's record, which is generated by your home state's Registry of Motor Vehicles. You'll also need to leave a refundable cash security deposit of approximately $350.

The Web site keeps an updated list of cars needing transport out of Boston, but getting back to Beantown is up to you—though, because the Auto Driveaway network is nationwide, you might be able to pick up another car in your destination city later and drive back to Boston for free.

ERideShare Boston Carpool Center
(618) 530–4842
www.erideshare.com/carpool.php?city=Boston

The Catch Most ride shares involve paying a share of gas costs.

Free membership in this carpooling Web site will give you access to the frequently updated list of carpooling opportunities, including both one-time road trips and regular commutes, plus access to ride shares to faraway cities. We're surprised by how many people list on this service. Remember to kick in for gas. The Web site also includes notes on safety.

HOUSE-SWAPPING SERVICES

Want to stay in an apartment in Paris? How about the Swiss Alps? Colorado? For free? Well, it's theoretically possible. It's called house swapping, and it's becoming all the rage for savvy travelers. By simply swapping your house (or apartment) with another family. Obviously there are risks when you open your home to someone you've never met (and can't supervise). But travelers who house-swap claim they quickly become addicted. Vacationing this way, they say, gets you entree into the locals' world, allowing you to experience a vacation destination in a much more intimate and complete way, as opposed to being holed up in a hotel. Most house-swapping services charge a small fee to list your home and browse the other house listings. Here are some services.

Craigslist
http://boston.craigslist.com/swp

These listings are free. But you need to proceed with caution, since there's no screening process whatsoever.

Home for Exchange
www.homeforexchange.com

The Catch $59 for one-year membership.

This service draws a lot of international members.

Home Link International
www.homelink-usa.org

The Catch Annual membership fee is $110.

The largest service, serving twenty-two different countries.

Intervac
www.intervacus.com

The Catch Annual fee $65 for U.S.-only swaps and $95 for U.S. and international swaps.

The oldest house-swapping service, founded in 1953.

CHEAP **RETREATS**

East Mountain Retreat Center
Lake Buel Road
Great Barrington
(413) 528–6617
www.eastretreat.org

The Catch Suggested donation $30 per day, which includes meals; $10 per night (no meals) requested of bicyclists and hikers. Reservations required.

Looking for real peace and quiet? This retreat, open from mid-April through mid-October (except closed late June and early July), is a silent retreat tucked away in a forest in the Berkshire Mountains. You'll be expected to cook your own meals, but food is provided. You'll get a private room with bedding and towels. But unless you're either talking to a guide or a teacher at the center or eating, it's expected that you will literally keep your mouth closed for the duration of your stay. The center suggests that you stay at least two days, but no longer than two weeks.

Kripalu Center for Yoga and Health

57 Interlaken Road
Stockbridge
(413) 448–3123
www.kripalu.org

The Catch If you contribute thirty-five hours of work per week, you gain access to all the center's amenities, plus room and board, for $50 a month.

Kripalu is the yoga lovers' retreat of choice in New England. The lovely, sprawling estate is on the line between Stockbridge and Lenox, Massachusetts, near Tanglewood, the summer home of the Boston Symphony Orchestra. Volunteers help keep the place looking good, feed paying guests, and clean bathrooms. But here's a secret: You can volunteer for one, two, or three months—depending which of two volunteer program you choose—and get discount use of the facilities! One program is pretty structured, with a strong yoga-educational component; the other is more laid-back, but does expect you to lend a hand around the place (as directed by your volunteer coordinator).

Rowe Camp and Conference Center

273 King's Highway Road
Rowe
(413) 339–4954
www.rowecenter.org

The Rowe Camp and Conference Center, run by a Unitarian Universalist minister, holds frequent weekend workshops and programs featuring some of the best minds in the country (folks like Grace Paley and Noam Chomsky have come in the past). They talk on subjects ranging from meditation to writing to baseball. Set on beautiful grounds in the Berkshire Hills of western Massachusetts, the center is open to anyone willing to put in a little elbow grease in exchange for free room and board. Between Labor Day and late June, there's a work-study sabbatical lasting from six weeks to a year, depending on your schedule; if you put in thirty-three hours of work during that time, you'll get free room and board and access to the conferences and workshops.

After late June, there's also a summer volunteer program, requiring at least twenty-eight hours of work per week in exchange for the free room and board. If you don't want to do *that* much work, they'll let you barter your services or skills, if they need 'em, for reduced rates on workshops and classes. But you'll still have to pay for room and board (subject to availability, and the rates vary).

Vipassana Meditation Center
386 Colrain-Shelburne Road
Shelburne Falls
(413) 625–2160
www.dhara.dhamma.org

The Catch *All students must apply and make reservations at least one month in advance.*

The ten-day silent meditation course offered at Vipassana can be rigorous in a minimalist way: you do no exercise, have no physical contact with others, hear no music, and, above all, may not speak. The focus is on silently meditating in complete isolation, using ancient Buddhist techniques. Donations are accepted, but only if you return for a second ten-day session, when you'll also be expected to prepare meals, keep the center running, and help new students complete their own courses.

FREEHAND:
FREE ART GALLERIES
AND EXHIBITS

*"My God! How terrible these money
questions are for an artist!"*

—PAUL GAUGUIN

There's absolutely no reason a Cheap Bastard should go overboard seeing art in (high-admission-fee-charging) museums alone—you can also find it for free displayed at plenty of art galleries, studios, artist cooperatives, and art schools. It doesn't cost a penny to browse through most of these treasure troves. Some galleries are tiny spaces that only showcase a few pieces at a time. Others are practically museums. While the bulk of the private galleries are located along or near Newbury Street in the heart of Back Bay, galleries are also springing up in less obvious locales—the South End, East Boston, Fort Point, Cambridge. Artists' communities have also sprouted up, many hosting annual open-studio events where you can find fresh, new artists doing fabulous work that's selling at "undiscovered artist" prices.

And it really helps to get plugged into this artistic community, because exhibition openings mean opening-night parties: some of the best social events in the city, free to attend, and most proferring free wine and/or beer, plus appetizers. My tip? When you visit a gallery you really like, ask to be added to their mailing list. Sure enough, you'll receive a postcard or e-mail invitation the next time new exhibitions, and the opening-night parties, hit the place.

PRIVATE **ART** GALLERIES

ACME Fine Art
38 Newbury Street, fourth floor (between Arlington and Berkeley Streets)
(617) 585–9551
www.acmefineart.com
Hours: Tuesday through Friday, 11:00 a.m. to 5:30 p.m., Saturday, 11:00 a.m. to 5:00 p.m. and by appointment.

This gallery features modern works, including abstract expressionism, Fauvism, Cubism, and surrealism, dating from 1900 through 1980.

Allston Skirt Gallery

65 Thayer Street
(617) 482–3652
www.allstonskirt.com
Hours: Wednesday through Saturday, 11:00 a.m. to 5:00 p.m. (Call ahead in August.)

This gallery features contemporary art in all media, from both established and emerging artists.

Alpha Gallery

38 Newbury Street
(617) 536–4465
www.alphagallery.com
Hours: Tuesday through Friday, 10:00 a.m. to 5:30 p.m.; Saturday, 11:00 a.m. to 5:30 p.m.

This spacious gallery exhibits multiple artists and focuses primarily on painting, although other media are represented. It holds frequent New Artist exhibitions but generally features mid-career and established artists. Don't miss their periodic special shows of master artists such as Pablo Picasso, Fairfield Porter, Max Beckmann, and Milton Avery.

Arden Gallery

129 Newbury Street
(617) 247–0610
www.ardengallery.com
Hours: Monday through Saturday, 11:00 a.m. to 5:30 p.m.

Arden represents contemporary living artists. Works vary from realistic portraits to abstracts to landscapes to still life.

Artana

355 Boylston Street
(857) 362–7474
www.artanagallery.com
Hours: Tuesday through Saturday, 10:00 a.m. to 6:00 p.m., Sunday noon to 4:00 p.m.

Newly relocated from Coolidge Corner in Cambridge to the theater district right downtown, Artana is on a mission to demystify and educate people about art. The gallery focuses on displaying collectible work created by accomplished New England artists.

Axelle Fine Arts Galerie Boston

91 Newbury Street
(617) 450–0700
www.axelle.com
Hours: Daily 10:00 a.m.

One of four Axelle galleries nationwide, this gallery represents talented contemporary European artists.

Axiom Gallery

141 Green Street (at MBTA station)
Jamaica Plain
(617) 676–5904
www.axiomart.org
Hours: During exhibitions only, open Wednesday and Thursday 6:00 to 9:00 p.m. and Saturday 2:00 to 5:00 p.m.

A collective, Axiom merged with and replaced the former Green Street gallery in Jamaica Plain, which had renovated and replaced an abandoned storefront in the Green Street MBTA station. Check the Web site for current exhibitions.

BAAK Gallery

35 Brattle Street
Cambridge
(617) 354–0407
www.baakgallery.com
Hours: Monday through Saturday, 10:30 a.m. to 8:00 p.m.; Sunday, 1:00 to 6:00 p.m.

Fine art mixed with fine jewelry (featuring conflict-free diamonds) has earned this gallery in Cambridge accolades from collectors, and awards from local magazines and newspapers.

Barbara Krakow Gallery

10 Newbury Street
(617) 262–4490
www.barbarakrakowgallery.com
Hours: Tuesday through Saturday, 10:00 a.m. to 5:30 p.m. except closed Saturday in July and August.

This gallery is known for its minimalist art collection as well as its conceptual installations, all done by regional and international artists.

Berenberg Gallery

4 Clarendon Street
(617) 536–0800
www.berenberggallery.com
Hours: Wednesday through Saturday, 11:00 a.m. to 6:00 p.m.

This small gallery, which shares space with a framing shop, presents the work of unconventional, sometimes marginalized artists who are institutionalized or have physical and/or emotional disabilities. The work is sometimes disturbing, always compelling, and spans all media except video.

Bernard Toale Gallery

450 Harrison Avenue
(617) 482–2477
www.bernardtoalegallery.com
Hours: Tuesday through Saturday, 10:30 a.m. to 5:30 p.m. except closed Saturday in July and open by appointment only in August.

This gallery features cutting-edge contemporary art in all media by internationally known as well as emerging artists.

Boston Center for the Arts

539 Tremont Street
(617) 426–8835
www.bcaonline.org
Hours: Wednesday and Sunday, noon to 5:00 p.m.; Thursday to Saturday, noon to 9:00 p.m.

The BCA presents about five large-scale exhibitions annually in its 2,200-square-foot Mills Gallery, including contemporary works by established and emerging local, regional, national, and international visual artists. During each show the center also schedules opportunities to get to know the artists, including opening receptions, talks, and other events.

Boston Sculptors Gallery

486 Harrison Avenue
(617) 482–7781
www.bostonsculptors.com
Hours: Tuesday through Saturday, 11:00 a.m. to 6:00 p.m.

The Boston Sculptors Gallery is a cooperative of three dozen participating sculptors, two of whom take over the space each month on a rotating basis.

The BSG has gained wide acclaim from art critics for its innovative approach and the quality of the work presented here since 1992.

Brickbottom Gallery
1 Fitchburg Street, C-111
Somerville
(617) 776–3410
www.brickbottomartists.com
Hours: Thursday through Saturday, noon to 5:00 p.m.

Brickbottom Gallery mounts professionally curated exhibitions of contemporary art. Its annual Open Studios, started in 1989, are among the oldest such offerings in Boston.

Bromfield Gallery
450 Harrison Avenue
(617) 451–3605
www.bromfieldgallery.com
Hours: Wednesday through Saturday, noon to 5:00 p.m.

This is the oldest artist-run cooperative gallery in Boston. Each member presents a solo show every two years. The shows often include pairings of visual arts with music, performance, and poetry.

Chase Gallery
129 Newbury Street
(617) 859–7222
www.chasegallery.com
Hours: Tuesday through Friday, 10:00 a.m. to 5:30 p.m.

Chase represents primarily local contemporary artists through rotating solo exhibits. It also handles resales.

Childs Gallery
169 Newbury Street
(617) 266–1108
www.childsgallery.com
Hours: Tuesday through Friday, 9:00 a.m. to 6:00 p.m.; Monday and Saturday, 10:00 a.m. to 5:00 p.m.

Childs Gallery wants you to buy art, and they'll stop at nothing, including trolling around someone's attic, to find it. Their collection is mostly older works, everything from Renaissance through the 1950s. You'll find both the classical and the obscure here.

DTR Modern Galleries
167 Newbury Street
(617) 424–9700
Hours: Monday through Thursday, 11:00 a.m. to 7:00 p.m.; Friday and Saturday, 11:00 a.m. to 8:00 p.m.; Sunday, 11:00 a.m. to 6:00 p.m.

Showcasing the works of twentieth-century masters, this is one of the best places in town to see the big names in their original format. Recent shows have included "the three Spaniards"—Miró, Picasso, and Dalí. They also show pop and surrealist art.

Fort Point Arts Community Gallery
300 Summer Street M1
(617) 423–4299
www.fortpointarts.org
Hours: Monday to Wednesday, 9:00 a.m. to 3:30 p.m., Thursday to Friday 9:00 a.m. to 10:00 p.m., Saturday 5:00 to 10:00 p.m.,

This gallery, located in the Artist Building in the Fort Point neighborhood, is a focal point of the artists' community in South Boston. The large exhibition space showcases Fort Point artists in all media, including large installations.

Galerie d'Orsay
33 Newbury Street
(617) 266–8001
www.galerie-dorsay.com
Hours: Monday through Saturday, 10:00 a.m. to 6:00 p.m.; Sunday, noon to 6:00 p.m.

Want to see some Rembrandt, Renoir, Toulouse-Lautrec, Pissarro, Picasso, Matisse, Chagall, or Miró? Drop by Galerie d'Orsay, which has more masters per square foot than nearly any other gallery in the city. They also feature works by contemporary painters, sculptors, and printmakers.

Gallery Kayafas

450 Harrison Avenue #61
(617) 482–0411
www.gallerykayafas.com
Hours: Tuesday through Saturday, 11:00 a.m. to 5:30 p.m.; August by
appointment only.

Kayafas specializes in fine art photography.

Gallery NAGA

67 Newbury Street
(617) 267–9060
www.gallerynaga.com
Hours: September to June, Tuesday through Saturday, 10:00 a.m. to 5:30
p.m. Call for summer hours.

Gallery NAGA is one of the most eclectic and diverse of the big-name galleries in town. Exhibits include painting, photography, prints, sculpture,
holography, and studio furniture.

Gallery @ The Piano Factory

791 Tremont Street
(617) 437–9365
http://galleryatthepianofactory.org
Hours: Saturday and Sunday, noon to 5:00 p.m. or by appointment. Call
ahead.

This gallery features the work of local artists in all media. Exhibitions rotate
monthly.

Hamill Gallery of African Art

2164 Washington Street
(617) 442–8204
www.hamillgallery.com
Hours: Thursday through Sunday, noon to 6:00 p.m.

Boston's only gallery of traditional African tribal art is a big, 7,000-square-
foot exhibition space, with work from seventy-five major tribal groups in
western and central Africa. It's an amazing place, unlike any other exhibit
space in the city. Works here include masks, figures, artifacts, textiles, jewelry, books, and posters.

Howard Yezerski Gallery

450 Harrison Avenue, #201
(617) 262–0550
www.howardyezerskigallery.com
Hours: Tuesday through Saturday, 10:00 a.m. to 5:30 p.m.; closed between Christmas and New Year's Day. Note: Call or e-mail for updated hours.

Relocating at press time to Harrison Street, this gallery features contemporary art, mixed media, prints, and oil paintings.

International Poster Gallery

205 Newbury Street
(617) 375–0076
www.internationalposter.com
Hours: Monday through Saturday, 10:00 a.m. to 6:00 p.m.; Sunday, noon to 6:00 p.m.

Now this is cool! (And not stuck-up—so to speak.) More than 10,000 vintage and modern posters reside at this gallery, including what might be one of the world's leading collections of Italian posters.

Judi Rotenberg Gallery

130 Newbury Street
(617) 437–1518
www.judirotenberg.com
Hours: Tuesday through Saturday, 10:00 a.m. to 6:00 p.m., Sunday 1:00 to 5:00 p.m.

One of the city's premier galleries, Rotenberg Gallery features early and mid-career contemporary artists working in all media, including video and installation projects.

Judy Ann Goldman Fine Art/Beth Urdang Gallery

14 Newbury Street
(617) 424–8468
www.judygoldmanfineart.com
Hours: Tuesday through Saturday, by appointment. Always call ahead.

This gallery focuses on contemporary artists and features acrylic and oil painters, installation artists, and photographers.

Kidder Smith Gallery

131 Newbury Street
(617) 424-6900
www.kiddersmithgallery.com
Hours: Tuesday through Saturday, 11:00 a.m. to 5:30 p.m.

The gallery holds solo exhibitions of painting and photography from mid-career contemporary, abstract, and representational artists.

Kingston Gallery

450 Harrison Avenue #43
(617) 423-4113
www.kingstongallery.com
Hours: Tuesday through Saturday, noon to 5:00 p.m.

Founded in 1982, Kingston Gallery is an artist-run exhibit space that shows emerging artists. Media include wool, paper, steel wool art, and photography.

Lanoue Fine Art

125 Newbury Street (mezzanine level)
(617) 262-4400
www.lanouefineart.com
Hours: Monday through Saturday, 10:00 a.m. to 6:00 p.m.; Sunday, noon to 5:00 p.m.

Mid-career and established contemporary artists in various media are the focus of Lanoue Fine Art, now in a new location on the same street. Works here include representational and abstract work by nationally and internationally renowned painters, sculptors, and printmakers.

L'Attitude Gallery

218 Newbury Street
(617) 927-4400
www.lattitudegallery.com
Hours: Monday through Saturday, 10:00 a.m. to 6:00 p.m.; Sunday, noon to 5:00 p.m.

Usable art, sculpture, and crafts—including glass, ceramics, wood, stone, mixed media, and textiles—are the focus at L'Attitude. The gallery presents more than seventy-five U.S. and international artists.

Mercury Gallery

8 Newbury Street (2nd floor)
(617) 859-0054
www.mercurygallery.com
Hours: Monday through Friday, 9:30 a.m. to 5:00 p.m., Saturday 9:30 a.m. to 5:30 p.m.

Expressionism rules at this comfortable gallery space, which resembles a plush living room and features artists in media such as pottery, photography, multimedia, and oil painting.

Mobilia Gallery

358 Huron Avenue
Cambridge
(617) 876-2109
www.mobilia-gallery.com
Hours: Tuesday through Friday, 11:00 a.m. to 6:00 p.m.; Saturday, 10:00 a.m. to 5:00 p.m.

For almost thirty years, this gallery has featured exciting wearable art and furniture, as well as jewelry, glass, ceramics, textile, and beadwork. Curated exhibits include paintings and mixed-media pieces.

Newbury Fine Arts

29 Newbury Street
(617) 536-0210
www.newburyfinearts.com
Hours: Monday through Saturday, 10:00 a.m. to 6:00 p.m., Sunday, noon to 5:00 p.m.

This gallery focuses on educating consumers and keeps a multi-artist, multi-genre exhibition on display at all times to expose visitors to a variety of styles and media.

Nielsen Gallery

179 Newbury Street
(617) 266-4835
www.nielsengallery.com
Hours: Tuesday through Saturday, 10:00 a.m. to 5:30 p.m.

Nielsen Gallery features contemporary painting and sculpture by nationally recognized artists.

OHT Gallery

450 Harrison Avenue #57
(617) 423–1677
www.ohtgallery.com
Hours: Tuesday through Saturday, 11:00 a.m. to 5:00 p.m.

OHT features emerging and mid-career contemporary painters from New York and Boston, with some national artists thrown into the mix.

OSP Gallery

450 Harrison Avenue #47
(617) 778–5265, extension 22
www.ospgallery.com
Hours: Monday through Saturday, 11:00 a.m. to 5:00 p.m.

On display at this gallery are emerging contemporary local and national artists working primarily on paper media.

Out of the Blue Art Gallery

106 Prospect Street
Cambridge
(617) 354–5287
www.outoftheblueartgallery.com
Hours: Daily noon to 8:00 p.m.

This non-curated gallery has been a welcome player on the local scene since 1996. It accepts contributions from all local artists, who pay a hanging fee to display their work here. Art ranges from photography to crafts. You're an artist? You're in luck: Volunteer your time here, and the fees are all waived for one show.

Pucker Gallery

171 Newbury Street
(617) 267–9473
www.puckergallery.com
Hours: Monday through Saturday, 10:00 a.m. to 5:30 p.m.; Sunday, 10:30 a.m. to 5:00 p.m.

The Puckers, Bernie and Sue, have been showcasing local and national artists in a variety of media—from watercolor and acrylic to photography and ceramic—since way back in 1967. Their vibrant approach to art still makes this gallery a key nexus point for the local arts scene today.

Robert Klein Gallery

38 Newbury Street (4th floor)
(617) 267–7997
www.robertkleingallery.com
Hours: Tuesday through Friday, 10:00 a.m. to 5:30 p.m.; Saturday, 11:00 a.m. to 5:00 p.m.

If you love photography, don't miss this gallery. Most work is by renowned nineteenth- and twentieth-century photographers. Alfred Steiglitz, Herb Ritts, Annie Leibowitz, or ManRay ring a bell? It doesn't get much better than that. Klein also exhibits an impressive array of contemporary photographers, too.

Victoria Munroe Fine Art

179 Newbury Street
(617) 523–0661
www.victoriamunroefineart.com
Hours: Tuesday through Saturday, 10:00 a.m. to 5:30 p.m.

This gallery offers a fascinating selection of nineteenth- and twentieth-century paintings, as well as a diverse collection of drawings, including eighteenth-, nineteenth-, and twentieth-century European and American architectural, engineering, decorative arts, garden design, and natural science drawings.

Vose Galleries of Boston

238 Newbury Street
(617) 536–6176
www.vosegalleries.com
Hours: Monday through Friday, 9:30 a.m. to 5:30 p.m.; Saturday, 10:00 a.m. to 5:30 p.m. (except closed Saturday in August).

Established in 1841 as an artist's supply store in Rhode Island, the Vose Galleries are the grande dame of Boston art galleries. This is the oldest family-owned art gallery in the United States, primarily exhibiting the work of American artists from the eighteenth, nineteenth, and early twentieth centuries. Several years ago the Vose also began showing contemporary (living) artists.

ART ASSOCIATIONS, UNIVERSITY GALLERIES, AND OTHER COLLECTIONS

Adams Gallery
David J. Sargent Hall
Suffolk University Law School
120 Tremont Street
www.suffolk.edu/offices/1104.html
Hours: Daily, 9:00 a.m. to 7:00 p.m.

This fun gallery at Suffolk University exhibits collections that revolve around historical themes relevant to life in Boston: the Red Sox, the Big Dig, the photography of the Boston Herald, the Boston Symphony Orchestra's 125th anniversary, and so forth. The university also presents lectures and discussions here related to the topics of the exhibits.

Cambridge Art Association Galleries
www.cambridgeart.org
Kathryn Schultz Gallery; 25 Lowell Street; Cambridge; (617) 876–0246
Hours: Tuesday through Saturday, 11:00 a.m. to 5:00 p.m.

University Place Gallery; 141 Mount Auburn Street; Cambridge;
Hours: Monday through Friday, 9:00 a.m. to 6:00 p.m. and Saturday, 9:00 a.m. to 1:00 p.m.

Today, the Cambridge Art Association consists of approximately 500 juried artist members—made up of photographers, printmakers, painters, sculptors, textile artists, and glassmakers—and a supporting group of Friend Members in its two galleries. The organization remains much the same as it was in the 1940s, with this mission: to enrich Cambridge by exhibiting art, supporting local artists, and creating opportunities for art education and art appreciation.

Cambridge Multicultural Arts Center

41 Second Street
Cambridge
(617) 577–1400
www.cmacusa.org
Hours: Monday through Friday, 10:00 a.m. to 6:00 p.m., and during special gallery events.

This local arts organization runs frequent exhibitions by local and national artists in various media. The CMAC also offers a variety of visual and performing arts–related programs for Cambridge residents and visitors.

Copley Society of Art

158 Newbury Street
(617) 536–5049
www.copleysociety.org
Hours: Tuesday through Saturday, 11:00 a.m. to 6:00 p.m.; Sunday and Monday, noon to 5:00 p.m.

The CoSo is the oldest nonprofit art association in the United States. It has 700 artist members nationwide (who must pass peer review to be admitted). CoSo mounts its members' exhibitions, runs educational outreach programs, holds workshops, and hosts lectures throughout the year to build an audience for its young and emerging artists.

New Art Center in Newton

61 Washington Park
Newtonville
(617) 964–3424
www.newartcenter.org
Hours: Monday through Friday, 9:00 a.m. to 5:00 p.m.; Sunday, 1:00 to 5:00 p.m.

Located in a renovated church in the village of Newtonville, this arts education organization offers beginning through advanced classes to children and adults. It also hosts frequent exhibitions of student artwork and has several juried shows throughout the year, including works of video, painting, installation, and sculpture.

School of the Museum of Fine Arts

230 The Fenway
www.smfa.edu/news_exhibitions/exhibitions/gallery_information.asp

You can see the art stars of tomorrow today in the many exhibitions mounted at MFA's art school annually. Some of these are solo shows by internationally renowned artists, some are group exhibits, and many are juried. There are alumni, current student, and faculty galleries. The art is contemporary, and all media are explored. The school is also affiliated with several other galleries. Here's a list.

Courtyard Gallery and Foster Gallery Museum of Fine Arts
465 Huntington Avenue; (617) 369–3718
Hours: Monday and Tuesday, 10:00 a.m. to 4:45 p.m., Wednesday to Friday, 10:00 a.m. to 9:45 p.m.; Saturday and Sunday, 10:00 a.m. to 5:45 p.m.

Grossman Gallery
School of the Museum of Fine Arts; 230 The Fenway; (617) 369–3718
Hours: Monday to Saturday, 10:00 a.m. to 5:00 p.m.; Thursday also to 8:00 p.m.

Mission Hill Building Gallery
160 Saint Alphonsus Street; (617) 427–7460
Hours: Monday through Friday, 10:00 a.m. to 4:30 p.m.

Society of Arts and Crafts

175 Newbury Street (second floor)
(617) 266–1810
www.societyofcrafts.org
Hours: Monday through Saturday, 10:00 a.m. to 6:00 p.m.; Sunday, noon to 5:00 p.m.

Incorporated in 1897, the Society of Arts and Crafts has been working to elevate the profile of craftsmen and -women for over a century, and its founders helped to fuel the Arts and Craft Movement. This gallery is a two-story space: The first floor is a retail gallery, and there's a more formal exhibition space up on the second floor. This organization goes out of its way to find new forms, and even exhibits types of work that might not be considered commercially viable by other galleries in town. There's some great sculpture and ceramic work here.

Tufts University Art Gallery

Aidekman Arts Center
40 Talbot Avenue
Medford
(617) 627–3518
Hours: Tuesday to Sunday, 10:00 a.m. to 5:00 p.m.; Thursday also to 8:00 p.m.

This gallery is affiliated with the School of the Museum of Fine Arts (see above).

Zeitgeist Gallery

186 Hampshire Street
Cambridge
(617) 876–6060
www.zeitgeist-gallery.org
Hours: Friday to Sunday, 1:00 to 7:00 p.m.

The Catch Most exhibits free, but some performances request a donation.

This cutting-edge art/performance/video gallery is an eclectic treasure that refuses to define itself. Zeitgeist has won accolades for its unique approach to the concept of art—one day it might feature a jazz guitarist, the next a sale of clothing designed for a coming era of global warming. Exhibits rotate frequently, and are intermixed with performances. Note that hours are limited: it's only open weekends. But it's well worth a visit.

OPEN **STUDIOS**

Open studios have become a rite of fall in Boston. That's when thousands of local artists throw open their studio doors and let the drawing-challenged masses into their inner sanctums. Open studios are an opportunity to see everything from accomplished masters to fledgling artists in their elements—and they're also a wonderful social scene (and a great way to meet your neighbors). Here is a list of artist organizations that hold open-studio events. Remember that they're usually held over a period of several days, usually a weekend, usually once or twice a year—though some organizations, like the SoWa Group, open members' studios as frequently as once per month.

Allston/Brighton Open Studios
Allston Arts District
(617) 254–3333
www.allstonarts.org

It's fitting that the only city in America named for an artist (Allston is named for the painter Washington Allston, who died in 1843 and is buried in Boston) holds an annual open-studio event for two days each winter. Started in 1987, it is one of the longest-running open-studio programs in the city, and the studios of the nearly forty artists who participate annually are within easy walking distance. In 2008, the event took place over two days in early November.

Charlestown Third Thursdays
Artist Group of Charlestown
523 Medford Street (near Sullivan Square)
Charlestown
(617) 241–0130
www.artistsgroupofcharlestown.com

Open studios are held at the Stove Factory on the third Thursday of April, May, June, September, October, and November.

Dorchester Open Studios
Dorchester Arts Collaborative
Dorchester
www.dorchesterartists.org

For two days in late October each year, you can tour local Dorchester artists' studios and visit group shows at locations like the Great Hall in Codman Square.

Fort Point Open Studios
Fort Point Arts Community
300 Summer Street M1
(617) 423–4299
www.fortpointarts.org

The artists of Fort Point have taught the city of Boston something about the transformative power of a strong art and culture community. Previously an industrial backwater, Fort Point has seen a cultural and architectural resurgence, thanks largely to the artists' presence; when developers started moving in, buying the buildings where artists had kept their studios, these artists banded together and staked a claim. There are now several designated artist live-work buildings in this neighborhood, which makes the Fort Point Open Studios one of the biggest and best. The event takes place over three days each October; there's also an annual art sale (December) and a three-day Art Walk event in May. Great community resource.

Jamaica Plain Open Studios
Jamaica Plain
(617) 524–3816
www.jpopenstudios.com

This two-day weekend event in late September has been going on for about fifteen years now. It's coordinated by the Jamaica Plain Arts Council and includes several juried shows, group shows at centrally located landmarks (such as the Unitarian Universalist Church), and artists' studios. Comprehensive studio location maps, a participant list, and information become available on the organization's Web site in early September.

Roslindale Open Studios
Roslindale
(617) 710–3811
www.roslindaleopenstudios.org

The newest addition to the open-studio scene got off to a great start in 2005, with almost thirty artists showing their work, and it's still going strong. The event spans two days in early November; there's a kickoff reception at the Longfellow House at 885 South Street.

South End Open Studios
United South End Artists, Inc.
South End
(617) 267–8862
www.useaboston.com/open_studios.htm

This two-day, weekend event in mid-September features tours through the wonderful artist studio complexes that line Washington and Harrison Streets.

SoWa Artists Guild First Fridays
450 Harrison Avenue
www.sowaartistsguild.com

On the first Friday of every month, from 5:00 to 8:30 p.m., there's a party going on at 450 Harrison Avenue, as visitors browse the fifteen galleries and fifty artists' studios packed into this artists' colony building. Free drinks and snacks are often provided for the masses. These evening events are very popular, and growing more so by the month.

CUT-RATE CULTURE:
MUSEUMS ON THE CHEAP

*"Clear out 800,000 people and preserve it
as a museum piece."*

—FRANK LLOYD WRIGHT,
ABOUT THE CITY OF BOSTON

A city with as much history as Boston is a bit of a museum in and of itself, as Mr. Frank Lloyd W. correctly noted. And our Boston forebears (Cheap Bastards that they were) never threw out anything, so our museums are today packed with their bequests: historic artifacts, masterpiece paintings, obscure curios. The city's history of invention, culture, creativity, and exploration is well documented in local museums, many of which are free to the public all the time—or at least have limited free hours.

ALWAYS-FREE MUSEUMS

Boston Fire Museum
344 Congress Street
(617) 482–1344
www.bostonfiremuseum.org
Hours: May through November, Saturday, 11:00 a.m. to 4:00 p.m. or by appointment.

This museum, in the suddenly hip Fort Point district, memorializes one of the oldest fire departments in the country. It's located in a restored firehouse that's been used since 1891. Exhibits include a hand-operated fire pump that dates to 1793, but remember: this museum is only open one day each week. Donations are accepted.

Commonwealth Museum
220 Morrissey Boulevard (across from the JFK Museum)
(617) 727–9268
www.sec.state.ma.us/mus/museum/index.htm
Hours: Monday through Friday, 9:00 a.m. to 5:00 p.m.; second and fourth Saturday of the month, 9:00 a.m. to 3:00 p.m.

This museum focuses on the history of the Commonwealth of Massachusetts, from the Puritans to the archaeology of the Central Artery Tunnel Project. It was closed at press time for an expansion; check the Web site and call before visiting.

Compton Gallery (of the MIT Museum)
Building 10, Room 150
77 Massachusetts Avenue
Cambridge
(617) 452–2111
http://web.mit.edu/museum/exhibitions/compton.html
Hours: Daily, 10:00 a.m. to 5:00 p.m.

This is a rotating exhibition space that highlights the work being done by students and professors working at and with MIT's various academic projects. Included is everything from photography, video art, and sketches to the technology itself.

Cyrus Dallin Art Museum
Jefferson Cutter House
1 Whittemore Park (corner of Massachusetts Avenue, Mystic Street, and Pleasant Street)
Arlington
(781) 641–0747
www.dallin.org
Hours: Tuesday to Sunday, noon to 4:00 p.m.

This museum is dedicated to the work of Cyrus Dallin, who created the famous statue of Paul Revere in the North End and the beautiful and moving Appeal to the Great Spirit—the statue of a Native American on a horse standing in front of the Museum of Fine Arts. It also chronicles many other works by Dallin, as well as his lifelong efforts to produce the Revere statue.

Davis Museum and Cultural Center
Wellesley College
106 Central Street
Wellesley
(781) 283–2051
www.davismuseum.wellesley.edu
Hours: Variable; call or check the Web site.

The Davis Museum and Cultural Center was founded in 1889 by the first president of Wellesley College. The museum offers rotating exhibitions of fine art and an active lecture, workshop, and educational program befitting an institution of higher learning.

Hart Nautical Gallery (of the MIT Museum)
Building 5
55 Massachusetts Avenue
Cambridge
(617) 253–5942
http://web.mit.edu/museum/exhibitions/hart.html
Hours: Daily, 10:00 a.m. to 5:00 p.m.

If you think ship models are cool, this is the place for you. The museum, started in 1922, showcases the work of MIT's Pratt School of Naval Architecture and Marine Engineering, which includes dozens of antique and current model ships.

Longyear Museum
1125 Boylston Street
Chestnut Hill
(617) 278–9000
www.longyear.org
Hours: Monday and Wednesday through Saturday, 10:00 a.m. to 4:00 p.m.; Sunday, 1:00 to 4:00 p.m.

The Longyear Museum is filled with exhibits and resources about the life and achievements of Mary Baker Eddy, founder of the Church of Christ, Scientist, and her early students.

McMullen Museum of Art
Devlin Hall (Room 108)
140 Commonwealth Avenue
Chestnut Hill
(617) 552–8587
www.bc.edu/bc_org/avp/cas/artmuseum/index.html
Hours: Monday to Friday 11:00 a.m. to 4:00 p.m.; Saturday and Sunday, noon to 5:00 p.m.

This Boston College museum features American, Italian, and Flemish paintings by the old masters, as well as three or four exhibits annually that highlight particular artists or themes, often revolving around explorations of religion or religious art.

MIT List Visual Arts Center

20 Ames Street (Building E15)
Cambridge
(617) 253–4680
http://listart.mit.edu
Hours: Variable but always closed Mondays and through the summer. Call ahead.

The List Visual Arts Center isn't just an art museum with a gallery. It's a collection of dozens of sculptures (by such renowned sculptors as Alexander Calder and Pablo Picasso), paintings, and installations throughout the MIT campus, including students' rooms, classrooms, and professors' and administrators' offices. The museum mounts five to eight exhibits a year in its museum gallery, but the real museum can be found by walking around and looking at all the public art the institute has amassed since it received its first donation of art from Standard Oil in 1950. That was followed in 1985 by a generous gift from Vera and Albert List that allowed the program to relocate to the first floor of a 1940 I. M. Pei-designed building, where its galleries are today.

Museum of Afro-American History

46 Joy Street
(617) 725–0022
www.afroammuseum.org
Hours: Monday through Saturday, 10:00 a.m. to 4:00 p.m.

The Catch Suggested donation is $5.00.

The Museum of Afro-American History is New England's largest museum dedicated to preserving, conserving, and interpreting the contributions of African Americans. The African Meeting House was the first African meetinghouse built in America, and the adjacent Abiel Smith School was the first building in the nation constructed for the sole purpose of housing a black public school. Today, the Abiel Smith School's galleries feature rotating exhibits as well as a museum store, which is open year-round.

Museum of Bad Art

Dedham Community Theater (basement level)
580 High Street
Dedham
(781) 444–6757
www.museumofbadart.org
Hours: Usually Sunday through Friday, 2:00 to 9:00 p.m.; Friday, Saturday, and holidays, 1:00 to 10:00 p.m.

It's so bad, it's good. Since 1995 the Museum of Bad Art has been astounding the art world with its ability to find absolutely the worst art available anywhere. To complete the experience, it is located in the basement of an old building, lit only by the unflattering glow of a large, humming fluorescent light fixture. Their permanent collection includes about 250 pieces, of which two dozen are exhibited at any one time. Which is more than enough.

National Heritage Museum

33 Marrett Road (intersection Route 2A and Massachusetts Avenue)
Lexington
(781) 861–6559
www.nationalheritagemuseum.org
Hours: Monday through Saturday, 10:00 a.m. to 5:00 p.m.; Sunday, noon to 5:00 p.m.

This museum has a selection of exhibits focusing on the history of our nation, with a special emphasis on New England. Past exhibits have described the history of the Freemason movement; collected household items from the past three centuries made in Massachusetts; and gone into detail on the Revolutionary War (one of the most crucial battles in the war took place in the Lexington/Concord area).

Perkins Museum

Howe Building (Maine Hall)
Perkins School for the Blind
175 North Beacon Street
Watertown
(617) 972–7767 (museum)
(617) 924–3434 (switchboard)
www.perkinsmuseum.org
Hours: Tuesday and Thursday, 2:00 to 4:00 p.m., September through July; in August call ahead for appointment.

The Perkins School for the Blind has been educating blind and deaf/blind students in the area for a long, long time; this museum, opened in 2004 to commemorate the school's 175th (yes, 175th) anniversary, charts the school's history and the history of educating vision-impaired students. It also tells the stories of those who founded the school—Samuel Gridley Howe and his wife Julia Ward Howe (she also wrote the words to "Battle Hymn of the Republic" in her free time, by the way!)—as well as some other celebrities who have been involved with the school. Interactive tactile, visual, and auditory exhibits are accessible to both blind and sighted visitors.

USS *Constitution* Museum
Building 22
Charlestown Navy Yard
Charlestown
(617) 426–1812
www.ussconstitutionmuseum.org
Hours: Mid-April through October, daily 9:00 a.m. to 6:00 p.m.; October 16 rest of the year, daily 10:00 a.m. to 5:00 p.m.

The Catch Donation requested but not required.

The USS *Constitution*, launched in 1797 and nicknamed "Old Ironsides" after the cannonballs of an attacking warship merely bounced off her triple-thick hardwood sides, is the oldest commissioned warship in the U.S. Navy. This interactive museum tracks the ship's history and the history of its military engagements and offers kid-focused learning exhibits about what life was like for sailors during the ship's heyday.

SNEAKING INTO MUSEUMS FOR FREE! LEGALLY!!

If you hold a valid Boston Public Library or Minuteman Library network card (see the Libraries chapter for lists of participating libraries), you can sometimes visit the best museums in Boston absolutely free—even when they're charging everyone else.

That's because both of these library systems make free museum passes available to anyone who asks. Needless to say, they're very hot tickets, but there *are* limits to the number of tickets issued. As a result, you must usually reserve your museum pass weeks before you intend to use it.

You can only reserve a pass four or fewer weeks in advance, and you must return the passes the same day you get them or first thing the next morning. You can reserve in person at the library or by phone. (See Appendix B for a list of branch locations.) Also, the person who *reserved* the pass must be the person who actually picks it *up*. Other rules apply, too. Ask when you call or visit. Still, it's one sweet deal!

Boston Public Library System Museum Pass
www.bpl.org/general/circulation/museum_passes.htm

The following museum passes are available from all Boston Public Library locations (except the Kirstein Business Branch). Listings state the number of people admitted and the discounted admission fee (where applicable).

- ✓ Children's Museum: up to six people, $2.00 per person fee
- ✓ Harvard Museum of Natural History: up to four people, $2.00 per person fee
- ✓ Museum of Fine Arts: up to two people, no fee
- ✓ Museum of Science: up to four people, no fee
- ✓ New England Aquarium (September through June only): up to four people, no fee
- ✓ Wheelock Family Theatre: restrictions apply; contact local branch for details

The following museum passes are available only at the library location(s) listed.

- ✓ Harvard Art Museums: Only at Brighton, Faneuil, Honan-Allston, and Jamaica Plain branches
- ✓ Isabella Stewart Gardner Museum: Only at Copley Square, Jamaica Plain, and West Roxbury branches
- ✓ John F. Kennedy Library and Museum: Only at Jamaica Plain branch
- ✓ Larz Anderson Auto Museum: Only at Jamaica Plain branch
- ✓ Zoo New England: Only at Connolly, Dudley, Egleston, Faneuil, Honan-Allston, Hyde Park, Orient Heights, Roslindale, and West Roxbury branches

Each of these branch locations offers one pass per day, per museum. All passes must be reserved by an adult with a valid library card at the branch or system—and *you must have no more than $10 in outstanding fines on your card.* Whoa, that's cold. Also, all children must be accompanied by an adult.

Cambridge Public Library System

www.eventkeeper.com/code/events.cfm?curorg=cambridge&curapp=passes

If you hold a valid Minuteman Library Network card (for a list of participating libraries, see the Libraries chapter), you can reserve free passes for certain local museums by calling Cambridge's central library (617–349–4044) or its Central Square Branch (617–349–4010). But you need to be sure passes are available. Check online first at the library's Museum Pass homepage (see above) to view daily availability of the passes, sorted by museum. How convenient is that?

You can reserve passes up to a month in advance. Here's a list of museum passes available, the number of people the pass will admit, and the discounted admission price, if applicable:

- ✓ Children's Museum: four people, $2.00 per person fee
- ✓ Franklin Park Zoos: two adults, four children, no fee
- ✓ Harvard Art Museum: free to all Cambridge Library cardholders
- ✓ Harvard Natural History Museum: free to all Cambridge Library cardholders
- ✓ Isabella Stewart Gardner Museum: four people Monday through Friday or two people Saturday or Sunday, $2.00 per person fee
- ✓ MIT Museums: four people, no fee
- ✓ Museum of Fine Art: two people, $5.00 per person fee
- ✓ Museum of Science: four people, no fee
- ✓ Peabody Essex Museum: two people, no fee
- ✓ Stone Zoo: two adults, four children, no fee
- ✓ Wheelock Family Theatre: one person (Friday and Saturday performances only), no fee

How You "May" Get into Museums Free

May is museum month in Boston. For some people. Specifically, those with Bank of America accounts or credit cards. Show a BoA card at the gate, and many museums that otherwise charge admission are free for you (and a guest!) thanks to the Museums on Us program. In 2008, participating institutions included the Museum of Fine Arts, Harvard's Museum of Natural History, and the DeCordova Museum and Sculpture Park in Lincoln. Assuming this promotion continues, you can check the Museum Month Web site (www.bankofamericapromotions.com/museums) for more info. Don't blame us if the program gets canceled, by the way—blame the economy.

SOMETIMES-FREE MUSEUMS

DeCordova Museum and Sculpture Park
51 Sandy Pond Road
Lincoln
(781) 259–8355
www.decordova.org
Hours: Main gallery Tuesday through Sunday, 11:00 a.m. to 5:00 p.m.; sculpture park daily year-round, sunrise to sunset

The Catch When it's free: The sculpture park is free whenever the gallery is closed. Also, the gallery is free to Lincoln residents and active-duty military personnel (and their dependents).

The DeCordova Museum is in the former home of Julian de Cordova, self-educated son of a Jamaican merchant who became a prominent local merchant himself. He deeded his home to the town of Lincoln and stipulated that it should be used as a museum after his death. The museum houses contemporary art and sculpture by living artists and focuses much of its efforts on educational workshops and programs. And here's the kicker: almost every Monday, the park is free and open to the public (because the gallery is closed). And if you're a Lincoln resident, or an active-duty military member? The gallery's always free, too.

Harvard Museum of Natural History

26 Oxford Street
Cambridge
(617) 495–3045
www.hmnh.harvard.edu
Hours: Daily 9:00 a.m. to 5:00 p.m.

The Catch Free entry does not apply to commercial tour groups.

The Catch When it's free: For Harvard members with ID, always; for Massachusetts residents, every Sunday 9:00 a.m. to noon (year-round) and Wednesday from September through May (the school year), 3:00 to 5:00 p.m.

The Harvard Museum of Natural History (HMNH), the public museum of Harvard University's three natural history academic institutions, explores the theory of evolution through its exhibits and specimens. It operates in tandem with the Peabody Museum of Archaeology and Ethnology (see below), so one admission ticket gets you into both! But if you're a Harvard student or staffer, you always walk in free. And if you're an official resident of Massachusetts—you probably are, if you're holding this book—you get in free Sunday morning (year-round) and Wednesday afternoon (during the school year from September through May).

Institute of Contemporary Art

100 Northern Avenue
(617) 478–3100
www.icaboston.org
Hours: Tuesday, Wednesday, Saturday, and Sunday, 10:00 a.m. to 5:00 p.m.; Thursday and Friday, 10:00 a.m. to 9:00 p.m.

The Catch When it's free: Thursday 5:00 to 9:00 p.m.; also free to families last Saturday of each month.

The ICA was the first art museum to be built in Boston in nearly a hundred years. The 65,000-square-foot building, featuring a cantilever that extends the building out over the waters of Boston Harbor, is already a Boston landmark. The museum explores contemporary art in all media, including performance and video. The new museum's focus is on making contemporary art inclusive through education, workshops, and interactive activities. And thanks to Target (the department store), Thursday nights are always free! True that. There's an additional promotion offered by the museum itself, as well: on the last Saturday of every month, families enter for free. Double true. Kids under seventeen always enter free, by the way.

Isabella Stewart Gardner Museum

280 The Fenway
(617) 566–1401
www.gardnermuseum.org
Hours: Tuesday through Sunday, 11:00 a.m. to 5:00 p.m.

The Catch When it's free: Always—if your name is Isabella.

The Catch When it's cheap: With a current student ID (58 percent discount).

Since 1903 the grande dame of Boston arts, Isabella Stewart Gardner, has been shocking, delighting, and astounding visitors with her unique and vast collection of art from around the world. Though Gardner no longer lives here (she died in 1924), the museum remains just as it was when she was alive—except for thirteen pieces of artwork and artifacts that were purloined in a sensational unsolved heist in 1990. Yet the paintings' empty frames still hang where they were! (That's because Gardner decreed that nothing in the museum can ever change position.) The courtyard garden here is one of the most beautiful, serene little green spaces in the entire city.

How it is free? Well, we must admit, this one is pretty tough to score: your name has to be Isabella! But if it is, you get in free for life. Kids under eighteen always get in free, too, if they come with a parent or guardian. There's a great hidden cheap deal here, as well. If you flash a currently valid student ID, you get a $7.00 discount off the usual $12.00 admission price. That means admission is just five bucks!

The MIT Museum

265 Massachusetts Avenue
Cambridge
(617) 253–4444
http://web.mit.edu/museum
Hours: Daily, 10:00 a.m. to 5:00 p.m.

The Catch When it's free: Sundays 10:00 a.m. to noon.

Home to renowned collections in science and technology, holography, architecture, and design, the MIT Museum makes science personal, accessible, and intriguing with constantly rotating exhibits. Go for the futuristic robot exhibit; stay for the cool photography of Harold Edgerton (whose famous high-speed photos of bullets going through various things never cease to mesmerize). Surprisingly, you can get in here—legally!—for free on Sunday morning between 10:00 a.m. and noon. Rise, shine, and go check it out; it's a fun place.

Museum of Fine Arts
465 Huntington Avenue
(617) 267–9300
www.mfa.org
Hours: Wednesday through Friday, 10:00 a.m. to 9:45 p.m.; Saturday through Tuesday, 10:00 a.m. to 4:45 p.m.

The Catch When it's free: Wednesdays, 4:00 to 9:45 p.m.

This is the granddaddy of Boston museums, with a mammoth collection of nearly every form of art, from nearly every century and country in which art was ever, er, created. Give yourself at least four hours to begin to scratch the surface of its vast holdings. It costs a pretty penny to get in here ($17 per adult at last check), but on Wednesday nights from 4:00 p.m. to closing (around 9:45 p.m.) it's free! Thank you, Citizens Bank Foundation!

The MFA's also free for children (age seven to seventeen) on weekdays after school (okay, technically, it's after 3:00 p.m.); every weekend; and on any public school holiday. Normally kids have to pay to get in, so this is another great reason to visit.

Peabody Museum of Archaeology and Ethnology
11 Divinity Avenue
Cambridge
(617) 496–1027
www.peabody.harvard.edu
Hours: Daily 9:00 a.m. to 5:00 p.m.

The Catch When it's free: For Harvard members with ID, always; for Massachusetts residents, every Sunday 9:00 a.m. to noon (year-round) and Wednesday from September through May (the school year), 3:00 to 5:00 p.m.

Founded in 1866, the Peabody Museum is one of the oldest museums in the world devoted to anthropology; it houses one of the most comprehensive records of human cultural history in the Western Hemisphere. Operated in tandem with the Harvard Museum of Natural History (see above), it also has the same free-entry policy. Harvard members with ID always enter for free. But so do Massachusetts residents (you're probably one) on Sunday morning from 9:00 a.m. to noon (year-round) and Wednesday afternoon (September through May only) from 3:00 to 5:00 p.m.

EXTREMELY **CHEAP** MUSEUMS

While many of our local museums charge $8.00 to $20.00 a head to get in, some museums offer welcome price breaks, especially for families. Some are cheap all the time, and others offer steeply discounted admission hours if you can come at the right time.

Adams National Historic Park
1250 Hancock Street (visitor center)
Quincy
(617) 770–1175
www.nps.gov/adam/index.htm
Hours: mid-April through mid-November, daily 9:00 a.m. to 5:00 p.m. (last tour at 3:15 p.m.)

Okay, this isn't exactly a museum, but it's even better than one: A collection of historic homes that together make up a historic park. You must join a guided tour in order to view these homes, where four generations of the Adams family lived in Quincy. You'll see the birthplaces of U.S. Presidents John Adams and John Quincy Adams; the English-style "Old House," where several generations of the Adams family also lived; and the Stone Library, which contains more than 14,000 historic volumes. Tours leave from the visitor center (note that the last tour leaves at 3:15 each day). There is a $5.00 per person charge to tour the homes—but it gets you into all of them, and for a seven-day period! How cool is that?

Blue Hills Trailside Museum
1904 Canton Avenue
Milton
(617) 333–0690
www.massaudubon.org/nature_connection/sanctuaries/blue_hills/index.php
Hours (museum): Wednesday through Sunday, 10:00 a.m. to 5:00 p.m.
Hours (museum grounds): Daily, sunrise to sunset
Admission: Museum, adults $3.00; seniors $2.00; children age three to twelve $1.50. Trails and grounds always free.

The Catch No pets are allowed on the museum grounds.

The Blue Hills Trailside Museum is the interpretive center for the state's 7,000-acre Blue Hills Reservation. It's managed by the Massachusetts Audubon Society. Indoor exhibits include displays featuring native wildlife such as wild turkeys, red-tailed hawks, and a snowy owl. Weekend programs on Saturday and Sunday, which are free with museum admission, include naturalist presentations about local wildlife, guided hikes, and other educational lectures. It's surprisingly inexpensive, too—just $3.00 max, and less if you're a senior or child.

Boston Children's Museum

300 Congress Street
(617) 426–8855
www.bostonkids.org
Hours: Daily 10:00 a.m. to 5:00 p.m., except Friday to 9:00 p.m.

The Catch Discount hours: Fridays, 4:00 to 9:00 p.m. ($1 per person)

For more than ninety years, this museum has featured interactive, educational exhibits that keep kids occupied and enthralled. Everything here is hands-on, and thanks to generosity of Target, Friday nights feature $1.00 admission (a 90 percent discount off the usual $10.00 fee!). Simply arrive after 4:00 p.m., plunk down your buck, and you're in.

Charles River Museum of Industry

154 Moody Street
Waltham
(781) 893–5410
www.crmi.org
Hours: Thursday to Saturday, 10:00 a.m. to 5:00 p.m.

The Catch Admission: adults $5.00; seniors and students $3.00; children under six, free.

Located in the Boston Manufacturing Company textile mill (built in 1814), this museum resides inside what's considered to be America's very first factory. The museum explores the evolution of industrial science through interactive exhibits and holdings of antique inventions such as steam engines, generators, timepieces, machine tools, bicycles, automobiles, and the like. There are also extensive biographies of famous inventors. The museum is a bargain at $3.00 to $5.00 per person.

Museum of the National Center for Afro-American Artists

300 Walnut Avenue
(617) 442–8614
www.ncaaa.org
Hours: Tuesday through Sunday, 1:00 to 5:00 p.m.

The Catch *Admission: Adults $4.00; seniors and students $3.00.*

Near Franklin Park and Jamaica Plain, this museum is the public face of the National Center for Afro-American Artists, which was founded by renowned local arts patron Elma Lewis. It's dedicated to the exhibition, collection, and criticism of black visual arts worldwide. From explorations of historical works to contemporary art, the museum's galleries are filled with paintings, sculpture, graphics, photography, and decorative arts that bring the black American experience into vivid perspective. And it never costs more than $4.00 per person.

ALMOST-FREE RANGE: LOW-COST ZOOS OF GREATER BOSTON

"My parents used to take me to the pet department and tell me it was a zoo."

—BILLY CONNOLLY

There aren't any free zoo options in the greater Boston area, but the city's two biggest and best (okay, only) zoos do offer some pretty sweet discounts. (The New England Aquarium, one of the most popular tourist destinations in the entire city, doesn't offer any free or reduced-price admission opportunities at all, though. Want to see a cool fish? Go to a restaurant in Chinatown and check the fish tanks.)

Franklin Park Zoo
1 Franklin Park Road
Dorchester
(617) 541–5466
www.zoonewengland.com
Hours: April to September, weekdays 10:00 a.m. to 5:00 p.m., weekends 10:00 a.m. to 6:00 p.m.; rest of the year, daily 10:00 a.m. to 4:00 p.m.

The Catch When it's free: If you have a current valid military ID

The Catch When it's cheap: Tickets are half-price on the first Saturday of each month, between 10:00 a.m. and noon.

Gorillas, giraffes, lions, tigers, and butterflies all peacefully coexist at the Franklin Park Zoo. The Tropical Forest is home to baby gorillas, pygmy hippopotamus, and free-flight birds; the Butterfly Landing is like walking into a fluttering dream—an enclosed tent where more than 1,000 butterflies live and fly freely. Serengeti Crossing is a multi-acre replica of the African plains, complete with ibex, wildebeest, zebra, and ostrich. And you can't leave without visiting Kalahari Kingdom, home to lions, giraffe, and other African wildlife.

Normal full-price admission is $12.00 for adults, $10.00 for seniors, and $7.00 for kids ages two to twelve—but those prices are slashed in *half* if you come on the first Saturday of the month and enter between 10:00 a.m. and noon! That's just $6.00 per adult and just $3.50 per excited kid. Great deal. Also, it's always free if you have a current valid military ID.

Stone Zoo

149 Pond Street
Stoneham
(781) 438–5100
www.zoonewengland.org
Hours: April to September, weekdays 10:00 a.m. to 5:00 p.m., weekends
10:00 a.m. to 6:00 p.m.; rest of the year, daily 10:00 a.m. to 4:00 p.m.

The Catch When it's free: If you have a current valid military ID

The twenty-six-acre Stone Zoo is ten minutes' drive north of Boston, and
worth the trip. This zoo hosts colobus monkeys, Canadian lynx, snow leop-
ards, Mexican gray wolves, flamingos, Arctic fox, spider monkeys, capybaras,
and more. The Treasures of the Sierra Madre exhibit has jaguars, cougars,
coyotes, and Gila monsters, while you can view hyacinth macaws, African
crested porcupines, emperor tamarins, Geoldi's monkeys, silvery-cheeked
hornbills, and more at Windows to the Wild. You get the picture.

Admission to the Stone isn't dirt-cheap, but it's borderline inexpensive:
It costs just $9.00 for adults, $8.00 for seniors, and $6.00 for kids ages two
to twelve to enter. That's not bad at all. And current members of the military
get in free anytime; bring your ID.

BOSTON GARDENING:
FREE AND CHEAP GARDENS

"The garden is the poor man's apothecary."

—GERMAN PROVERB

As the home of world-renowned landscape architect Frederick Law Olmsted, Boston has a long history of shaping nature to its designs. From the first public garden in the country to the last remaining World War II Victory Garden, this city is a flower lover's paradise. You can get in on the horticulture act yourself by joining one of the many community gardens that have sprung up in vacant lots throughout Boston. Plus, there are tons of free gardening classes to get you started.

FREE AND CHEAP PUBLIC GARDENS

Arnold Arboretum

125 Arborway
Jamaica Plain
(617) 524–1718
www.arboretum.harvard.edu
Hours: Grounds open daily, sunrise to sunset; visitor center weekdays 9:00 a.m. to 4:00 p.m., Saturdays 10:00 a.m. to 4:00 p.m., Sundays noon to 4:00 p.m.

The Catch Donations accepted.

This is Boston's premier garden experience. The free-to-visit Arnold Arboretum has been providing Bostonians an oasis from the city since it was bequeathed to Harvard in 1872. It's home to thousands of species of flowering plants, shrubs, and trees and one of the most impressive Bonsai collections in New England. Each Mother's Day, the park hosts a Lilac Festival, which draws thousands (it's also the only day when picnicking is allowed in the park). Trails, both paved and gravel, wind throughout, bringing visitors around ponds and streams, into stands of pines, and through gardens planted in rhododendrons, roses, and the like. The Hunnewell Building houses the arboretum's library and archives.

Back Bay Fens

From Boylston Street overpass at Charlesgate to Longwood Medical area
www.emeraldnecklace.org/parks/back-bay-fens

The Fens was once a foul-smelling tidal creek, until Olmsted's plans reshaped the land surrounding the Muddy River, which became a freshwater creek when the Charles River was dammed in 1910. The Fens is now home to parks, meandering trails, and gorgeous gardens, including the oldest remaining World War II Victory Garden in the United States (Plots cost $20; information at www.fenwayvictorygardens.com.) The Kelleher Rose Garden here contains more than 200 varieties of roses in a wonderfully tended and landscaped display. The Fens is entirely free to the public, but avoid this park at night.

Boston Public Garden

Bounded by Arlington, Beacon, Charles, and Boylston Streets
www.friendsofthepublicgarden.org

The Public Garden was the first botanical garden in the United States, and you can't miss it—it's right in the center of the city, across the street from the Boston Common (in fact, many tourists and locals are fooled into thinking this is another part of the Common). Swan boats glide across a twenty-four-acre lagoon, and meticulously tended rose gardens spring to life each spring; in fact, the city's gardeners plant an ever-changing rotation of seasonal flowering plants. It's a very popular spot for wedding photos, picnics, and hanging out on benches under mammoth weeping willows.

Gore Place

52 Gore Street
Waltham
(781) 894–2798
www.goreplace.org
Hours: Grounds open daily, sunrise to sunset.

The Catch Admission fees charged for tours of the home. Grounds always free, except during special events when grounds are closed to public.

No, not Al Gore's place. This former summer home of the seventh governor of Massachusetts, Christopher Gore, hosts acres of gardens and lawns fashioned largely on traditional European landscaping ideals (as opposed to the fastidious and abundant English gardens that were all the rage at that time). Gore's elegantly furnished mansion has been called the Monticello of the North; architectural historians consider it the most significant Federal-period mansion in New England. It costs a lot to tour the mansion, but nada to wander the glorious open grounds.

Harvard University Botanical Museum Glass Flower Collection
26 Oxford Street
Cambridge
(617) 495–3045
www.hmnh.harvard.edu/on_exhibit/the_glass_flowers.html

The Catch *Normal museum admission fees $9.00 per adult, $7.00 seniors and students, $6.00 children age three to eighteen.*

This is more a "virtual" garden than a real one, because the flowers are entirely made of glass. But they sure are pretty. Beginning in 1886, German glass artisan Leopold Blaschka and his son Rudolph worked to create this magnificent display of glass flowers. They worked at it for more than fifty years, and today Harvard's Botanical Museum proudly displays 3,000 of their works of art, representing nearly 850 species. (Elizabeth and Mary Ware bought the collection and donated it to Harvard.) When it's cold and snowy, coming here is like walking through a permanent spring—minus the allergic reactions, of course. Best of all, the Botanical Museum is free for Massachusetts residents on Wednesday from 3:00 to 5:00 p.m. (September through May only) and on Sunday morning from 9:00 a.m. to noon (year-round).

Lyman Estate Greenhouses
185 Lyman Street
Waltham
(781) 891–1985
www.spnea.org/visit/homes/lyman_estate_greenhouses.htm
Hours: Mid-December to mid-July, Wednesday to Sunday 9:30 a.m. to 4:00 p.m. (to 7:00 p.m. Thursdays); rest of the year, Wednesday to Saturday 9:30 a.m. to 4:00 p.m. (to 7:00 p.m. Thursdays).

The Catch *Suggested donation $6.00, but you can enter for free if you want. Guided tours always $6.00.*

This thirty-seven-acre country estate was designed in the late 1790s following traditional English style, and the three large greenhouses were constructed in 1804 to house exotic and hard-to-find fruits to feed the Lyman family; they're some of the oldest greenhouses in the United States, filled with heirloom fruits and plants. The Grape House contains exotic fruit trees, while the Camellia House is filled with flowering camellias (obviously); a world-renowned orchid collection graces still another greenhouse. There are frequent plant sales, and guided tours of the greenhouses ($6.00) are also offered on the first Wednesday of each month.

MAKING **THE** BEST **OF** THINGS: CEMETERIES AS **PARKLANDS**

Once upon a time, cemeteries in this country served as de facto public gardens and social gathering places—they were designed more like parks than mausoleums. People actually came not only to pay respect but to take long walks or slow drives, have picnics, or read a books under trees. Although this might seem a little creepy in this day and age, a (free!) trip to either of the city's two historic garden cemeteries is guaranteed to change your mind about getting the best use out of . . . well, a no-win situation.

Forest Hills Cemetery
95 Forest Hills Avenue
Jamaica Plain
(617) 524–0128
www.foresthillscemetery.com
www.foresthillstrust.org
Hours: Daily, 8:30 a.m. to dusk.

Talk about a great hidden parkland destination: this is it. Listed on the National Register of Historic Places, Forest Hills Cemetery was designed and built in 1848 on 250 acres in the heart of the city, near the Arnold Arboretum and Franklin Park. It's renowned not only for its abundant gardens and the famous people buried here (including William Lloyd Garrison and Eugene O'Neill), but also for sculpture pieces such as Martin Milmore's 1867 work The Citizen Soldier, a memorial for local soldiers who died in the Civil War. They provide maps, brochures, and books about the cemetery in the cemetery office. There's even a sculpture pathway here! It's practically a museum of outdoor art. The Forest Hills Educational Trust hosts juried exhibitions of sculpture here frequently, and free guided walking tours take place on the last Sunday of each month.

Mount Auburn Cemetery

580 Mt. Auburn Street
Cambridge
(617) 547–7105
www.mountauburn.org
Hours: May through August, daily 8:00 a.m. to 7:00 p.m.; rest of the year,
daily 8:00 a.m. to 5:00 p.m.

Based on the plan of Père Lachaise Cemetery in Paris, Mount Auburn Cemetery is simply an incredible place; you'll almost forget that it's a cemetery. The design was laid out in 1831 (by a group of amateur landscape architects!), and today it's a designated National Historic Landmark. The cemetery includes an impressive collection of more than 5,000 trees spread across 175 acres of hills, dells, ponds, woodlands, and clearings. The landscape styles here include Victorian-era plantings, contemporary gardens, natural woodlands, and formal ornamental gardens. There are also hundreds of ornamental sculptures, chapels, bridges, and lookouts. Who's buried here? A who's-who roll-call of Boston society from the past: members of the Cabot and Lowell families, Julia Ward Howe, Mary Baker Eddy, Oliver Wendell Holmes, and the artist Winslow Homer, among many others.

The group Friends of the Mount Auburn Cemetery hosts frequent tours on various aspects of the cemetery's history, art, architecture, and horticulture; check the Web site for events calendars. And please follow the house rules—no pets, no bikes inside the cemetery's walls (you can lock up at the gate), no picnics or inline skating, and no gravestone rubbing. Also, you need to apply for a permit to take photographs.

GARDENING **AT** NIGHT: **JOINING** A **COMMUNITY** GARDEN

Boston Natural Areas Network

62 Summer Street (second floor)
(617) 542–7696
www.bostonnatural.org/communitygardens.htm

Surprisingly, there are more than 250 community gardens scattered in neighborhoods throughout Boston. These are collective gardens containing smaller plots each "owned" and tended to by locals with the gardening bug—but without enough space in their own backyard to plant a true garden. Each of these garden oases is administered by its own nonprofit organization, but the Boston Natural Areas Network helps organize these tiny groups, centralize their administration, and advertise new plot openings. Many of the garden groups charge a small plot fee; figure $20 annually (though some have a sliding scale that depends on your income). Not only are these gardens a great way to exercise your green thumb and grow almost-free fresh food for your table, but they're also a great place to learn tips and tricks from more experienced gardeners. The BNAN even presents musical concerts at some gardens in the summer.

BNAN also holds workshops on how to start, fund, and administer your own community garden, and offers a number of free gardening education workshops throughout the year, including a good master gardeners' class. (This class is free, but the educational materials used in it cost $35.) For a complete calendar of BNAN's community garden–related events, visit the BNAN Web site.

APPENDIX A:

CHEAP **DATES** THAT **STILL** PACK A (**ROMANTIC**) PUNCH

"I've been asked to say a couple of words about my husband, Fang. How about short and cheap?"

—PHYLLIS DILLER

Cheap dates don't have to be bad dates; in fact, they might even be so much fun that your partner might forget little or no money changed hands. I'm not promising they'll forget. I'm just saying.

The "It Must Be Magic" Date: Nothing sets the mood faster than having someone pull a $20 bill out from behind your ear. The sense of mystery that a little sleight of hand produces can't help but infuse the rest of the evening. So head for the Hong Kong restaurant on Massachusetts Avenue in Harvard Square on a Tuesday night and watch the close-up magic show from 7:00 to 8:00 p.m. in the lounge on the second floor (it's known as the Mystery Lounge). (See the "Cheap Laughs" chapter of this book for more funny bone–tickling date ideas.)

The "Hold Me Closer, Tiny Dancer" Date: What is hotter than watching two people dance the dance of love, the tango? Find your way to the Tango by Moonlight event held on the Weeks Pedestrian Bridge (near Harvard Square) at 7:30 p.m. on any full-moon night during the summer. If you're *really* brave, go early with your date and take a quick dance lesson together. (If that doesn't help you two kids to get to know each other fast, I don't know what will.) In winter, there's a different kind of dancing happening at the weekly MIT Lindy Hop Society Dances, held at the MIT Student Center Wednesday nights. For more information on both events, see the "Free (and Free-Form) Dance" chapter.

The "Sunset, Celluloid, and Thou" Date: It's a variation on a tried-and-true winner theme (the old-timey drive-in), except it won't cost you a cent. On any Friday night, pack a picnic and go to Rowes Wharf by the Boston Harbor Hotel, where you can see a classic movie for free just as the glow of sunset fades over the harbor. If the breeze is a little too brisk, check out a film inside instead, such as at the Boston Public Library's Copley Square branch. A film is screened at the library's Rabb Lecture Hall almost every night of the week, often documentaries, foreign films, or other hip flicks that don't play in regular cinemas at all—thus making you appear even *more* cultured and intelligent than you already (or truly) are. For more ideas on ways to get your honey into the dark for free, see the "Celluloid Zeroes" film chapter.

The "Phat Cats (and Kittens)" Date: If your beloved has even hinted that he or she likes music, you simply must go to Wally's Cafe, the oldest and best jazz club in the city.

The vibe here is laid-back, the clientele is diverse, the admission is free(!), and you'll look like a swingin', in-the-know, music aficionado. Finger-snapping optional. And just think of the big brownie points you'll score if some famous musician shows up unannounced and takes the stage with the band—it happens all the time here. Your date might talk about this for years. If you don't blow it. For more info on ways to impress your little music lover, see the "Bargain Beats" music chapter.

The "Thinking Man's" Date: Got nothing intelligent to say? Not so smooth with the ladies (or gents)? No sweat; let someone *else* do the talking instead. You can rub elbows with some of the city's leading literati thanks to the Four Stories Reading Series in the Enormous Room (yes, it's really called that) on the first Monday of every month during winter. In between readings, you can lounge (in other words: snuggle) on big comfy couches and listen to the funky song stylings of the night's guest deejay. Before you know it, you'll have tons to talk about. When Four Stories is on hiatus during the summer months, check out the rousing political debates the Ford Hall Forum's lecture series (held at various venues around the city)—and schedule a long walk right after the lecture so you two can fully explore your feelings . . . about the debate, of course. For more ideas on ways to liven up the conversation, check out the "Free Verse" readings and lectures chapter of this book.

The "Night of a Thousand Flavors" Date: Dating a foodie? You're in the right town. Head over to Faneuil Hall Marketplace on the first Wednesday evening of every month for A Taste of Quincy Market, when every food store in the cavernous downtown marketplace puts out (no pun intended) free samples for you to taste. If you can make it through even half the samples available, you can skip over dinner and go straight to after-dinner drinks. Or other festivities (wink, wink). For more free meals, happy hours, and samples, check out the "There Is Such a Thing As a Free Lunch" chapter.

The "Loaf of Bread, Jug of Wine" Date: Is there anything more romantic than sharing a glass of fine wine with the object of your affection? Yup—sharing fine *free* wine with the object of your obsession . . . affection. *Affection*. The Wine Gallery in Kenmore Square will let you sample a variety of high-end wines from its "Wine Jukebox," an automatic wine-sample dispenser that's almost as much fun as the wine itself. It's also a great way to find out if your date is drawn more to high-end wines (in which case you might want to reconsider the whole relationship? Kidding!) or good-value, moderate, and inexpensive offerings (grab hold and don't let go!). The "Free Spirits" chapter of this book lists plenty more free wine-tasting opportunities throughout the city, too.

The "Likes Long Walks on the Beach" Date: Castle Island is that perfect place to take that "long walk on a beach" people are always talking about in their lame personal ads. (Not that we'd ever go that route. No way.) The island, which isn't really an island anymore, is surrounded by a smooth walkway that connects with the walkway along the beaches of South Boston. You could literally walk for hours around Dorchester Bay and finish up on sloping grassy hills next to Fort Independence. If the wind is right, you can even lie on your backs and watch airplanes landing at Logan across the harbor. Imagine where the planes are coming from. Imagine where you two crazy kids are headed on your next holiday in search of warm surf . . . you get the picture. See the "Exercising Your Right to Cheapness" chapter on fitness, fun, and games for more on Boston's best free beaches and parks.

APPENDIX B:

PUBLIC **LIBRARY** AND **BRANCH** LOCATIONS

Arlington Public Library
www.robbinslibrary.org

Robbins Main Library, 700 Massachusetts Avenue; (781) 316–3200;
Edith M. Fox Branch, 175 Massachusetts Avenue; (781) 316–3198

Boston Public Library
ww.bpl.org/branches

This huge urban library system has three dozen neighborhood branches (at this writing), each with distinctive architecture, holdings, and events: the Grove Hall branch in Roxbury, for instance, has jazz events and especially strong holdings of African-American literature. Here are all the branches; check BPL's "neighborhood branches" Web site (see above) or call a branch directly for weekly opening hours.

Alliston/Brighton
Brighton Branch Library, 40 Academy Hill Road; (617) 782–6032
Faneuil Branch Library, 419 Faneuil Street; (617) 782–6705
Honan-Allston Branch Library, 300 North Harvard Street; (617) 787–6313

Boston (Downtown)
Kirstein Business Branch Library, 20 City Hall Avenue; (617) 523–0860
West End Branch Library, 151 Cambridge Street; (617) 523–3957

Charlestown
Charlestown Branch Library, 179 Main Street; (617) 242–1248

Dorchester
Adams Street Branch Library, 690 Adams Street; (617) 436–6900
Codman Square Branch Library, 690 Washington Street; (617) 436–8214
Fields Corner Branch Library, 1520 Dorchester Avenue; (617) 436–2155

Lower Mills Branch Library, 27 Richmond Street; (617) 298–7841
Uphams Corner Branch Library, 500 Columbia Road; (617) 265–0139

East Boston
East Boston Branch Library, 276 Meridian Street; (617) 569–0271
Orient Heights Branch Library, 18 Barnes Avenue; (617) 567–2516

Hyde Park
Hyde Park Branch Library, 35 Harvard Avenue; (617) 361–2524

Jamaica Plain
Connolly Branch Library, 433 Centre Street; (617) 522–1960
Jamaica Plain Branch Library, 12 Sedgwick Street; (617) 524–2053

Mattapan
Mattapan Branch Library, 10 Hazelton Street; (617) 298–9218

North End
North End Branch Library, 25 Parmenter Street; (617) 227–8135

Roslindale
Roslindale Branch Library, 4238 Washington Street; (617) 323–2343

Roxbury
Dudley Branch Library, 65 Warren Street; (617) 442–6186
Egleston Square Branch Library, 2044 Columbus Avenue;
(617) 445–4340
Parker Hill Branch Library, 1497 Tremont Street; (617) 427–3820

South Boston
South Boston Branch Library, 646 East Broadway; (617) 268–0180
Washington Village Branch, 1226 Columbia Road; (617) 269–7239

South End
South End Branch Library, 685 Tremont Street; (617) 536–8241

West Roxbury
West Roxbury Branch, 1961 Centre Street; (617) 325–3147

Brookline Public Library
www.brooklinelibrary.org

Main Library, 361 Washington Street; (617) 730–2370
Coolidge Corner Branch Library, 31 Pleasant Street; (617) 730–2380
Putterham Branch, 959 West Roxbury Parkway, Chestnut Hill;
(617) 730–2385

Cambridge Public Library
www.ci.cambridge.ma.us/~cpl

Main Branch, 359 Broadway; (617) 349–4040
Boudreau Branch, 245 Concord Avenue; (617) 349–4017
Central Square Branch, 45 Pearl Street; (617) 349–4010
Collins Branch, 64 Aberdeen Avenue; (617) 349–4021
O'Connell Branch, 48 Sixth Street; (617) 349–4019
O'Neill Branch, 70 Rindge Avenue; (617) 349–4023
Valente Branch, 826 Cambridge Street; (617) 349–4015

Everett Public Library
www.noblenet.org/everett

Parlin Memorial Library, 410 Broadway; (617) 394–2300
Shute Memorial Library, 781 Broadway; (617) 394–2308

Milton Public Library
www.miltonlibrary.org

Main Library, 476 Canton Avenue; (617) 698–5757
East Milton Branch, 334 Edgehill Road; (617) 898–4961
Kidder Branch, 101 Blue Hills Parkway; (617) 698–5757

Needham Public Library
www.needhamma.gov

1139 Highland Avenue; (781) 455–7559

Newton Free Library
www.ci.newton.ma.us/library/default.asp

Main Library, 330 Homer Street; (617) 796–1360

Auburndale Branch, 375 Auburn Street; (617) 552–7158

Waban Branch, 1608 Beacon Street; (617) 552–7166

Somerville Public Library
www.somervillepubliclibrary.org

79 Highland Avenue; (617) 623–5000

Thomas Crane Public Library (Quincy)
www.thomascranelibrary.org

Main Library, 40 Washington Street; (617) 376–1300

Adams Shore Branch, 519 Sea Street; (617) 376–1325 (adult),
(617) 376–1326 (children)

North Quincy Branch, 381 Hancock Street; (617) 376–1320 (adult),
(617) 376–1321 (children)

Wollaston Branch, 41 Beale Street; (617) 376–1330

APPENDIX C:

BOSTON **COMMUNITY** **CENTER** LOCATIONS

Some of these community centers are run by independent community organizations, others by the Boston Centers for Youth & Families. Hours, membership fees, and programming can change without notice, so call ahead if you're interested in a specific program listed here to be sure it's still offered. Most of these centers charge less than $50 for an annual family membership—and that gives you access to all their programs.

ALLSTON/BRIGHTON
Jackson/Mann Community Center
500 Cambridge Street
(617) 635–5153

After-school programs, child care, basketball, volleyball, ceramics, gym, karate, volunteer program, recreation activities, special-needs program (Camp Joy), summer program, street workers, GED, ABE and ESL, girls' programs, Boston Youth Connection Program.

CHARLESTOWN
Bunker Hill Street at Doherty Playground
(617) 635–5173

Outdoor pool open during the summer months.

Charlestown Community Center
255 Medford Street
(617) 635–5169

Basketball, volleyball, swimming, field trips, volunteer programs, recreation activities, gym, pool, Tiny Tots program, child care, Youth Connection Program, special-needs program (Camp Joy), summer day program, girls' programs, summer pool program, Clougherty Pool (run by Charlestown Community Centers).

Kent Community Center

50 Bunker Hill Street
(617) 635–5177

Preschool child care, tutoring, recreation activities, child care programs.

CHINATOWN

Boston Chinatown Neighborhood Community Center

885 Washington Street
(617) 635–5129

Child care, tutoring and enrichment programs, after-school programs, summer programs, full recreation program, pool.

DORCHESTER

Cleveland Community Center

11 Charles Street
(617) 635–5141

Tutoring program, basketball, recreation activities, gym, Youth Connection Program, day camp, Youth Challenge Program.

Holland Community Center

85 Olney Street
(617) 635–5144

Basketball, volleyball, swimming, karate, softball, weightlifting, exercise class, recreation activities, gym, pool, after-school tutoring, Boston Youth Connection Program, girls' program, summer day program, volunteer and mentoring programs, special events.

Marshall Community Center

35 Westville Street
(617) 635–5148

School-age after-school program, preschool program, recreation activities, Youth Connection Program, swimming lessons and programs, summer day program, summer pool program.

Murphy Community Center
1 Worrell Street
(617) 635–5150

Child care, tennis, volleyball, basketball, swimming, ceramics, quilting, crafts, computers, volunteer program, recreation activities, gym, pool, nursery school program, special-needs program (Camp Joy), tutoring, baseball clinics, summer day program, summer pool program.

Perkins Community Center
155 Talbot Avenue
(617) 635–5146

Basketball, volleyball, swimming, karate, softball, weightlifting, exercise classes, tutoring, arts, theater, plays and shows, volunteer and mentoring programs, recreation activities, gym, pool, girls' programs, after-school child care, school reentry program, after-school tutoring, special-needs program (Camp Joy), adult education, bike program, weekend camping (summer only), summer day program, summer pool program.

EAST BOSTON
Harborside Community Center
312 Border Street
(617) 635–5114

Street hockey, soccer, swimming, swim team, gym, Kid's Club, Saturday Fallout program, baton twirling, Teen Center, special-needs program (Camp Joy), after-school tutoring, Youth Connection Program, volunteer programs, dances, business skills program, ESL, GED and CASA testing, outdoor skate park, summer pool program, summer day program.

Orient Heights Community Center
86 Boardman Street
(617) 635–5120

Senior citizen drop-in, reading program, many recreational leagues and programs including wheelchair basketball, teen trip night, arts and crafts, movie night, special events, summer day program, and more.

Paris Street Community Center

112 Paris Street
(617) 635–5125

Weightlifting, karate, basketball, aerobics, track, arts and crafts, volunteer program, girls' program, senior citizen bingo, Boston Youth Connection Program, drama hour, racquetball, cardiovascular room, cake decorating, summer day program.

Paris Street Pool

113 Paris Street
(617) 635–5122

Swimming, swim classes for ages three through adult, lifeguard certification, swim team, summer pool program.

HYDE PARK
Hyde Park Community Center

1179 River Street
(617) 635–5178

Line dance and evening ceramics for adults, choral group, computer lessons, ESOL, GED, after-school tutoring, Saturday art and tutoring classes, gymnastics, various athletic leagues and activities, volunteer and mentoring programs, Boston Youth Connection Program, chess club, Double Dutch Jump Rope Club, girls' dance step club, teen explorer club, special events, summer day program.

JAMAICA PLAIN
Agassiz Community Center

20 Child Street
(617) 635–5191

Basketball, drug and alcohol counseling, alternative education (reading/math), computer programs, recreation activities, gym, after-school programs, summer day program, volunteer and mentoring programs, Boston Youth Connection Program.

Curtis Hall Community Center
20 South Street
(617) 635–5193

Volleyball, basketball, swimming and swim lessons, lifeguard training, water aerobics, weightlifting, recreation activities, pool, JP for Fours Pre-School, volunteer and mentoring programs, senior fitness, computer classes, summer pool program.

English High Community Center
144 McBride Street
(617) 635–5244

Basketball, soccer, karate, weightlifting, computers, adult education program (ESOL and GED), recreation activities, gym, teen program, summer day program.

Hennigan Community Center
200 Heath Street
(617) 635–5198

Basketball, swimming, tutoring, teen center, high school and college guidance help, recreation activities, gym, pool, after-school programs, Boston Youth Connection Program, teen tutorial computer program, summer pool and day programs.

MATTAPAN
Gallivan Community Center
61 Woodruff Way
(617) 635–5252

Recreational and educational activities, social programs, Osco Study Club, computer program, support groups, Boston Youth Connection Program, summer day program.

Mattahunt Community Center
100 Hebron Street
(617) 635–5159

Basketball, swimming, weightlifting, drop-in center for teens, reading and math classes, volunteer and mentoring programs, recreation activities, gym, pool, after-school child care, after-school tutoring, Boston Youth Connection Program, special-needs program (Camp Joy), aerobics classes, entrepreneurship program, summer pool program, summer day programs.

Mildred Avenue Community Center
1-5 Mildred Avenue
(617) 635–1328

Gym, exercise studio/weight room, classrooms, dance studio, community rooms, computer room, senior center with kitchenette, swimming pool, recording studio, summer pool program, summer day programs.

NORTH END
Mirabella Pool
(run by the Nazzaro Community Center)
475R Commercial Street
(617) 635–1276

Open during the summer months.

Nazzaro Community Center
30 North Bennet Street
(617) 635–5166

Basketball, weightlifting, open gym, tutoring, drop-in center, peer leadership program, volunteer program, recreation activities, gym, pool (Mirabella pool), baseball, swimming lessons, summer day program for ages five to eleven, Boston Youth Connection Program, active senior center.

ROSLINDALE
Archdale Community Center
125 Brookway Road
(617) 635–5256

Recreational and educational activities, social programs, day care, support groups, girls' program, family literacy, after-school tutoring program, school-age child care, Boston Youth Connection Program, G.I.V.E. boys' program, Computer Learning Center, Archdale Steppers, summer day program.

Flaherty Pool
(run by Boston Centers for Youth & Families)
160 Florence Street
(617) 635–5181

Swimming activities and programs, swim league, open and lap swim.

Roslindale Community Center
6 Cummins Highway
(617) 635–5185

Gym activities, volunteer program, recreation activities, Tiny Tots program,
after-school tutoring, summer day program, GED, teen/youth council,
Roslindale Adventures for Youth trips, Marion Shea Computer Center.

ROXBURY
Madison Park Community Center
55 New Dudley Street
(617) 635–5209

Recreational and social programs, gym, pool, sports leagues, girls' tennis,
teen room, after-school reading/math tutoring, Rainbow Reading/Math program, Madison Park Red Sox Rookie League program, summer day program.

Mason Pool
(run by Boston Centers for Youth & Families)
176 Norfolk Avenue
(617) 635–5241

Adult lap swim, adult lessons, community lessons, swim team, lifeguard
training/junior lifeguard training, lifeguard team, synchronized swimming,
water aerobics, water polo.

Orchard Gardens Community Center
2 Dearborn Street
(617) 635–5240

Gym, martial arts, youth baseball, reading program, Boston Youth Connection Program, workshops, summer day program.

Shelburne Community Center
2730 Washington Street
(617) 635–5213

Basketball, judo, billiards, recreation activities, gym, after-school tutoring, volunteer and mentoring programs, summer camp, swimming, sports, field trips, tutoring, cultural activities, computer room, aerobics, girls' program, summer day program.

Thomas Johnson Community Center
(Mission Hill Community Centers)
68 Annunciation Road
(617) 635–5212

Basketball, arts and crafts, movie hour, recreation activities, gym, volunteer program.

Tobin Community Center (Mission Hill Community Centers)
1481 Tremont Street
(617) 635–5216

Basketball and other sport leagues, sports camps, summer day program, teen center, special events, field trips, and more.

Vine Street Community Center
339 Dudley Street
(617) 635–1285

Senior center; teen center; child care center; recreational, educational, and social programs; summer day programs.

SOUTH BOSTON
Condon Community Center
200 D Street
(617) 635–5100

Basketball, swimming, soccer, volunteer program, recreation activities, gym, pool, after-school tutoring, special-needs program (Camp Joy), computer skills training, before-school program, summer day program, summer pool program.

Curley Community Center
1663 Columbia Road
(617) 635–5104

Volleyball, handball, horseshoes, aerobics, racquetball, volunteer program, recreation activities, gym, weight room, Tiny Tots program.

Tynan Community Center
650 East 4th Street
(617) 635–5110

Basketball, volleyball, street hockey, arts and crafts, ceramics, girls' program, volunteer program, recreation activities, gym, after-school tutoring, Boston Youth Connection Program, day camp, summer day programs.

Walsh Community Center
535 East Broadway (behind South Boston Courthouse)
(617) 635–5640

Basketball, boxing, street hockey, roller hockey, tennis, volleyball, summer day programs.

SOUTH END
Blackstone Community Center
50 West Brookline Street
(617) 635–5162

Boston Youth Connection Program, gymnastics, basketball, self-defense, recreation activities, gym, pool, after-school child care, after-school tutoring, volunteer and mentoring programs, streetworkers, GED (also in Spanish) and ESL, girls' soccer, Saturday intensive ESL, babysitting for educational programs, food share, summer pool program, summer day programs.

WEST ROXBURY
Draper Pool (run by Boston Centers for Youth & Families)
5279 Washington Street
(617) 635–5021

Adult lap swim, adult lessons, community swim lessons, swim team, lifeguard training and junior lifeguard training, lifeguard team, water aerobics, water polo.

Ohrenberger Community Center
175 West Boundary Road
(617) 635–5183

Floor hockey, gymnastics, basketball, drama, arts, soccer, roller-skating, volunteer program, recreation activities, gym, after-school child care, nursery school program, Boston Youth Connection Program, computer classes, special-needs program (Camp Joy), tutoring program, summer day program.

Roche Family Community Center
1716 Centre Street
(617) 635–5066

Senior center, senior lunch program, teen center, girls' basketball league, computer room, gym activities, Boston Youth Connection Program, summer day program.

West Roxbury Community Center
West Roxbury High School
1205 VFW Parkway
(617) 635–5190

Basketball, swimming, quilting, sewing, typing, arts and crafts, volunteer program, recreation activities, gym, swimming pool, special-needs program (Camp Joy), Boston Youth Connection Program, summer day program, summer pool program.

APPENDIX D:

BOSTON **COMMUNITY** **LEARNING** CENTERS

Here's a list of Boston's community learning centers. They offer after-school programs and educational opportunities for students, and sometimes adult evening classes as well.

ALLSTON/BRIGHTON

Gardner School CLC, 30 Athol Street, Allston; (617) 635–8365
Garfield School CLC, 95 Beechcroft Street, Brighton; (617) 635–6323
Hamilton School CLC, 198 Strathmore Road, Brighton; (617) 635–5269
Jackson/Mann School CLC, 40 Armington Street, Allston; (617) 635–5153

BOSTON

Quincy School CLC, 885 Washington Street; (617) 635–5135

DORCHESTER

Dever School CLC, 325 Mount Vernon Street; (617) 695–2300
Holland School CLC, 71 Pleasant Street; (617) 635–5144
Lee School CLC, 155 Talbot Avenue; (617) 635–6339
Marshall School CLC, 35 Westville Street; (617) 971–0066
Murphy School CLC, 1 Worrell Street; (617) 635–8781

EAST BOSTON

Guild School CLC, 195 Leyden Street; (617) 567–3249
Otis School CLC, 218 Marion Street; (617) 635–8372

JAMAICA PLAIN

Curley School CLC, 40 Pershing Street; (617) 427–5300
Young Achievers CLC, 25 Walk Hill Street; (617) 635–6804

MATTAPAN

Mattahunt School CLC, 100 Hebron Street; (617) 296–6089
Taylor School CLC, 1060 Morton Avenue; (617) 635–5252

ROSLINDALE

Bates Elementary School CLC, 426 Beech Street; (617) 469–5151
Sumner School CLC, 15 Basile Street; (617) 635–8131

ROXBURY

Hernandez School CLC, 61 School Street; (617) 635–8187
Mason School CLC, 150 Norfolk Avenue; (617) 635–8405

INDEX

Best Western Terrace Inn, 73
Beth Israel Deaconess Medical Center, 155–56
Beth Urdang Gallery, 247
Big Moves Boston, 39
Big Sky Bread Co., 94
bike paths, 176–78
Black Rose, The, 4
Blacksmith House, 67
Blackstone Community Center, 300
Blaine School, The, 116
Blanchards Wine and Spirits, 102, 104
Bloomingdales, 120
Blue Hill Meteorological Observatory Library, 186
Blue Hills Reservation, 169
Blue Hills Trailside Museum, 272–73
Blue Man Group, 25
blues music, 8–10
boardinghouses, 71–72
boating, 178
Bojack Academy of Beauty Culture, 116
bookstore readings, 61–63
Boomerang's, 146
BoSoma Dance Company, 40
Bostix Ticket Booths, 35–36
Boston African American National Historic Site, 214
Boston Animal Control, 203
Boston Athenæum, 188–89, 227
Boston Backpackers, 72
Boston Ballet, 124–25
Boston Center for the Arts, 243
Boston Centers for Youth & Families (BCYF), 122, 174–75
Boston Children's Museum, 135, 273
Boston Chinatown Neighborhood Community Center, 293
Boston Clinical Trials and Medical Research, Inc., 156
Boston Common, 171, 208
    Frog Pond, 132
    Visitor Center, 232
Boston Community Learning Centers, 123
Boston Conservatory, 16, 40
Boston Courant, 196
Boston Dance Alliance, 45
Boston Fair Housing Commission Metrolist, 76
Boston Fire Museum, 260
Boston Globe, 229
Boston Haitian Reporter, 198
Boston Harbor Hotel, movies at, 56, 286
Boston Harbor Islands, 173–74, 223–24
Boston Housing Authority, 76–77
Boston International Comedy and Movie Festival, 50
Boston International Hostel, 72
Boston Library Consortium, The, 192
Boston Lyric Opera, 10
Boston Medical Center, 156, 160, 164
Boston Metro, 198
Boston Nanny Centre, 81
Boston National Historic Park, 214–15
Boston Natural Areas Network, 224, 283–84
Boston Nature Center and Wildlife Sanctuary, 169–70
Boston Parents' Paper, 198
Boston Parks and Recreation Department, 133
Boston Phoenix, 198–99
Boston Public Garden, 171–72, 280
Swan Boats, 178
Boston Public Library, 185
    art and architecture tour of, 228
    Associates of the Boston Public Library, 86
    branch locations, 288–89
    free films at, 53–54, 286
    Homework Assistance Program, 123–24
    Kids Cinema, 126–27
    kids' story hours, 141

ABOUT THE AUTHOR

Born and bred in rural Massachusetts, Kris Frieswick has lived in Boston on and off since she graduated from Emerson College in 1985. She is a freelance journalist and humor columnist and has won numerous awards for her work in various genres. She is a regular contributor to the *Boston Globe Magazine,* the *Economist, Worth* magazine, *Arrive* magazine, Southwest Airlines's *Spirit* magazine, *Boston* magazine, and many others. For five years, she wrote a regular humor column for the *Phoenix* newspapers, a chain of alternative weeklies based in Boston. Her humor columns have appeared in two humor anthologies, and she's done numerous interviews on television and radio. She has also dabbled in standup monologue at famous comedy clubs the Lizard Lounge and the Hong Kong, both in Cambridge.

Kris and her husband Andrew Robinson live in Boston's South End, the sixth Boston neighborhood that she has called home. She's an avid traveler, skier, cyclist, cook, and bargainista whose proudest Cheap moment was convincing a deli clerk to grind up a leg of lamb and sell it to her for the price of hamburger. The memory still gives her goose bumps.